THE SOUTH-WE

A LANDSCAPE HISTORY

Published by

Ashbourne Hall, Cokayne Ave
Ashbourne, Derbyshire, DE6 1EJ England
Tel: (01335) 347349 Fax: (01335) 347303
e-mail: landmark@clara.net

1st Edition

13 ISBN: 978-1-84306-357-5

10 ISBN: 1-84306-357-3

British Library Cataloguing in Publication Data: a catalogue record for this book is
available from the British Library.

Print: Cromwell Press Ltd

Design by: Mark Titterton

Edited by: Ian Howe

Front Cover: Looking towards Blackclough.

Back Cover Main: Reef limestone hills of the Upper Dove.

Back Cover Bottom Left: Jenkin Chapel.

Back cover Bottom Middle: Green road near Allmeadows Farm, Algreave.

Back cover Bottom Right: Goyt Bridge now rebuilt higher up the River Goyt.

Page 1: A Dispute map of 1599 between John Claye and
William Gilbert showing 'Ryve Edge Whear sclates are gotten'.

Page 3: The 1759 Macclesfield – Buxton turnpike descends to Burbage.
CHPR embankment middle ground.

Photographs by the author unless otherwise stated

THE SOUTH-WEST PEAK

A LANDSCAPE HISTORY

Landmark Publishing

CONTENTS

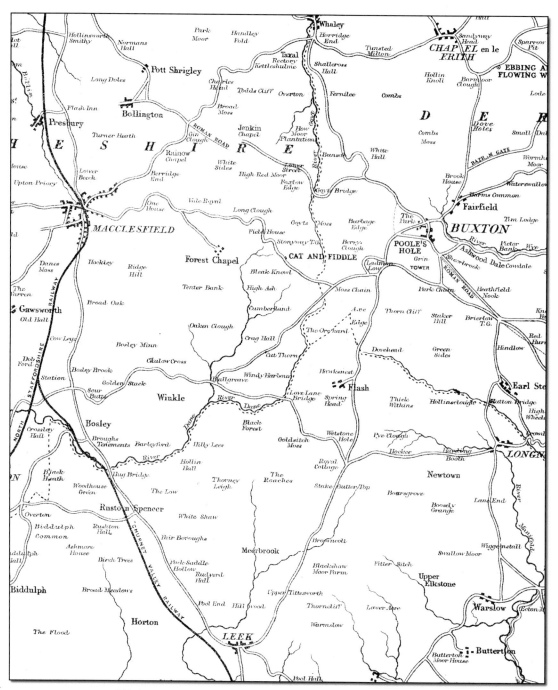

This book covers the area bounded by Leek, Buxton, Chapel-en-le-Frith and Macclesfield.
The map is taken from *The Buxton Guide*, 1868. Some spellings have changed, eg 'Winkle'.

PREFACE

A work such as this must draw heavily upon the experience of others. No one person can hope to be an expert in all the specialised subjects included in these pages. Their interdisciplinary character, however, has afforded me the pleasure of making vital excursions into some subjects with which I was hitherto quite unfamiliar. It was always my intention to use a 'broad brush' in compiling this guide but I have occasionally been lured into detail. Working in the South-West Peak for the past 18 years has given me an abiding interest and fascination with the relationships between the land and its people. I have discovered new ways of looking at this landscape and coming to an understanding of older technologies, communication routes and industrial processes that were previously unfamiliar. Placing them into their wider social and historical perspective has been a rewarding task. My hope is that this book will appeal to the general reader and also to those with an interest in local history.

Whilst attempting to trace the origins of early routes across the landscape, where sometimes much of great antiquity has survived the plough, I realised that one must begin in the library rather than the field, using aerial photographs, travellers' records, place-names, current archaeological evidence, old maps and documents. Old maps will occasionally reveal clues to ancient routes but documentary evidence is not always available. Nevertheless, a vital key to understanding is to go and look. Much information can be deduced from the physical evidence sometimes unavailable from other sources or which may previously have been misinterpreted.

I am aware of gaps, inevitable oversimplification and the many pitfalls hidden in evidence but I trust I have avoided major errors and succeeded in giving a reasonably clear outline of this history – a considerable quantity of which, I am also aware, remains unearthed. I have used my own fieldwork and research and drawn freely on the latest reliable published and unpublished work of others. I sincerely hope adequate recognition of this has been given. I would like to express my gratitude to people living in the area for their comments and willingness to share local knowledge.

I also wish to most warmly thank those of my friends with expertise in some of the subjects touched upon, for their interest, constructive criticism, generous loan of material and contributions so generously given, directly or indirectly to the formulation of this book.

ACKNOWLEDGEMENTS

I am particularly grateful to John Barnatt for finding the time to read an early draft of my text and provide me with constructive criticism and firm encouragement to continue.

My close friend and colleague Margaret Black who shares my enthusiasm for the landscape and its history, has also shared much of the fieldwork and research. Her steady reasoning, home baking and flasks of tea have lifted spirits on many occasions.

I have been fortunate to have enjoyed the friendship and enabling support of Brian Rich. Brian has unstintingly shared his considerable knowledge of local history, generally pushed me along and provided a constant stream of up-to-date source information. His contribution to the formulation of this book has been invaluable

The Peak District National Park's Archaeological Service were unfailingly helpful, as were the Local Studies Libraries at Macclesfield, Matlock, Buxton and Whaley Bridge. The staff were always patient in unearthing scraps of information that had eluded me, or suggested an appropriate line of approach..

Others who have generously loaned material, shared information or given help include; Harry Ball, Alison Bramwell, Susan Gawkroger, Geoff Howe, Roger Norton and Nicholas Sumner.

Eric Wood, 2007

PART ONE
PREHISTORY TO THE NORMAN CONQUEST

Chapter 1. INTRODUCTION AND BACKGROUND

Although general historical background information is provided and landscapes are described, this book concentrates mainly on the specific topics of settlement patterns, land use, industry, communication and travel from prehistory to the early 20th century.

The geographical area under consideration is on the south-western side of the Peak District National Park and is divided between North-East Cheshire, North Staffordshire and North-West Derbyshire. It comprises all or parts of the civil parishes of Leekfrith, Heathylee, Hollinsclough, Quarnford, Hartington Upper Quarter, Taxal, Macclesfield Forest and Wildboarclough, Sutton, Wincle, Rainow, Pott Shrigley, Kettleshulme, Lyme Handley and Chapel-en-le Frith.

LOCAL SETTLEMENT PATTERNS

With the exception of one or two villages, the overall settlement pattern is of scattered hamlets and individual farmsteads. Many can still be seen today, standing out in small groups or alone among the fields – some perhaps established when the commons were enclosed in the 1700s and early 1800s. However, some isolated farms are a lot older. In much of the South-West Peak, the land was not sufficiently fertile to establish village communities in the medieval period. Here an older way of life, based on these scattered farms and hamlets, continued through to today. Even though much of this area is at the very threshold of subsistence agriculture and very thinly populated, it has experienced considerable industrial development in the past followed by decline and, by the 19th century, population drift to the nearby towns. Every stage of human history and change has left its mark: the prehistoric barrows and monuments, the subsequent invasion and colonisation by European

and Scandinavian peoples, the encroachment of medieval farmers into the hunting forests followed by the early-modern rebuilding of farmsteads and settlements with their developing industry and trade. Later came the mechanisation of simple water-powered mills, and the extension of quarrying, limeburning and coal mining – all to supply the local industries and those beyond. With the growth of these small industries came the canals, the early turnpike roads and the steam engine. From the 1830s the railways arrived, just when the area's industrial significance had begun to decline. With an improved transport infrastructure, self-sufficiency became less important. Food could now be imported easily and many arable fields were given over to pasture and meadow. This enabled some farmers to respond to opportunities to sell dairy produce and milk to the nearby developing industrial towns.

The economy of the area today is based chiefly on stock rearing (sheep and cattle) but it would be a mistake to search much of it for completely self-sufficient communities relying wholly on agriculture, especially in the past. By 1620, in areas where farms had been built and land taken in from the constantly shrinking medieval hunting forest, a report by Derbyshire JPs shows that miners digging coal, iron ore and lead outnumbered agricultural workers. Those families with non-viable agricultural holdings could sustain themselves through industrial activity and 'carrying'. Nineteenth-century census returns reveal that agriculture was seldom the sole employer. Dual or multiple occupations given in these returns as part-time with farmer include: button-maker, silk worker, miner, mason, quarry man, limeburner, lime getter, blacksmith, wheelwright, butcher, plasterer, carrier, peddler, gunpowder labourer, cordwainer (shoe maker), gamekeeper and publican. A great range of industries was practised here among the hill farms, no doubt creating a particular society quite unlike that of today.

High-altitude settlement in Flash, for example, one of the highest villages in England where the soils are acid and heavy, was only possible because of a dual economy. The whole area around the southern rim of the Axe Edge watershed in the parish of Quarnford contains the ruins of farms, cottages, field walls, low earthworks, abandoned quarries and worked-out mines with their associated structures. There are derelict mills and the grassed-over remnants of old turnpike roads.

Bank and ditch boundary Pye Clough, Heathylee.

Trains of packhorses have created many of the deep curving grooves across the hills. In the river valleys at Wildboarclough, Rainow, Gradbach, Kettleshulme, Goytsbridge, Fernilee and along the upper Dane, various water-powered industries once flourished and then declined, revealing similar settlement and abandonment patterns. Much of the region, including the high and lonely moors, still contains the evidence of past industrialism. Today, such features are perceived as adding to the richness of the landscape. It is an area with a wonderfully diverse historic heritage. In the past, generations of people who thought and worked in ways different from us had struggled to wrest a living from these often uncompromising environments. Their persistence has produced the landscape we admire so much today.

BOUNDARIES, ANCIENT AND MODERN

Before the deliberate use of specially erected marked or dated stones on prescribed boundaries, prominent natural features would have been utilised. These might be cut-marks on trees, springs, rivers, the more obvious large boulders, oak and holly trees – but particularly thorn trees; hardy, long-lived and not easily toppled by winter gales. Indeed, the thorn is the most commonly occurring boundary marker in surviving Anglo-Saxon charters. Man-made linear features would include simple traditional paths and tracks, field boundaries of all sorts including banks and ditches and any clearly artificial lines across open land. Dating of bank and ditch earthworks is difficult. They could have been constructed at any time between the medieval period and the 19th century.

The early church divided its territories into basic ecclesiastical units known as *parishes*, each with a parish church or dependent chapel. Their boundaries were completed by the late 12th century and the general parish map then remained remarkably stable until the Reformation. Parish boundaries were chosen with care, perhaps to coincide with those of a landed estate whose boundaries were possibly descendants of a Romano/British property or even a prehistoric territory. Boundaries followed topographical features such as watercourses, ridgetops or linear features; perhaps Roman roads or even older informal highways. It should be borne in mind, however, that not all of these parish boundaries, many of which were laid down perhaps a thousand years ago, have remained unaltered. Parishes varied in area, some including many townships dispersed over many miles. The term 'parish' has been used of two quite distinct units of administration since an Act of Parliament in 1894; the *civil parish* (CP) on the one hand and the *ecclesiastical parish* on the other. It is the boundaries of the civil parishes that are portrayed on modern large-scale Ordnance Survey maps, not those of their ecclesiastical namesakes, though civil parish and ecclesiastical parish could and often did coincide. Before the late 1800s, the *manor*, a precise area controlled by a lord, was often the most important unit of local administration (see Chapter 5).

In the 17th century large parishes could be divided for poor-law purposes into their constituent *townships* – these being the ancient secular administrative units of a rural community as defined for the purposes of fiscal and judicial administration. A northern English phenomenon was the *quarter*, a subdivision of the parish sometimes coinciding with a township and often maintaining its own highways – although some did not. In the Peak District, Hartington CP is still subdivided into Middle Quarter, Town Quarter, Nether Quarter and the large subdivision Hartington Upper Quarter, which encompasses much of the northern part of the South-West Peak.

BEATING THE BOUNDS

The age-old ritual of 'beating the bounds' was once known in every English parish and involved walking either to a critical point on the parish boundary or along its line, beating with sticks. There were several reasons for this activity, often undertaken with enthusiasm by whole communities. Before the provision of reliable maps and with a populace that was largely illiterate, the whereabouts of these boundaries needed to be memorised and checks were made that boundary sharers had not moved prominent markers. Beating the bounds took place in Rogation Week, the time between the fifth Sunday after Easter and Ascension Day. Led by local officials – the parson, the constable of a township or the steward of the court of a manor – the procession was perhaps enjoyed by the communities as a time of freedom from work and an opportunity to celebrate. These occasions, often accompanied by liberal quantities of food and drink, became very disorderly and were forbidden at the Reformation although Royal charters, issued during the reigns of Elizabeth I and Charles II, requiring this ancient custom to be carried out annually, are still undertaken and enjoyed by many present-day local communities.

The South-West Peak contains a rich but sometimes forgotten legacy of route and boundary markers both ancient and modern; many associated with tenure or ownership. Some will indicate where the feet of countless generations of countrymen have trudged along the limits of their lands, ritually 'beating the bounds'.

A BOUNDARY DISPUTE

Boundary disputes were most likely to occur across land beyond the limits of a community's enclosed farmland. The following example is probably typical of its time. In a boundary dispute of the manor or lordship of Warnforde (Quarnford), claimed by Sir John Savage in c.1564, the bounds are described in a plea to Sir Nicholas Bacon:

'Showeth unto your lordship your orator Sir John Savage of Clyfton county Chester, knight, that his father, Sir John Savage of Clyfton was seisin [in lawful possession] of the manor or lordship of Warnforde county Stafford. After his death the manor descended to your orator as his son and heir, who entered into and was seisin of the same.

'But about 20 March 6ELIZABETH Sir Humfrey Bradbourne, Sir Thomas Fitzharbert, Sir Folke Greville, Knights, John Draycote, Vincenty Moundy, Peter Leycester esquires and ----- Jackson yeomen have wrongfully entered into a parcel of the said manor [Quarnford] being within these bounds, that is to say, from Gratbach Clough ascending to Goodsichfall following the water [the Black Brook] to the Colepyttes, and ascending after the said water to Gybter House and from thence to Edders Greenhed, and so following the height of Morych to the black hole, and so following the height of blake banke descending to the water to Wylde Eeye and from thence to the three meerstones at Gamon Grenehed and so the blacke stone in Axen from thence to the Setstone in the Mosse and from the Setstone following to the three sheres at the Dane hed, and from thence descending after the water to the fall in Gratbach. They claim this said parcil of the manor of Austonfylde, and take the profits to their own use. Your orator prays that your witnesses may be examined who can prove his title to the said parcel of land. He also prays that a writ of subpena may be directed to the said Sir Humfry Bradbourne and the others.'

The dispute was probably over access to coal around the Fyrestone Brook and under Orchard Common (see Chapter 10, Three Shires Head).

Because of the work of the Ordnance Survey and ongoing research into local place-names, we can take this joint evidence and reconstruct the 16th-century manorial boundaries of the above dispute on the modern map. They prove to be almost identical to the parish and county boundaries of today's Quarnford.

Fivestones (SK028699) Axe Edge Moor.

Gratbache Clough is Great Valley – the wooded valley of the Black Brook; Goodsichfall is Goldsitch Moss; the colepyttes obviously refers to early mining here; Gybter House will be Gib Tor Farm; Edders Greenhed will be Adders Green; Morych will be the Morridge Top east of Downsdale or Roundhill and blake banke exists as Blackbank from where the stream is crossed to 'Wylde Eeye'. The farm here was Neelde Yee in 1455. It then became Needle Eye (a hole in a rock pillar?) but the letter 'N' of Needle was subsequently copied as a 'W'. Further transcriptions rendered the name as Nield Lye. The farm is now called Nield Bank. The three meerstones (boundary stones) at or near Gamon Grenehed are shown on Christopher Saxton's 1577 county map of Staffordshire. Today they are represented by one meerstone (SK 034 678) on a mound in a field south-west of Gamballs Green (Gambus Greve, 1501) behind the Travellers Rest inn at Flash, where the county boundary is picked up below Dove Head Farm.

These stones are a red herring with regard to the 'three sheres at the Dane hed' (see Chapter 10) and have a different significance. They were on the boundary between Hollinsclough and Quarnford, where a possibility exists that the boundary of Heathylee also came to this point to provide a meeting for the three townships.

The 'Setstone in the Mosse' on a later dispute map of 1673 between the Earl of Derby and Sir John Harpur, appears to be near 'the Head of the Dane where

Three Shires meet' i.e. Cheeks Hill. The 'blacke stone in Axen', which might be an unknown or missing stone near Axe Edge End, has become the Elliot Stone; a position approximating to Five Stones (SK 0259 6937) is called The Moor Stones and that of the 'meerstones' now becomes the Mare Stone!

The isolated outcrop of Fivestones north of Drystone Edge (Tristor Edge on a 16th/17th-century map) was a boundary marker in a long-running dispute from the 16th to the 19th centuries between Quarnford (in the ancient parish of Alstonefield, Staffordshire) and Hartington (Derbyshire). The largest of the stones is inscribed with the capital letters Q and H. Fivestones is however, not lost like the previously quoted 'Setstone in the Mosse'.

LOCAL MAPS

The various dotted lines shown on Ordnance Survey maps, that mark the boundaries of counties, parishes and other units of local administration, create complex patterns across the South-West Peak. This intriguing pattern has generally been a stable element in the landscape where many such boundaries are proving to be of great antiquity – in some cases, the most durable legacy from Anglo-Saxon England and perhaps earlier.

The OS One-Inch, Six-Inch and Twenty-Five-Inch series of maps published in the 19th century are invaluable tools to the local historian. They reveal the

Reef limestone hills of the Upper Dove.

local administrative boundaries in great detail, showing counties, hundreds, wapentakes (the Scandinavian equivalent of the Saxon 'hundred'), boroughs and the civil parishes that in many cases are the old manors and sometimes the traditional townships (but only where they later *became* the civil parishes). These older maps have provided the basis from which today's excellent but less detailed 1:25,000 'Explorer', 'Pathfinder' and 'Outdoor Leisure' series were produced. It is from these later maps that the Grid References throughout this book are taken.

GEOLOGY OF THE PEAK DISTRICT

The Peak District's oldest exposed rocks are sedimentary limestones from the Carboniferous Limestone series formed over 300 million years ago and deposited over a period of about 20 million years in a shallow tropical sea. The slow, persistent sedimentation of marine creatures on the sea floor created these deeply bedded limestones. Angular hills such as those east of the upper River Dove like Hollins Hill, Chrome, Parkhouse and High Wheeldon are parts of hard coral limestone reefs that formed, became buckled and were then left stranded by pressure and time.

With a change in marine conditions, tides and drainage shifted and other sediments were formed; mudstones and shales and the sandstones we now recognise as Gritstones or Millstone Grits laid down one upon another. These strata have also been subjected to pressure, faulting and erosion to leave perpendicular edges and terraces down the eastern and western sides of the National Park. Uplift and erosion in the centre of the region combined to reveal the exposed underlying limestone plateau. In between the two are dales and valleys often characterised by softer shales that have eroded far more quickly than the surrounding rock.

LOCAL GEOLOGY AND LAND USE

Apart from its limestone eastern margins, the geology of the South-West Peak is characterised by shales and sandstones – commonly called gritstones of the Millstone Grit series. These were formed from the depositions of mud and sand – part of a delta where in low swampy ground that often flooded, huge seed ferns and giant horsetails created the coal forest of the Upper Carboniferous period, named after the great coal-bearing strata. In all these rocks are found the fossilised remains of plants and simple marine and freshwater animals. It must be appreciated that due to continental drift towards the end of the Carboniferous period, Western Europe was positioned

Windgather Rocks (SJ995783).

near to the Earth's equator. Later still these gritstones were folded and tilted by gigantic earth movements to form downward dips or synclines. One such dip is called the Goyt Syncline. Today, some rivers of the area follow lines of geological weakness at the base of this syncline.

Glaciation, climate and erosion have all given the South-West Peak its particular range of landforms, soils and drainage patterns. Gritstone beds are much more impervious to water than the limestone plateau and therefore the higher landscapes are characterised by badly drained peat moorland broken up by drainage channels known as 'cloughs'. These cloughs are in turn served by minor eroded channels of 'hags' (banks) and 'groughs' (gullies). The harder gritstone outcrops have formed imposing escarpments or 'edges', such as Combs and Windgather in the north and Hen Cloud, Ramshaw Rocks and The Roaches in the south. These provide a dramatic contrast to the rolling uplands.

The landscape comprises both open and enclosed moorland, moorland fringe and settled valley pasture. Lying between the farmland of the surrounding valleys and the uplands are areas called 'intakes', where tenants have progressively enclosed and improved 'waste' adjoining their farmland, sometimes at a much earlier date than the wholesale Parliamentary Enclosures of the late 18th and early 19th

centuries. This was known as 'taking-in', hence the name 'intake' for these small-scale arrangements often undertaken by agreement between tenants and landowners. Some of these intakes are now part of the improved farmland, while others that were not sustainable have fallen out of use, their earth banks or walls left to decay.

Although we no longer associate much of this landscape with arable farming, in earlier centuries oats (the climate was too wet and cold to grow wheat), barley, rye, peas and beans were necessary and commonplace crops. In times of war, production of crops was sometimes compulsory. Below a height of 350m the soil responds well to liming and where cattle and sheep are grazed together, fertility and grassland maintenance are good. Given today's climate, cultivation and soil improvement above 350m is difficult. Coarse grasses provide only rough grazing while mosses, heather and bilberry have conspired over centuries to form acidic peat. Individual farms and whole communities have exploited these upland peat deposits as a primary source of fuel. Such areas are suitable only for sheep grazing by breeds that are adapted to the cooler climate. This grazing has prevented regeneration of trees, whilst the management of heather moors for grouse populations is still undertaken for the benefit of commercial gun sport. In general terms, this is a sparsely populated area of isolated farms, rolling hills, wild and open moorland and rushing streams, some having cut deeply through the peat and soft shales.

THE GROUSE MOORS

Because the relative value of sheep grazing as against grouse shooting materially changed, some land-owners have managed or leased their moorland for grouse shooting. This activity is still carried on today by landowners, farmers and shooting syndicates. It involves regular and controlled sheep grazing, the introduction and maintenance of artificial drainage and the periodic burning of blocks of vegetation to ensure the dominance of the tougher plant species, e.g. heather. This has ensured the retention of today's characteristic land cover, maintaining an ideal habitat for Red Grouse at the expense of biodiversity. To afford undemanding access to the butts (shooters' positions) by 'the guns', vehicle tracks have been constructed. A good example of this in the upper Goyt Valley is the track from the bottom of Goyts Lane crossing Wildmoorstone Brook and curving up into Wild Moor towards the line of butts (SK 016 745).

MODERN LANDSCAPE CHANGES

Major and significant changes were to come in the early 20th century. With rising populations and the consequent need for more drinking water, plus a demand from heavier industries as the country began to re-arm itself to face the threat of World War II, some rivers of the South-West Peak were dammed to create reservoirs. This has resulted in the enclosed land of the watersheds becoming permanent pasture, some of which is slowly reverting to moorland at its upper margins. Some hillsides that had been treeless since prehistory have been planted with huge blocks of alien conifers where, today, old buildings and walls show that such land was formerly farmed. Some of these farmsteads were abandoned and remain as poignant ruins. Others were demolished entirely due to the demands of water supply and the then perceived need to keep streams free of pollution from domestic and farm effluent, prohibition being placed on the keeping of any animals other than sheep. Water-gathering grounds that have been depopulated this way include 1,000 acres around Lamaload Reservoir by 1964, the large area around the twin reservoirs of Fernilee and Errwood in the upper Goyt Valley by 1938 and 1967 respectively and, by 1929, an

area around Trentabank Reservoir a few kilometres to the south-west. Sadly, this resulted in the families that had lived and worked here for generations being cruelly uprooted and scattered.

During the latter part of the 20th century, and increasingly today because of ongoing changes in agricultural emphases and the rise of conservation initiatives, many farms have been made into residences only, with the land being either sold or leased to neighbouring farmers. In the past, farmers helped their neighbours, pooling labour and equipment for sowing and harvesting. Nowadays, there is an increased loss of traditional countryside where many farms are run on a part-time basis and few people are seen working in the fields except at haymaking.

THE AXE EDGE WATERSHED

Receiving an average of over 140cm of rain a year, Axe Edge Moor, with its summit at 551m, is one of the major watersheds of England and the source of five rivers. The River Dove rises at Dove Head below the A53 Buxton to Leek road where, just to the south, the River Manifold rises near Flash Head. Both rivers drain to the south to flow eventually into the River Trent and the North Sea. The River Goyt, rising in the grits and shales just south of the Cat and Fiddle Inn, flows north through Whaley Bridge and Stockport, collecting the rivers Tame and Etherow before turning west into the Irish Sea as the mighty Mersey. The River Dane springs from the very heart of the moor and is joined by the Clough Brook, which collects waters from the Stake Clough and Wildboar-clough areas, to meander slowly westwards onto the Cheshire plain towards the River Weaver. The River Wye rises above Cold Springs Farm near the B5004 and also on the Axe Edge watershed above Burbage. These combine and flow through Buxton before turning eastwards towards Ashford and Bakewell through the deep limestone gorge.

AXE EDGE MOOR AND ITS ROADS

During the 18th and 19th centuries the relatively isolated small town of Buxton became transformed by an improved roads network created by Turnpike Trusts – each Trust empowered to charge tolls on specified lengths of road and borrow money for their maintenance and improvement. This book describes the development of these roads through the town and across the South-West Peak, providing communication with the large industrial towns of Manchester and Stockport and the smaller industrial towns of Macclesfield, Leek and Congleton. Also described are route changes brought about by increased traffic, the tolls and tollgates, some of the financial problems and the development of transport methods from the packhorse to the arrival of the railways (see Chapter 18).

The Axe Edge and Goyts Moss moorland west of the town of Buxton was to present many difficulties to the turnpike road builders. There is severe weather exposure, steep-sided valleys and the headwaters of rivers in peat up to 2m deep. They could either dig down to bedrock or float the foundations on bundles of wood or heather. The early turnpike builder John Metcalf used the latter technique on some of his road constructions, as had the Romans many centuries earlier. The Leek and Buxton turnpike had to cross a ridge at 500m. Both the earlier and the later versions of the Macclesfield and Buxton turnpike reached 510m at the position now occupied by the Cat and Fiddle Inn, with the Congleton and Buxton turnpike crossing Axe Edge Moor at 475m. Tolls could be charged for the maintenance and improvement of these roads that were built primarily in response to pressures on an increasingly outmoded packhorse system struggling to meet demands for the local mineral resources, particularly lime and coal. Small-scale mining of coal for domestic fuel and casual limeburning for agricultural improvement were to be increasingly undertaken on a new commercial basis. The huge requirement for agricultural lime created during this period was matched by a need for lime mortars for the building of new houses and factories, and lime for a new chemical industry. Rising demands for stone for building, for enclosure walls, paving, road surfaces and railtrack ballast, provoked increased development of those quarries that were accessible by the turnpikes and some, later, by the railways.

The principal landowners in the study area were the Earls of Derby, the Harpur (later Harpur-Crewe) family and the Dukes of Devonshire. From the 1780s, the large Devonshire estate was using the enormous profits from its Ecton copper mine to develop the village of Buxton into a 'spa' to rival Bath, thus increasing the need for all these raw materials and for an efficient transport system to enable the leisured classes to come to Buxton and 'take the waters'. The rapid development of the town would not have been possible without the improved access provided by these roads. With its fine hotels, pump rooms, assembly rooms, coffee shops, reading rooms, clubs and, later, twin railway stations, Buxton was to become a town where the fashionable aristocracy of the late 18th and 19th centuries could spend the summer season.

THE OLD ROUTE NAMES

The current classification of roads, tracks and paths – some public, some concessionary, some private and others merely traditional – is outside the requirement of this guide but their older names are interesting. The Anglo-Saxon settlers used the word *straet* (street) from the Latin term *via strata* (paved road) to describe Roman roads – but the translation is only sound when in association with a *major* settlement-name *on or near* a Roman road. For less important routes, the more general word *way* from the Old English *weg* was used. It is still in use in such words as byway, wayfarer, right of way, and to 'ask the way'. Roads are sometimes referred to in Saxon charters as *heiweg*, a highway, *haehstraet*, obviously high street, and *portweg*, a portage way to market and, by an extension of meaning, any great thoroughfare.

The Scandinavian settlers of northern England used the Old Norse *gate* or *gata* to mean an opening, or any type of road or track. The names of many old routes in the Peak District include the element 'gate', e.g. Cut Gate, Torgate, Gun Gate, Stoney Gate and Chapel Gate. The very similar Old English *geat* was a word that meant a bar or barrier that could be opened. The word *lane*, which usually denoted a less important track enclosed by woods or fields, was in use by the 13th century. These were sometimes named after the traders who used them or their occupations. Some lanes acquired descriptive names like Back Lane, High Lane, Long Lane and Dirty Lane. The new word *road* seldom appeared in local documentation before the 17th century and even now has not entirely replaced the usage of the former names. It might have become popular after John Ogilby's atlas *Britannia* was published in 1675 (see Chapter 18). Long, straight roads are rare, perhaps either Roman or medieval in origin, or else have followed the lines of boundary walls at the time of formal enclosure. As a general rule, the wider a road the more recent it is, although some older roads have been subsequently widened.

Chapter 2. PREHISTORY

EARLY HABITATION

There have probably been people in the Peak District for the last half-million years or so, early populations retreating and advancing with the movements of ice sheets across several ice ages and warmer intervals. Neanderthals and other early Stone Age, or Palaeolithic, people, travelled in small nomadic groups. They made temporary camps in caves but more commonly out in the open, from where they searched out and hunted the migrating herds of horse, bison and reindeer. The best evidence for these hunter-gatherers comes from caves, where we find long-bladed flint tools and the bone fragments of both animals and people who had either been brought to the caves as the prey of carnivores, were temporary occupants, or had briefly sheltered.

In the Cresswell Crags gorge near Worksop, Nottinghamshire, what is believed to be the first Ice Age figurative cave art (we already had carvings on bone) to be found in Britain was revealed in 2003. The strikingly powerful engravings, some in bas-relief, including bison, horses, bears, deer and water birds, were cut into the walls and roofs of the caves. They are thought to be between 13,000 and 14,000 years old, sometime towards the end of the last ice age, and can be dated stylistically to the same period as continental cave art. The engravings may have been of particular significance to the prehistoric people of the area, perhaps creating an intimate relationship with the animals they hunted. This site, on the very edge of the Peak District at the very limits of the ice sheets, is currently the most northerly place on earth where such cave art has been found.

THE MESOLITHIC PERIOD (10,000–4,500 BC)

Following the end of the last major glacial episode about 10,000 years ago, the tundra belt comprising alpine species such as dwarf birch and juniper retreated north after the glaciers and was replaced by thick forests. Worked stone fragments, small local chert arrow barbs and a few flint blades from further afield are the only dateable evidence of these later, Mesolithic people. These small groups adapted to dramatic changes in the environment by adopting new hunting strategies to follow the movement of animals and birds to supplement their largely vegetarian diet of berries, roots and nuts. They appear to have settled briefly at differing locations in temporary camps that were perhaps seasonal or occupied during short-term food-gathering trips, where they may have held meetings and ceremonies.

THE FIRST SETTLERS, THE NEOLITHIC FARMERS (4,500–2,000 BC)

As the ice caps melted, the 'land bridge' between what we term the British Isles and the Continent was finally broken around 8,000 BC. Until that happened, communities ranged freely back and forth in step with the cycles of warmer and colder conditions. With climate changes and perhaps a landscape that now supported less game, traditional hunting strategies became unsustainable, leading to the gradual adoption of farming and settlement by these people from around 4,500 BC.

Stone tools, either lost or discarded, are the most common evidence of these people and although such tools are found throughout the region wherever soils have been disturbed, evidence for Neolithic activity here in the South-West Peak may well be under-represented. Nevertheless, Neolithic local settlers established a community on a shelf of land recently known as the Lismore Fields, an area west of Buxton below the Burbage ridge. Their settlement, discovered in the 1980s, provided dramatic confirmation that Neolithic activity was not confined to the limestone plateau. The settlement was near to a spring and stream, the River Wye, where rare evidence of rectangular buildings with central hearths was revealed. Stone tools, flakes from a polished Cumbrian axe, plain but well-made Grimston Ware pottery and some traces of the settlers' crops and diet radiocarbon dated to around 3,500 BC was also unearthed. Using fire and axes, the community would have created clearings in the surrounding forest for crops and for herding domesticated animals whose grazing prevented forest regrowth. Chert and flints were fashioned into a variety of sharp tools and weapons for hunting. Because fine-grained stone for polished axes, and

The Bull Ring, Dove Holes.

flints to make superior tools and weapons, did not occur naturally near their area, these people, or individuals within the group, were exchanging items with neighbouring groups. This is a surprisingly effective method of trade where items can travel hundreds of miles in a few months. A Late Neolithic flint thumb-scraper together with production waste was found in the upper Goyt Valley in 2003. Scatters of flintwork from the Late Mesolithic period may indicate occupation of the Lismore Fields site at an even earlier date. The settlement site is now covered by a modern housing estate.

In the Late Neolithic period (2,500–2,000 BC), indicating collective will and cooperation at tribal level, the dramatic 90m-diameter henge monument at Dove Holes (SK 079 783) known as The Bull Ring was created. It remains a near-circular construction of stone and earth banks with internal ditches and two causewayed entrances; very similar both in size and design to the Arbor Low monument south of Monyash but robbed of any stone settings in the 18th century. Local communities and perhaps others from the wider region, travelling in from their settlements on a variety of convenient connecting routes, would have gathered at this very important site. Quarries, sports fields, a cemetery and the village of Dove Holes now surround the henge.

THE BRONZE AGE (2,000–800 BC)

During the Bronze Age, the basic economy of herding and tillage continued but now in a more sustained way. This was the time of the introduction of the smelting of useful metallic ores, particularly bronze, an alloy of nine parts copper to one of tin. The ores are not found everywhere and the knowledge required to work them is complex. Tin, for example, does not occur anywhere in the Peak District. Nineteenth-century antiquarian digging and recent archaeological surveys point to early copper ore extraction in nearby mines at Ecton in Staffordshire and at Alderley Edge in Cheshire, where stone mining hammers and bone picks have been linked to Bronze Age activity. Recent investigations in the Ecton copper mines has revealed evidence of a digging tool made from an antler tine radiocarbon dated to the early Bronze Age, indicating that these miners were able to follow the brightly coloured copper minerals deep underground. To remove hard rock, they would have used fire setting, whose basic application involves burning wood fires against the rock face, causing it to weaken. In some cases sudden water quenching may have been used to increase the heat-fracturing effect. Rock could then be removed by exploiting any fracture weakness to prise out the heat-shattered fragments. The rock around the copper mineral was then laboriously removed with stone hammers and anvils and the mineral fragments sorted out into a concentrate for further treatment. Although such evidence for prehistoric copper smelting in Britain is rare, it is possible that in many instances the final production of copper took place well away from the mines.

There is a similar lack of evidence for bronze smelting sites in the Peak District. It may be that ores, metals or tools were being traded and/or bronze artefacts found here were imported from elsewhere in Britain, reflecting the broader webs of contact and communication. Bronze swords and axes were often utilised for tokens of prestige. Such items could be decorated, placed in graves, or, if necessary, reworked. Materials such as flint, however, were highly efficient and durable, were cheap to produce and were used extensively well into the late Iron Age, by which time iron had replaced bronze as the most important metal in the manufacture of tools and weapons.

During the Bronze Age, the local people built their round barrows containing the bones of their ancestors, some on the summits of the South-West Peak's western-facing hills. These monuments, many surviving like beacons in the more recent landscape, proclaim 'this land is taken'.

Standing Stones and Burial Mounds

Few, if any, barrows or stone circles were built after 1500 BC. Although stone circles associated with the Bronze Age period are as yet undiscovered in the South-West Peak, there are a small number of standing stones erected singly, called 'monoliths'. These may have been used to mark territorial boundaries and trackways, although they may have had a religious function. Some standing stones may have been erected during the Neolithic Period and many were probably erected much later. Virtually nothing is known of any underlying beliefs that might be associated with either the impressive henges or the standing stones. There are scheduled Bronze Age burial mounds on hilltops at many places in the South-West Peak.

Bronze Age standing stone — 'The Murder Stone', (SJ98438110).

THE IRON AGE

In Britain, the Iron Age dates from c.800 BC and is characterised by the emergence of regional tribal kingdoms and the use of iron, overlapping at first with Bronze Age traditions. The iron ores were usually mined by the opencast method and smelted in bowl or shaft furnaces using greater heat than had been necessary for bronze. Iron then rapidly replaced bronze for all kinds of usage – especially tools and weapons. The Iron Age is now considered to end after the Roman invasion in AD 43, but with its traditions persisting long after this date. In the Peak District the climate was deteriorating, becoming cooler and wetter, and any exposed farming communities and fields at the edges of the gritstone moors were abandoned. Although archaeological evidence for prehistoric individual settlements beyond the Bronze Age had once proved elusive, we now know that the Gardom's Edge settlement (centred at SK 275 730) and, by inference, many others on the Peak District's Eastern Moors, span both the Bronze Age and much of the Iron Age. At these locations during this period, there was an increase in the visibility and intensity of farming, with pottery finds of the same type as those found at the Mam Tor hilltop enclosure.

Immediately south of Taxal in the comparatively sheltered upper Goyt Valley, there is just the possibility that areas of small irregular walled fields still in use today may indicate an Iron Age or Romano-British farming presence – firstly the seasonal herders and then more sustained farming. However, the only obvious and certain physical reminder today of any prehistoric farming in the whole of the South-West Peak is the wide scatter of burial mounds.

HILLTOP ENCLOSURES (HILLFORTS)

From the Iron Age period in the Peak District, there are the nine hilltop enclosures, the so-called 'hillforts'. They are difficult to understand because lack of archaeological evidence hides much of the chronology and character of their use. Many have their origins in the final stages of the Bronze Age, persisting until the first millennium AD and the Iron Age. Some may be older. These enigmatic constructions seem to represent two themes: Settlement and Defence.

Many hillforts did witness sporadic occupation but this was extremely varied – many have had little or no occupation at all. Some were large, others small, some may have held buildings – these variations suggesting that they were obviously not used in the same ways or over the same time. Hillforts were constructed in some landscapes that were already settled, providing a focus for a wider community rather than a centre for the elite or dominant. Perhaps they were established in places that had a history of gatherings – people meeting for reasons of trade, to renew kinships, to make agreements or settle disputes. Perhaps these dramatic monuments were a constant reminder of the broader social pattern.

A LOCAL HILLFORT, CASTLE NAZE

In common with the other hillforts, the promontory enclosure of Castle Naze on Combs Moss (SK 054 785) at the edge of the study area is assumed to have had a number of construction phases. It relied on natural steep defence around much of its perimeter, whilst at its point of weakness on the land-mass side, it has a man-made defence in the form of a double rampart and ditch. These astonishing earthworks, which make such a bold visible statement, certainly suggest inter-group tensions at some time and the need to construct a refuge against the threat of physical attack. However, as with other Peak District hillforts, evidence of attack or destruction is either flimsy or absent.

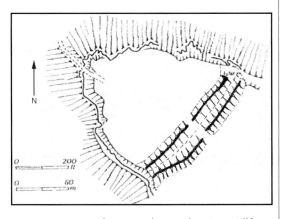

Castle Naze, The Combs Moss Hillfort.

Castle Naze itself is approached by a deep hollow-way leading up to the entrance at the north-east end of the ramparts. From its hairpin turn, because of shallower soil eroded to bedrock in places, the final rising 100 metres of the hollow-way has become less pronounced. The narrow, flattened terraced appearance may have been made by the boots of modern walkers anxious both to view the fort and to avoid the wet, rushy bottom of the final part of the climb.

The excavated central breach of the large earth banks may have been a defendable, gated way through to wider pasture for valuable cattle or horses held within the enclosure long before the climate deteriorated. A recent archaeological survey proposes this central breach to have been used as a through-route by post-medieval pack teams arriving through the north-east entrance. Although this might imply some evidence of passage both on the moor and within the enclosure itself, very little is apparent. With the exception of a group of sub-circular stone-getting pits near the promontory point, the interior is a feature-less grassy triangle of about two acres. At 440m above sea level the enclosure holds a magnificent situation on a gritstone headland and remains largely uninvestigated (see plan).

What little amount of excavation there has been at these Peak District hilltop sites is leading to suggestions that a few had been abandoned by 500 BC. Some will retain the buried remains of such features as workshops, hearths, querns, storage pits and the postholes and foundations of buildings. In 1873, Romano-British pottery and an early 4th-century AD coin of Emperor Constantine were found at Castle Naze.

PREHISTORIC TRAVEL

Many travel routes created by prehistoric people have been surmised. A simple, general term for what would have become, over many centuries, a complex network of such routes would be 'trackways'.

The truth is that despite much speculation, we do not have any real clues as to the location of prehistoric trackways. Suggestions that have been made usually fall into the speculative category – perhaps based on unwarranted assumptions as to the nature of trade and travel at that time. A few routes would have been travelled widely but where they went is totally open at a regional scale. For long-distance travel, however, it is clear that people found it easier to travel by boat along coastlines and the larger rivers. From Neolithic times onwards, for example, we can find many specific cultural links along the western seaboard from Scotland to Cornwall. These overshadow any links east–west across land where early travel across virgin territory, much of it thick forest, would have been unimaginably difficult. In hilly districts such as the South-West Peak it is likely that any trackways were confined by topography rather than precise direction; travellers perhaps using convenient ridgeways to provide a clear unobstructed view of the ongoing route and then dropping down to easier and more sheltered ways picked out in the first place by herds of animals either migrating, pursued, or driven from one grazing ground to another. Subsequent routes, including those of the medieval period, probably followed these unplanned but convenient tracks but little documentary evidence exists.

The route chosen by a nomadic band of Stone Age hunters and that by a later packhorse carrier may have been quite different but would have had a common link. That link would have been the need to find the easiest route, given that the topography was known and the local weather could be roughly predicted. A dry valley floor or a terraced way along a scarp slope above the floodplain appears to have been generally preferred by men and animals over thousands of years.

Those who have walked along The Tors ridge overlooking the Todd Brook valley between Shining Tor (SJ 995 738) and Pym Chair, when the prevailing westerly has 'some north in it', will appreciate why the packhorse trains followed a sheltered route, creating hollow-ways along the east-facing flank of this airy crest. The fine aesthetic qualities of today's ridge footpath would have held little appeal for these traders and carriers.

WAYMARKERS

Nothing for certain is known about any waymarkers used by prehistoric people as aids to travel. Any existing markers will inevitably be from differing periods, some undoubtedly going back to prehistory but perhaps no longer recognisable as such. Here and there across the landscape, tall, hoary old solitary stone pillars, some pierced by holes for rustic poles, still provoke controversial explanations for their presence. Were some originally ancient 'standing stones', or are they merely the survivors from pairs of old, roughly cut gateposts separated by necessity and the arrival of wider, mechanised farm machinery? We would need to know whether this stone pillar was manufactured as a gatepost or is second-hand. Might an old route itself be a landscape feature that subsequently had a stone marker erected alongside it or was the old track heading for the marker?

To obtain raw materials for the manufacture of tools and weapons, prehistoric people would have found it necessary to travel considerable distances to either seek out or trade the chert and flints and, later, the metallic ores for smelting. Any waymarkers they may have used would have been of limited use. Only local groups would have known their meaning – strangers might see the signs but were unlikely to have realised their importance.

Topographical features are likely to have been used as 'signposts'. These would have been given names suggesting their shape, size or individual significance. A few of the origins of these names will have come down to us from as far back as the native Britons, while many can be traced to Anglo-Saxon and, to a lesser extent in the Peak District, the Scandinavian settlers. With the further incursion of people of Scandinavian origins (the Normans) into Britain in 1066 – this time by people who no longer spoke Norse – we now find occasional place-names having their origins in a dialect of French such as a remnant of the phrase *en le*, as in Chapel-en-le-Frith.

Although some major overland routes across England had evolved in the Iron Age, it was not until the arrival of a Roman road network that lengthy journeys could have been made with any great confidence. Tax collectors, troops and wealthy families might undertake such journeys but most people were tied to their settlements. Because later Saxon and medieval societies had a less developed idea of national communications, they would have used what remained of the Roman network and any local tracks, all of which were susceptible to the vagaries of the climate. At a local level in the South-West Peak, the late-Saxon pillar crosses may have given some guidance.

Gatepost or Standing Stone?
Farmland west of Combs Moss.

Chapter 3. INVASION AND SETTLEMENT

INTRODUCTION

Julius Caesar had led military expeditions into Britain in 55 and 54 BC and there had been some contacts with the Roman world, mainly through trade. Britain was successfully invaded by the Romans in AD 43. They were the first invaders of Britain to document their occupation and from this time historians have access to a written history about these islands with references to specific tribes and specific places including the Peak District – although they remain, of course, an invader's view. Throughout the whole Roman period, this written history is episodic and patchy and therefore we cannot reconstruct society on the basis of it. The invasion is now seen to have been exploitative and brutal; suppressing the identities of the peoples it conquered, portraying them as ignorant savages – which clearly they were not. The Britons had sophisticated iron weapons, tools and well-developed wheeled vehicles, while their artists and craftsmen could compete with anything offered by the ancient world. Many aspects of Iron Age/Romano-British life would have continued right through to post-Roman times.

ROMAN OCCUPATION OF THE PEAK DISTRICT

The Peak District may have come under permanent Roman occupation around AD 80, sometime during Agricola's campaign against a tribal people of the area, the Brigantes. Control apparently came quickly and one suspects that the accepted image of the *pax Romana* may well be a very distorted one. There was no uniformity of Roman occupation, so we can only speculate about its overall impact on the region. It was a new order that would have worked to the advantage of a few and to the detriment of most.

The Peak District's Roman military forts were part of a wider network frequently sited to control communication routes. These forts were linked by roads and were often to acquire local civil settlements or *vici*, arranged around them to support the military. Initially, forts were constructed of earth and turf ramparts, with palisading, gates and towers in timber, although from the late 1st century these were replaced by stone. We know little in detail but the establishment of auxiliary forts and dependent *vici* of *Navio* at Brough-on-Noe (c.AD 75) and *Ardotalia* at Glossop (c.AD 78), for example, may well be what we would recognise as urban. This represented a new way of living, although beyond the influence of the *vicus* there would probably be continuity of tribal life where local farmers now had to pay taxes, either in kind or in the new coinage. The Brough and Glossop forts (with others in the wider region) were abandoned by the military at various points in the 2nd century during the Antonine campaigns and occupation in southern Scotland, at which time the total garrison of Britain peaked at about 30,000 men. The reoccupation of the Brough fort in the mid-late 2nd century, perhaps to provide military supervision of the lead industry, marked the onset of continuous occupation through to the mid-late 4th century, although its *vicus* only remained continuously occupied from establishment up to the mid-3rd century. The Glossop *vicus* was deserted when the Ardotalia fort was abandoned – and remained so.

Primary reasons for Roman occupation of the Peak District were: (a) to further the imperial ambitions of Emperor Claudius by subjugating the British as the legions pushed north; and (b) to exploit the region's agricultural potential and mineral wealth including copper, silver, coal and lead. Lead in particular appears to have been in demand, extraction and processing perhaps operating as a dual economy with farming for a few communities. Silver, sometimes associated with lead ore, was used in Roman coinage. Lead from Wirksworth, Carsington (and possibly Brough-on-Noe) was an export item, ingots having been found close to the Roman port of Petuaria, now Brough-on-Humber. The Derbyshire ingots or 'pigs' of lead stamped with the Roman letters *LVT* or *LVTVD*, or in one case *LVTVDARES*, are thought to represent a shortened name-form of the documented *Lutudarum*, the so-called Roman lead administrative centre of the area, possibly near Carsington although the site is now lost. The lead would have been shipped from Petuaria to other coastal centres and exported out across the Empire.

ROMAN BUXTON

The Romans would have been attracted to Buxton because it potentially represents a civilian settlement that developed around a Romano/Celtic religious cult centred upon natural hot and cold springs. Today, the Georgian Crescent building probably covers the site of the Roman baths. In this area during the 17th and 18th centuries discoveries were made of lead-lined baths, red plaster and building remains in the sediments which surround the area of St Anne's well. In the 18th century, a structure was found which has been interpreted as a probable classical temple – one of only three known from Britain. This lends tangible support to the interpretation of Buxton as the 'Bath of the North'.

The overall character and extent of civilian settlement, and whether this was in association with a military installation or not, remains obscure. Archaeological fieldwork over the last two decades at suggested locations in the town, including excavations on and around the Silverlands plateau and at Mill Cliff, has failed to establish a long-speculated military installation, suggesting that if this Roman settlement identified as *Aquae Arnimetiae* (c.AD 75) had a fort, it was located elsewhere.

Any further remains of *Aquae Arnimetiae* still lie under the modern town. The Roman name 'Aquae' denotes a spring; 'Arnimetiae', the local Celtic goddess Arnimetia, is a name meaning 'of the sacred grove'. Roman civilians left abundant evidence of their appreciation of Buxton's thermal waters. Offerings to deities dating from the 1st to the 4th centuries, including bronze bracelets, lead tablets and over 200 coins, are displayed in a reconstructed shrine in Buxton Museum.

ROMANO-BRITISH SETTLEMENT

Although permanent domestic settlement during the Roman period was mainly in typical Iron Age circular or ovoid huts (roundhouses), caves probably fulfilled a variety of roles in the context of Romano-British life. Archaeological investigation of over twenty caves in the Peak District, most on the limestone plateau, has revealed evidence of an essentially domestic (perhaps seasonal) function or occupation; a few have additional metalworking refuse. Evidence from some caves, however, lends support to the interpretation of these as rural shrines or sanctuaries – mysterious 'places apart' to be visited where votive offerings could be deposited. Some fissure caves appear to have been a focus for burial.

At the public show cave, Poole's Cavern, Buxton,

archaeological material recovered suggests some Bronze Age and Iron Age occupation. However, the majority of the finds point to human usage between the late 1st and 3rd centuries, during which time Roman Buxton, which may have been a local market centre, was likely to have been a major attraction for troops and traders in north-west England. Finds indicate that bronze-working was practised within Poole's Cavern or nearby. Some finds may have been stored here but worked elsewhere. Evidence also survives of lead-casting by the 'lost wax' method. The cave material recovered and recorded does not indicate that cave occupants were shepherds or peasants – in fact many of the finds of pottery, glass, iron, lead and bronze reflect Roman tastes and access to quality products. Such finds include manicure sets, brooches, fine pins, wine jars, Samian tableware, needles, nails, spindle whorls, bangles, rings, earrings, buckles, knives and spear heads. Recent interpretation of the site suggests it to have been essentially domestic but with additional refuse from metalworkers' activities.

The Romano-British rural populations of the Peak District are likely to have been descendants of people living in the region during later prehistory. Mixed farming, perhaps with an emphasis on pasturing, was the dominant type of community that may have been largely indifferent or unreceptive to Roman civil culture. Their experience was perhaps one of Roman military culture. The mining of lead does not seem to have influenced the distribution of any early Romano-British rural settlement or colonisation of the Peak District, nor is there any evidence that the search for lead or of smelting sites was a governing factor in any subsequent settlement locations. There are in fact perilously few secure instances where Roman mining of lead can actually be demonstrated. As with the coal mining, those areas that attracted the Romano-British lead miner probably attracted medieval and later miners for the same reasons – ease of access and quality.

During a recent archaeological survey (1998–2000) where over 140 known or potential Romano-British settlement sites were recorded, 22 sites are considered to be definitely Roman in date while another 61 are probably Roman by comparison with the dated sites.

The nature of the settlements varies from isolated buildings to nucleated 'villages'. Animal bones found at these sites indicate that sheep, goats and cattle were reared and the households, communities and fields were all defined by boundaries, sometimes walls built on larger stones known as orthostats.

With the exception of one settlement site in Wildboarclough in the study area, a few north of Bamford and others on the eastern fringe of the Peak National Park, all on the gritstone margins, the majority of the sites are on the southern half of the limestone plateau. They are on land that is now seen as 'marginal', most favouring a southerly aspect near to running water. Of the 22 sites definitely dated to the Romano-British period, 20 are sites that may also have earlier or later occupational histories.

Immediately east of Buxton along the River Wye are three of these sites. The Chee Tor field system (which can be comfortably viewed from the Millers Dale to Wormhill road) at SK 127 732; the Burrs well-preserved nucleated settlement at Chelmorton (SK 106 714); and the site at Cow Low (SK 101 727) with its field systems and building platforms, are all near public footpaths. Closer visits might be arranged by asking permission from landowners.

All these sites on the limestone appear to be only a fragment of the original extent of Romano-British settlement and potentially more settlements lie hidden under existing villages, farmsteads and pasture fields. This absence may be due simply to lack of archaeological fieldwork.

The traditional use of the study area landscape, especially for grazing sheep – probably from as early as the Bronze Age – will not have escaped the notice of the Roman administration. Indeed, the Romano-British settlement earthwork of 40m x 36m at SJ 989 693 in Wildboarclough suggests that other such sites are yet to be discovered.

ROMAN ROADS

Even before the Roman invasion, Britain was criss-crossed by thousands of miles of trackways. Many of these were to local destinations but there were also long-distance routes. The Romans would no doubt use some of these prehistoric trackways, although there is no proven contemporary use of any in the study area – the precise routes are in any case difficult to determine. Map and place-name evidence can sometimes indicate a general line.

Initially planned as fast military roads to enable the legions to move quickly to suppress trouble anywhere in their newly conquered territories, the major Roman roads were laid out by surveyors and engineers. Roman roads carried troops, goods, and, equally important, information. Because of these strategic considerations, except where the terrain made this impractical or for example where they wished to take advantage of a particular river crossing, Roman military roads were built in straight sections between sighting points, some echoed in major routes today. Alongside the hundreds of miles of Roman roads there were also many thousands of miles of less well-constructed minor connecting roads, some surviving from before the Roman conquest, others no doubt created in response to changing needs during the occupation.

FORDS AND BRIDGES

Despite having introduced the semicircular arch, the Romans left no surviving arched road bridges in Britain although occasional Roman riverbank abutments have survived to form springing for a later-constructed arch. It is assumed that as an occupying power they would have mainly utilised shallow fording points, finding bridges perhaps too vulnerable but building these where there was no practical alternative. Any such bridges were probably constructed either in stone or wood, or as a wooden roadway supported on stone piers. Where rivers were wide, ferries were used.

PEAK DISTRICT ROMAN ROADS

Only well-authenticated stretches of Roman roads are described. The pattern of Roman communication roads in highland areas, including the north and west of Britain, is uncertain and it therefore seems likely that many of the Peak District Roman roads were less substantial in construction, perhaps most being unmetalled tracks that received attention only when the need arose. Undoubtedly some Roman roads fell into disuse but, on the other hand, many will have survived in part, with later diversions to take account of new economic realities. Many sections of Roman road have of course been ploughed out or lost either through erosion or burial under peat and may never be proven.

BUXTON TO BROUGH-ON-NOE

Short stretches of road between the settlement at Buxton and the fort called Navio at Brough-on-Noe follow the course of a Roman road subsequently named Batham Gate and referred to in 1400 as 'the road to the Baths'. In 1572, a Dr Jones described the road as 'an high way forced over the moors, all paved, of such antiquity as none can express called Bathgate'. From its junction with the A6, 2km south of Dove Holes, sections of a route, although interrupted through heavily quarried areas, can be followed towards Bradwell Moor as low banks across fields and along modern minor roads through Peak Dale, Small Dale and Dam Dale. The final approach to the Brough-on-Noe fort at the confluence of the River Noe and the Bradwell Brook remains unproven, as does the likely alignment of an ongoing road to Templeborough to the east of Sheffield.

'THE STREET', DERBY TO MANCHESTER (VIA BUXTON)

This Roman road, the most prominent one across the Peak District, is presumed to be from Little Chester or *Derventio* (Derby) to *Mamucium* (Manchester) via Brassington and Buxton. Although the first known documentary evidence of the name, 'Le Streate', occurs in 1415, the name may have been in common use for centuries. The road is described below as two sections.

SECTION 1. DERBY TO BUXTON

The course of the 18km of The Street north of Derby is still uncertain but from Brassington northwards towards Buxton, with the exception of a 2-mile diversion at Pomeroy (SK 118 677) to avoid the steep gradients of Sterndale Moor, the modern Ashbourne to Buxton A515 closely shadows straight sections of The Street along the watershed between the Dove and the Wye. Parts of the present-day county and parish boundaries, not all of which will be unaltered from the formation of the parishes, can also be seen to coincide with, or closely follow, the line of the Roman road. Just north of Brierlow Bar, The Street continues to Buxton, parallel to the A515 and a field's width west. To enable the known course of The Street to be followed easily, the 1:25,000 OS White Peak map conveniently shows the current administrative boundaries, often following the 'Roman Road' for many miles and depicting it with the appropriate pecked lines. Clearly, where a parish boundary follows a Roman road, its present line is most likely to postdate the construction of the road. This line also looks to have provided the Parliamentary Commissioners in the late 18th/early 19th century with a convenient 'enclosures' boundary between communities.

The alignment of 'The Street.' north of Buxton.

SECTION 2. BUXTON TO MANCHESTER

Leaving Buxton to the north-west, the alignment of The Street is picked up beyond Cold Springs Farm (SK 044 745) as a narrow tarmacked lane flanked by hollow-ways leaving the A5004. From here the lane, marked as 'Roman Road' on current OS maps, surely represents a rationalisation of this route when it was improved and turnpiked between Whaley Bridge and Buxton in 1724 (see Chapter 18).

At the White Hall Centre the old hollow-ways of The Street diverge to the west of the turnpike but can be picked up again climbing a steep bank at SK 028 765 to a boundary wall. Beyond this wall they almost disappear across improved pasture but reappear in steep rough grassland west of Hanging Rock (Hanging Stone 1640) situated at SK 027 767. The actual line of the Roman road is of course uncertain but may well follow Elnor Lane into Shallcross. From Shallcross the line of the final 22km section of The Street is thought to remain west of the A6, eventually climbing through Whaley Bridge to follow Longside on the eastern contours of Black Hill and then on to Disley, Hazel Grove, Stockport and Manchester.

BROUGH-ON-NOE TO GLOSSOP

A Roman road linked the forts of *Navio* at Brough and *Ardotalia* at Glossop. A direct line between the forts is blocked by the bulk of Kinder Scout so the Roman surveyors are likely to have used the Noe and Woodlands valleys, crossing lower terrain north of the main hill mass at the head of the Snake Pass. The old paved route to Glossop (Doctor's Gate) still in evidence here is no longer considered to be Roman in origin.

Large proportions of the Roman road will be lost either through erosion and landslip or will have disappeared under the peat. The probable alignment of other sections of this road are indicated on the current Peak District OS Dark Peak map as 'Roman Road'.

A ROMAN ROAD FROM BUXTON TO THE SOUTH-WEST?

Apart from some road-straightening at Upper Hulme and Cisterns Clough, the present Leek to Buxton (A53) road follows exactly the line of the late-18th-century Leek and Buxton turnpike. The current OS map, however, shows a straight section of this road (popularly thought to be making for the auxiliary fort at Chesterton, Staffs.) as 'Roman Road', but this is unlikely. Much of the A53 runs through unimproved moorland and the complete absence of adjacent linear hollows indicating *any* ancient or previous route along this line has always suggested that the turnpike was an entirely new cut.

A ROMAN ROAD FROM BUXTON TO THE WEST?

An old road (Goyts Lane) branches north-west from the A5004 above Longhill Farm at SK 032 752. From where it emerges from the drowned hamlet of Goytsbridge (SK 012 756) in the upper Goyt Valley it is known as 'The Street' and runs with old braided hollow-ways towards Pym Chair, with the highest portion that crosses boggy ground shown on the 1880 six-inch OS map as 'Embridge Causeway'.

The name 'Street' has resulted in suggestions that this was an alternative alignment of the Roman 'Street' from Derby to Manchester, where from Pym Chair it perhaps forded the Todd Brook before ascending the tortuous Bank Lane (known locally as The Corkscrew) aiming for Rainow and Bollington (see Chapter 9). 'Street', however, was a word used in medieval times to denote a road of some importance but not necessarily one of Roman origin (see introduction to this chapter). A detailed archaeological field survey completed in 1994 suggests 'The Street' across the upper Goyt Valley to be 'probably medieval'. No evidence has been produced to suggest that a Roman road ever ran westwards from Buxton.

MILESTONES

Records for the Roman period can often reveal references to major roads across their empire having large cylindrical stones placed at mile intervals. Some of these stones were uninscribed; others gave route distances and occasionally a dedication now often illegible. Not surprisingly, given the relatively less developed societies that ensued, very few remain *in situ*. Buxton museum has what may be the lower portion of a Roman guidepost or milestone found in 1856 in a garden at Silverlands near the old Upper Buxton Railway Station and displaying the word *ANAVIO*. However, no other milestones have been found for certain anywhere in the Peak District, suggesting that either such roads were of relatively minor importance or that Roman milestones have yet to be unearthed. The 1994 OS map of Roman Britain gives a national tally of 37 milestones. There are no Peak District milestones depicted on the current edition of this map.

ROMAN WITHDRAWAL

Faced with continuing tribal unrest and concerned by unfolding events in Europe and Rome, the occupying army and its administration were, by the beginning of the 5th century, recalled on various pretexts, leaving 'Britannia' with a Romano-British administration to manage local affairs. Britain now remained bereft of adequate defence and became easy prey to a variety of foreign raiders. The Britons therefore found it necessary to take up arms in their own defence. From this point, the Peak District military forts and the Buxton spa settlement of *Aquae Arnimetiae* appear to have been abandoned.

ANGLO-SAXON SETTLEMENT

Even at a national level, little is known of the Romano-British after the Romans departed, nor of the arrival of the first Anglo-Saxon settlers who were to depose the British ruling elite. This Anglo-Saxon 'invasion' was really more a spread of ideas than of actual people. The whole of the long Anglo-Saxon Period (a convenient label), dating from the breakdown of Roman rule and institutions and lasting until the Norman Conquest in 1066, has been dramatically named as the *Dark Ages*. This is now seen as both a misnomer and an oversimplification. There was no total collapse of the economy and, in any case, the so-called *Dark Ages* lasted only until the mid to late Saxon period during which, from the second half of the 7th century, society was becoming more hierarchical and conversion of the Mercian aristocracy to Christianity began. From this time, we find the gradual emergence and cultural development of regional English kingdoms.

SETTLEMENT OF THE PEAK DISTRICT

Very little is known of the native Britons of the Peak District. They may have been displaced in the 5th or 6th centuries either by immigration, or by intermarriage perhaps with settlers of an extremely diverse origin, who may have had more culturally in common with each other (particularly in relation to religion or language) than with any Britons. Even if the British of the region were in a numerical majority, their survival would probably have depended on the political and cultural allegiances of the elite groups and the influence on the culture that this had. There is a paucity of charters (usually boundary perambulations) for the South-West Peak to provide evidence for either British or Anglo-Saxon life before William the Conqueror's Domesday survey of 1086.

Pre-Anglian place-names are useful to demonstrate the British presence in this region. The name Eccles, derived through Latin from the Greek word for church, is found at Hope, and between nearby Whaley Bridge and Chapel-en-le-Frith where we find Top Eccles Farm, Eccles Road, Eccles Pike, Eccles Fold and Eccles House. The survival of the names probably indicates well-established late Roman and post-Roman communities in that area.

From the 9th century the Scandinavians, once highly mobile raiders, were arriving in far larger numbers to settle. Rather than fighting any established settlers for better land, they seem to have been quite prepared to settle inferior land, determined to become conciliatory colonists. By the 11th century, much of the northern half of England between the Roman Watling Street and the Humber, including Derbyshire (but not Cheshire or Staffordshire) was, on and off, under the political control of the Danes. Known as Danelaw, this was in effect an Anglo-Danish area where neither specific Danish nor English law applied. Although the lack of distinctive Scandinavian place-names suggests this settlement was very uneven with only minimal direct impact on the whole of the Peak District, we find that some Anglo-Saxon families were using Scandinavian personal names for their children.

Two unique defining documents relating to the Peak District survive for this period. The earlier is the *Tribal Hidage*, probably compiled in the second half of the 7th century. It lists all the provinces and client kingdoms that paid tribute to the kingdom of Mercia. This identifies the '*Pecsaetna*' or 'People of the Peak', an upland people; probably a semi-autonomous elite group focused on the limestone plateau. In the later *Anglo-Saxon Chronicle* of 924 (a source of pro-Alfred propaganda), an area called '*Peac Lond*' is defined. It might be considered as the first mention of the Peak District.

LOCAL ANGLO-SAXON SETTLEMENT

Recognisable burials from the Anglo-Saxon period suggest that conversion of this society to Christianity was both prolonged and uneven. Some of their graves became increasingly flat and no longer accompanied with grave goods, making dating and identification difficult. Burials undertaken by other Anglo-Saxon groups, however, suggest some retention of earlier beliefs and rituals, including the accompanying of such burials with grave goods.

On the nearby limestone plateau, some Bronze Age burial mounds have been found to contain Anglian burials or artefacts probably placed there out of ancestral respect and acting as territorial markers – with a significant number of later barrows, e.g. Benty Grange (SK 146 643) between Monyash and Harting-ton, a typical Anglian barrow high on a ridge.

Although some gritstone shelves of the South-West Peak have Bronze Age burial mounds, some contain-ing Roman coins, no single excavation has revealed their re-use by Anglo-Saxons. Indeed, the lack of early Anglo-Saxon settlement evidence presents a problem akin to that previously described for the Iron Age. Pre-sumably some people would have settled here dur-ing this period, perhaps below the very high ground where such barrows are found. Any surviving *British* enclaves, however, may have occupied outlying parts of the Anglian estates, while the elite groups were buried in the richer limestone heartlands. British enclaves are likely finally to have been fully absorbed into mainstream Anglo-Saxon society with the expan-sion of the kingdom of Mercia in the 8th century.

During the Christian period, Anglo-Saxon culture is mainly confirmed through such tangible evidence as the stone crosses which have survived from the later Anglo-Saxon period (see Chapter 4). None of the study area churches reveal recognisable Anglo-Saxon fabric.

ROADS

Despite a continuity of settlement, indisputable proof for any road building by the Anglo-Saxons is only slight throughout the whole of England. However, some charters (there are disappointingly few for the Peak District, usually perambulations of boundaries) do record a charge on local *thegns* (noblemen) to keep bridges in good repair, but without mention-ing any routes leading to them. Together with sur-viving sections of the Roman network, any routes in existence at this time would have been quite informal and no different than those from prehistory. In a few places in the study area where the land has remained largely undisturbed, a few routes from this period *might* exist as faint hollow-ways with an occasional guidestone or cross. In farmed areas there would be prescribed worn trackways (not necessarily fixed) that were governed by the positions of hedges, ditches, banks and walls where the indigenous people and any newly arrived settlers from Europe and Scandina-via lived and farmed. As with today's farmland, these were areas where others didn't trespass.

AN INLAND PORT

As early as the Anglo-Saxon period there had been a port at Torksey on the east bank of the Trent sixty miles from the sea. Torksey was a trans-shipment point for Lincoln, ten miles to the south-east, to which it was joined by a Roman canal – the Foss Dyke. Along these navigable waterways, goods to and from inland markets including those of the Peak District could be shipped. From Roman times there were periods of silting-up and neglect and periods of energetic clean-ing – usually corresponding to changes in commercial activity, particularly that of the wool market when, in the late 13th century, Boston replaced Lincoln as the staple (duty free) market for wool. The later decline in wool export when fulled cloth became available in England may also have reduced the movement of ships to and from Lincoln along the Foss Dyke.

The Anglo-Saxon *burh* of Torksey, which by the late 10th century housed King Aethelred's mint, was once a flourishing town rivalling Lincoln in importance and size, but with the post-conquest development of Boston at the mouth of the River Witham, it began to decline. Right up to the first half of the 14th century, much of the lead and wool from the Peak District would have passed through Torksey.

Chapter 4. THE ANGLO-SAXON CROSSES

INTRODUCTION

Perhaps the most compelling expressions of early Christian art to survive in the Peak District are the large, stylistically linked stone churchyard crosses at, for example, Eyam, Bakewell and Bradbourne. Although we do not know where or when these crosses were originally erected, recent research into regional groupings of so-called Anglo-Saxon stone monuments suggests that these were pre-conquest crosses erected in the 9th century during the Viking occupation of north-east Mercia, owing their geographical coherence to former areas of land occupied by the *Pecsaetna*. These *Primary group* crosses are characterised by naturalistic vine-scroll illustrative panels with some symbols and figures having a clear Christian content. When newly carved and perhaps painted in bright colours they would surely have been seen as remarkable sculptures. Some of the decorative carving provides important insight into the artistic traditions, religious beliefs and perhaps superstitions of the Scandinavian settlers of the area. These crosses were certainly objects of veneration, weapons in the fight against evil, places of prayer, votive offerings for the living or memorials to commemorate the life of a saint. All these functions were linked by a belief in the cross's real power.

A *Secondary group* of simple pillar crosses (see below), found at remote locations, display little or no decoration. There is, then, a diversity of styles, locations and, probably, differing distributions. It seems likely that there would have been as many crosses erected *outside* churchyards as there were within – but when these remote crosses actually became redundant, we have no idea.

A number of surviving cylindrical pillar crosses that are common to northern England can be found on the more remote uplands of the South-West Peak, often occupying sites rising up to the high moors. Recently published papers as to the origins of this Secondary group suggests their distribution pattern to have corresponded to either:

(a) A boundary expansion by settlers into marginal land around the western Peak District in the earlier part of the 10th century, or

(b) Almost all originating from the large medieval parish of Prestbury, Cheshire, which although having shrunk by the middle of the medieval period, still encompassed 33 townships in the centre and south of the 'hundred' of Macclesfield and included Sutton Downes (now Higher Sutton), Wincle, Bollington, Hurdsfield, Kettleshulme, Lyme Handley, Macclesfield, Macclesfield Forest, Pott Shrigley, Prestbury, Rainow, Sutton and Wildboarclough. These Secondary group crosses are suggested to be 9th- or 10th-century products originally sited on the boundaries of these ecclesiastical land-holdings, some subsequently moved.

The surviving pillar crosses have plain, cylindrical or slightly ovoid shafts which usually end in a single or double roll surmounted by a tapering square section and topped by the integral cross head. The cross heads, either cruciform or 'wheel' shaped, appear disproportionately small and are badly damaged or missing. Sometimes cross shafts appear as pairs set into sockets in a single stone base but reasons for this remain unclear.

Some crosses certainly appear to be, or have been, markers on old parish boundaries crossing hilltops, or along difficult remote routes – although they may have been in their original positions when these boundaries were set out. It is known that carved and painted timber crosses were also set up in similar locations but of course none survive. Prior to the erection of the Norman stone churches, these crosses, often described as Mercian in style, may at one time have indicated a location for preaching and provided a station for processions. Having existed for so many centuries, they probably changed their purpose and significance through time as succeeding generations interpreted them, or moved and used them in ways that met their own needs.

Broken cross shafts and cross heads found in the medieval fabric of regional churches sometimes turn up during restoration work. The parish churches of Leek, Alstonefield and Bakewell, for example, have pre-conquest cross shafts erected close to the buildings and collections of cross fragments either visible in the existing fabric, or recovered during restorations and displayed within the building. This would seem to reflect the importance of these three locations as Christian centres where perhaps several crosses had once been erected. Or, possibly such 'mother churches' had become focal centres for crosses returned as venerable relics made redundant at newly built churches or chapels in the wider countryside.

LOCAL PRE-CONQUEST CROSSES

THE BOW STONES (SJ 973 813)

Alongside an ancient track (now part of the Gritstone Way long-distance path), on the boundary of the National Trust Lyme Park Estate, can be found the truncated cylindrical shafts of two gritstone Secondary group crosses known as the Bow Stones. They have a single collar, above which there is a suggestion of interlace decoration, with post-medieval, deeply incised survey (?) marks and the initials HL (Henry Legh?). They resemble other pillar crosses of the area. These shafts, dismantled at some time in the past, are popularly thought to have been discovered in the 17th century in a field at Disley. They were then claimed by the Legh family of Lyme, cemented as a pair into a large stone block and moved to their present position.

In the churchyard of St Mary's Church, Disley, is a large rectangular stone pierced through by two circular sockets. This again is popularly thought, despite

the obvious large discrepancy between shaft and socket diameters, to be the original base of the Bow Stones. Two mutilated cross heads found buried over a mile from Lyme Hall on Whaley Moor in the 19th century were at the time suggested by local historians to be the heads of the Bow Stones (see below). They are available for examination in the family chapel at Lyme Hall but although of contemporary design do not appear to be of the same gritstone.

THE WHALEY MOOR PLAGUE STONE, OR DIPPING STONE (SJ 9955 8172)

This eroded gritstone block has two shallow rectangular holes on its upper face thought to be sockets for two crosses. It appears to have been carved from earthfast rock where possible toolmarks are visible. In the unlikely event that this is a cross base of *any* origin, then to hold two heavy upright stone crosses the sockets would have needed to be considerably deeper and the plinth set on level ground. This enigmatic stone on sloping ground has perhaps never had any connection with crosses. It is only 150m both from a sharp angle in the civil parish boundary separating Lyme Handley and Disley and from the county boundary between Cheshire and Derbyshire at a point where the Todd Brook rises – so is it a boundary stone?

A very similar stone with two shallow rectangular holes can be found in the churchyard of St Mary's Church, Bolsterstone, South Yorkshire. A variety of explanations for such stone blocks has been provided

The Bow Stones.

The Whaley Moor Stone.

by 18th- and 19th-century local historians and anti-quarians but it is of course possible that the Bolster-stone block, together with the one at Disley church, are merely discarded pieces of old church masonry whose function has long been forgotten. The Disley twin-holed block may have been utilised long ago as a conservation repository within the safety of the churchyard for the shafts of two rediscovered crosses thrown down centuries before. The suggested but unlikely crossheads of the Bow Stones were discovered somewhere upslope of the Dipping Stone.

THE MACCLESFIELD WEST PARK CROSSES

A further branch of the Legh family residing at Ridge Hall in Sutton, Macclesfield, were persuaded to gift three Secondary group shafts to the Macclesfield West Park in 1858. They appear to have been collected together from remote ridge-top positions around Sutton, to form a group in the grounds of Ridge Hall (Farm), possibly for their best protection, but now stand incongruously amongst the Macclesfield West Park children's swings and are without dignity. Typically, they have missing crossheads and faint interlace decoration on their upper faces.

The Macclesfield West Park Crosses.

Cleulow Cross.

CLEULOW (OR CLULOW) CROSS (SJ 9520 6740)

Set on its artificial-looking mound north of Wincle immediately above a prominent old hollow-way, this well-preserved Secondary group cross, still with a portion of the small crosshead attached, was undoubtedly used for centuries as a marker by those travelling between Macclesfield and Leek. The 9ft Cleulow cross sits snugly in the 20in diameter socket of its original (?) base. Above the double collar, the tapering upper portion is strongly chamfered and has no decoration. Before the trees were planted (the plantation appears on a map of 1870) it would certainly have been in a prominent position. It stands above the point where the A54 and the Sutton to Wincle roads intersect. This cross and the three from Ridge Hill Farm (now in Macclesfield West Park) probably marked a boundary or a trackway along these hills on the edge of the Cheshire Plain.

THE SWYTHAMLEY CROSS (SJ 9699 6483)

This Secondary group cross might perhaps have been moved a number of times. It could be called The Wincle Cross, as it was removed from the yard of

Wincle Grange, Cheshire, in 1874 and resited in a paved courtyard west of nearby Swythamley Hall. A modern odd-looking crosshead now surmounts the typical squared-off plain upper section.

THE SHALLCROSS

Four crosses once stood along the alignment of the Old Road between Buxton and Shallcross. The crosses are shown on a map from 1640 and are named Rough Low Cross, Womans Cross, Wainstones Cross and Shallcross. Thirty-five years later, John Ogilby's strip road map, produced for Charles II, shows an illustration of a hilltop cross near a place called 'Shawcross Hall'. No other crosses are shown along the line of the road, suggesting these may have been removed during the Civil Wars. At SK 0163 7965, a Secondary group cross, converted into a pillar used to mount a sundial and displaying modern initials HL (see Bow Stones), with a possible date 1720, is perhaps the Shallcross (or Shawcross). It was rediscovered at the beginning of the 20th century at Fernilee Hall and has been set up by the roadside within a rebuilt pinfold near to its more likely original location in Shallcross village. The upper portion above the double collar shows faint signs of carving.

Residents of the village remember a square stone block with a circular hole by the roadside at a junction of parish boundaries at SK 029 771. It has now disappeared but may have been the base of the Wainstones Cross. Of the Rough Low Cross, only the parish boundary line remains as a possible clue to its likely position, while the junction of a footpath and the old road at SK 033 763 near to White Hall has been suggested as a site for the missing Womans Cross.

THE PYM CHAIR CROSS

In 1978 fragments of an Anglo-Saxon period cross, found by the main west–east trade route across the study area near to Pym Chair in the upper Goyt Valley, are now in the Sheffield City Museum. A large and heavy stone, possibly with a squared socket but now broken in two, can be found near to the road at Pym Chair (SJ 9957 7670). Being sited on old parish boundaries of Whaley Bridge, Kettleshulme and

The Shallcross.

Rainow it would have been a bold marker in this high position. The large broken stone, which was described in the late 19th century as 'intact', bears the initials PC and a benchmark arrow (see photo) but these were probably carved in the 19th century. The name first appears in 1611 as 'Pim's chayre', probably derived from the Middle English personal name *Pimme* (Old English *Pymma*) and 'a chair', perhaps referring to the nearby rocks.

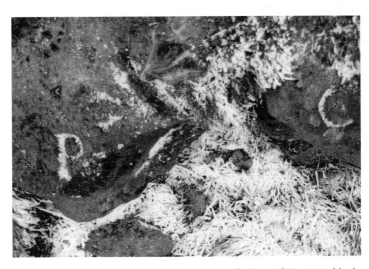

The Pym Chair stone block.

The modern-era resiting of some of the more remote Secondary group crosses of the area, sometimes in groups on private land, suggests their positions may have been dictated by fashionable romanticism as well as a worthy desire to save these impressive symbols in stone for posterity. Landscapes, and perhaps items within them, were held by the elite of the 18th and 19th centuries as items to be bought, sold or accumulated.

POST-CONQUEST CROSSES

As with the Anglo-Saxon crosses, many post-conquest crosses displaying an equal diversity of styles and locations still survive, perhaps continuing the same traditions. Some at remote locations were erected to indicate a boundary such as where, for example,

The Wheston Cross.

Lady Cross on the Peak District's Eastern Moors is on the boundary of land given to Beauchief Abbey. Some indicate pre-turnpike routes, while others can be found indicating town and village markets at Macclesfield, Buxton, Chapel-en-le-Frith, Longnor, Monyash and Leek.

Just outside the study area high on the limestone plateau north-east of Buxton lies the old farming settlement of Wheston. Inside an enclosure, a fine example of a 15th-century cross stands just off the road at SK 1315 7645. It has carved representations of the Nativity and a very powerful Crucifixion although the facial features have been carefully mutilated in an act of zealous vandalism, possibly in the mid-1500s. Like the nearby cross at Foolow, it is probably connected with the nearby mother church at Eyam, where it would have acted as a focal point for village celebrations, rustic sports and pastimes and a central place to gather for a whole variety of secular and religious observations and proclamations, including 'beating the bounds' (see Chapter 1).

Many crosses of this period are square or rectangular in section and where a mortised cross-head has been removed from the shaft tenon (reminiscent of carpentry) there often remains a knob of eroded stone.

The removal and defacing of images, including crosses, was ordered by Edward VI in 1548 during the religious upheavals of the time, whilst almost 100 years later, during the English Civil Wars, a Parliamentary Act of 1643 ordered the removal and destruction of crosses in public places. This throwing down of so many crosses must surely have caused distress to many people who regarded them as important symbols in their lives. Some crosses were discreetly moved and hidden until a change in political climate or the easing of Puritan bigotry made it safe to re-erect them. Sometimes only the base, or base and stump of the shaft remain, while many of the shafts were secretly buried and await rediscovery. More recently, when commons and moors were enclosed for grouse management, prominent crosses were perhaps removed by landowners to hide clear indications of ancient rights of way. It seems remarkable that despite such mutilation and destruction so many crosses have survived. One of the best-preserved surviving round-shafted crosses can be examined in the churchyard of St Edward's Parish Church, Leek.

PART TWO

FROM MEDIEVAL TIMES

Chapter 5. THE EARLY MIDDLE AGES

INTRODUCTION

By the 10th century, England had been divided into unequal areas of land or 'shires', later to be called 'counties'. These were subdivided into relatively unstable areas called 'hundreds' or, under Danish administration, 'wapentakes' – again of unequal size but each having its own public court used by the local populations to hear disputes and misdemeanours. The 'hundred', which was also a taxation unit, may have originated as a territory consisting of roughly one hundred families. The term 'wapentake' is derived from the Scandinavian word *vapnatak* (literally, 'weapon-take'), referring to the brandishing of weapons at a meeting of armed warriors when decisions were proclaimed by a clash of spears.

Despite persistent raids, ongoing settlement and, at times, some political control by Vikings, a unified England had become an integrated part of Europe and was enjoying considerable prosperity until 1066 when the arrival of Duke William of Normandy as military conqueror brought immediate social, political and cultural changes.

William was determined to bring the country into obedience. He declared himself ruler of all the land in England, replacing most, but not all, of the Anglo-Saxon hierarchy with a tough new foreign aristocracy, with himself at the head of a government of exceptional effectiveness. For the common people, 1066 generally speaking was business as usual but under new management. They carried on the timeless rhythms of agriculture and social routine, speaking their native English language. There were still shires and hundreds, the common and open field system remained the same, courts still heard pleas regarding such matters as common rights and the Saxon principle of servile tenure was a system gladly accepted and continued by the Normans.

THE DOMESDAY SURVEY

A census describing English society was compiled using a set of standard statistical details. Known as the Domesday Book (by analogy from the Day of Judgement) it can perhaps be best understood as providing a final decision as to who owned how much of the relative resources within a region. Although much of Domesday was available to William's commissioners from existing Shire Court written accounts, it was nevertheless an invaluable survey of the whole of England south of the Tees and the Westmorland fells – the limits of practical rule achieved by the 10th-century Anglo-Saxon kings. The survey was partly undertaken to discover how much cultivated land there was, what it was worth and who held it, rightfully or wrongfully. It was rushed to near-completion by commissioners (the king was very ill), shire by shire, hundred by hundred in 1086 and produced for William I by Michaelmas 1087, twenty years after his arrival as Conqueror. Although Domesday was designed for fiscal purposes, to protect and to increase the king's revenue, quite simply William I needed to know the essential facts about his kingdom, how it was peopled, and with what sort of men. By this time, a Norman hierarchical system of tenure and service was fully established. All estates were fiefs and every piece of land was held from somebody else in a chain that started from the king, who, together with the earls, bishops, abbots and barons held most of the land. These tenants-in-chief were required to render military service and swear fealty and obedience. The king of course was answerable only to God. The Crown owned 17% of the land in England at this time and was the largest single estate.

Domesday, perhaps surprisingly, fails to show entries for any known permanent settlements in the study area. This suggests that (for a variety of reasons) either abandonment had occurred, or the area was so thinly populated at the time of the survey that tax collection was considered pointless. Some places, however, are likely to have been included in the Domesday entries for better-known nearby settlements.

WORKING OXEN

Oxen have been one of the most important sources of motive power in the British countryside. For thousands of years they cultivated the land and transported people and goods. Trained to work, the domestic ox has left a lasting mark on our language, landscape and culture but has now almost totally disappeared from the United Kingdom.

It is not until the Neolithic period in Britain that we find evidence for a separate domestic ox. From the time of the Roman occupation, the ox was established as the primary traction animal on the farm. In Saxon times, agriculture was almost totally geared to the ox, while in William I's Domesday Survey his commissioners were estimating the size and value of land holdings in terms of the ox. Land was reckoned by the amount a team of eight oxen could work in a year – the *carucate*, which in area ranged from about four to seven hectares. Smallholdings were measured in eighth parts of a carucate called *oxgangs* or *bovates*, equivalent to what a single ox could work in a year. The elongated, reversed S-shaped ridges and furrows that are the result of the oxen's work can occasionally be seen on land that changed long ago from arable to pasture – and has remained as such ever since. This swirling pattern of parallel ploughing occurred because the long, heavy plough teams of four to eight oxen, yoked in pairs, had to start to make their turn well before the end of the furrow. Even a four-ox team could be 12 metres long. In places, the pasture of the upper Dove still retains striking evidence of this wide, medieval-type ridge and furrow ploughing that continued to be used and modified in some parishes into the 18th or even 19th centuries where traditional strips continued in use.

A whole system of measurement was derived from the working ox. A *furlong* was the length of a furrow that a team might be expected to pull without a pause. One furlong (furrow long) equals 220yds (201metres). It comprises 10 *chains*; one chain equals 22yds (20.1 metres) and equals 4 *poles*. The pole – also called a *rod* or *perch*, was the notional length of the driving pole used to urge the animals.

The physical structure of the ox made it easier to harness than the horse because it was possible to place a yoke across the shoulders of a pair of oxen so that they could push against it and pull a plough or wagon. The longer, upward shape of a horse's neck inhibited the use of such a yoke for pulling. The introduction of the horse-collar and the horseshoe, allied to the development of heavier and stronger horses during the later medieval period, was to see oxen gradually replaced by horse teams which could do the same work more efficiently with a consequent increase in productivity. However, even with land enclosures and a growing awareness that farming was in revolution, the ox continued to play a small part as a draught animal on farms and in transport well into the 18th century. By this time, there were growing improvements in hard road surfaces that suited the hooves of horses but not the cloven feet of oxen. Oxen, with their complicated digestive systems, were worked for only part of the day, while a horse functions well on concentrated high-energy food that can be provided at the start and finish of a whole day's work. Apart from the economic arguments, perhaps it was the sheer appeal of horses and the fondness of people for them that eventually spelt the end for oxen. Oxen have done much haulage work over the last 2,000 years. Until the advent of the canal and railway systems they were the main movers of heavy loads. They even played a part in the early days of the tramways and railways before reliable locomotives were introduced.

SETTLEMENT AND COMMUNITY

THE MANOR AND THE OPEN FIELD

By the end of the 11th century, political, commercial and social stability were returning with rural England subdivided into *manors* granted by the crown to a 'lord'. The manor was a basic economic unit consisting of a lord's *demesne* (domain) and lands worked by bond tenants. The lord controlled the population, who were expected to provide services to him in return for his protection. These services could be quite complex. The tenants might either pay rent, work the lord's share of the open field together with their own share or/and give so many days' work according to their status, in the erection and maintenance of any public structure such as roads and bridges, the church and the mill. If the manor was within the area of a hunting forest, the lord was required to provide men to assist at the time of the hunt.

The basic medieval *open field* system consisted of several open fields surrounded by a ditch and bank. This area was divided into unenclosed narrow cultivation strips that were all farmed as a co-operative effort by both owners and tenants. Usually closest to the settlement, these were the most fertile soils for growing crops for food. Disputes were dealt with at the manorial court, where the tenants also met to decide which strips were to remain fallow and where and when animals could be grazed in the woods and open pasture around the fringes of the parish. Here the tenants enjoyed common rights to take wood and peat for fuel and collect wild foods. Society at this time was predominantly rural, with only about ten per cent of the population living in towns.

KNOWN ORIGINS OF LOCAL SETTLEMENT PATTERNS

During the 12th and 13th centuries the climate improved and the population increased. To feed this increasing population more land was cleared for crops but overuse brought about a deterioration of the soil condition. By the beginning of the 14th century, there came a huge worsening of the climate. Wet weather brought about liver fluke on pasture and sheep numbers declined alarmingly. With poor grain harvests, coastal flooding and a weakening of the general health of the population, there came a nationwide famine. A whole series of plagues, including the so-called Black Death, then drastically reduced populations.

After 1350, land in the Peak District became more freely available to the surviving tenants and there developed a tendency to rationalise individual holdings into groups. This was followed by a regional growth in livestock farming, particularly in sheep and wool production, and by the acceleration of bank and ditch earthworks and drystone wall enclosures to control grazing. Part of the huge wealth generated by this wool trade was used to fund the building of new stone churches and bridges and to make much-needed improvements to the roads.

With peasant migration ceasing to be restricted by landlords, a considerable amount of redistribution of settlement occurred as many people tried to move to more promising areas. The emergent settlement pattern in the South-West Peak was one of dispersed hamlets, farms and enclosures, a few with open fields and strips close to township centres where cereals, peas, beans and necessary root crops were grown. Any surviving woodland in the valleys was used for building, fuel and timber. Open areas were given over to meadow and pasture. The moorland, which would have provided some rough grazing, probably remained unoccupied. From here on, the feudal system of the manor gradually died out, with lords becoming landowners of large estates and local people their tenants. Many such leases were either extended or would become permanent. More recently, many large estates have been broken up and the land sold. An example of this is the break-up of the Harpur-Crewe Estate that was a large landowner in the South-West Peak.

RAINOW (SJ 950 760)

Rainow, in common with other settlements in the study area, does not appear in the Domesday record. Although it is possible that no permanent settlement had been made, it may be that it was included in the entries for Macclesfield; one of those areas of Cheshire particularly targeted for an uprising and destroyed in the winter of 1069–70 by William I. The first recorded dwelling in Rainow parish occurs in a mid-12th-century reference to a Richard Davenport who was granted the tenement of the One House and was given the office of Supreme Forester (see Chapter 6). In a rental from 1380, thirty dwellings are quoted in Rainow which would have comprised both houses and farms, some perhaps in the small secretive hamlet of Rainowlow to the north of today's main village.

The lords of the Manor and Forest of Macclesfield exploited the high grounds of Harrop, Saltersford and Shutlingslow by creating large pastures, which, perhaps as the climate deteriorated in the 14th century, were being leased out.

Seventeenth-century Rainow, still within the Manor and Forest of Macclesfield, comprised Saltersford, Harrop and Rainow itself, where there ensued some consolidation of the earlier small-scale settlement by enclosure from waste and by grants of common land into individual ownership. By the 1660s, Rainow had a population of 500 within its 109 households. This expansion was due to continuing Common enclosures throughout the 17th to 19th centuries – although Rainow was never subject to enclosure by Acts of Parliament (see also Chapter 15, Rainow Mill).

QUARNFORD (SK 002 662)

The first mention of the settlement of Quarnford (not the 17th-century township of Quarnford) appears as Quernford in 1227, where 'Peter the clerk' created 'a park', probably for growing rich herbage for cattle. Peter was succeeded by his grandson Hugh le Despencer, a member of the Earl of Chester's household, who fenced this park to exclude cattle. The size and location of the 'park' are not known. Hugh held what became called the manor of Quarnford by 1321. In 1308, Thomas de Audley is known to have had vaccaries (cattle farms) at Birchenbooth further up the Dane. Birchenbooth (SK 006 677) was one of the earliest recorded settlements in the parish of Quarnford. In 1327, the Crown assigned the manors of Quarnford, Rushton Spencer and Alstonefield to Sir Roger Swynnerton. In 1347 there is mention of the 'vaccaries de Miggele' (Midgely).

The name Quernford is derived from (OE) *cweorn* or millstone; the ford was probably over the Dane near Manor Farm (formerly Quarnford Farm, c.1597). The large establishment of Manor Farm, a mainly 19th-century farmhouse, is apparently on the site of the original Quarnford settlement. In the mid-15th century, John Savage acquired Quarnford and Rushton. There are records of early coal mining here and the sale of a farm and cottage in 1597.

By the late 16th century, there is evidence for a few substantial farms down the Dane at *Gradbache*, one possibly an earlier version of Gradbach Old Hall from as early as 1374. There was certainly a house on the site by the early 1630s. By 1613, when Quarnford appears to come under the jurisdiction of Alstonefield manor court, a 'surveyor of the highways' was appointed. From 1615 this office, now styled as a 'headborough' (a deputy of the parish constable), continued sometimes jointly with Hollinsclough until at least 1775.

FLASH (SK 026 672)

Evidence for early settlement here seems limited to a document suggesting that by 1597 Flash (probably a more important settlement at nearby Flash Bottom) had at least five houses. During the 18th century pedlars and hawkers, whose goods consisted chiefly of silk ribbons from Leek, buttons from Macclesfield and smallwares from Manchester, settled the area. The present village of huddled weather-worn cottages seems to have grown up around a church built

in 1744 but rebuilt in 1901. Nonconformity was, as with many such hill villages of the area, very strong. Dissenters sometimes registered houses for meeting and worship and a Methodist Chapel was built in 1784. The chapel, which closed in 1974, was later converted into a house.

By the mid-18th century, many of the women and girls of the village and surrounding area were involved in button-making by hand. Although only one was recorded in 1841, there were 30 by 1861. In 1834, the Traveller's Rest may have been the scene of an attempt to establish a trade union for the female button-makers of the area. The promoters were brought to trial at Stafford, where the defendants were lectured by the judge and then released.

TAXAL (SK 006 798)

The name *Tackeshale* occurs c.1251 and again in 1273 as *Tackishalche* in an Inquisition post-mortem. Possibly 'valley or recess held on lease by Tak or Tatuc' from ME *tak* plus OE *halh*. In 1285 Erdil had staked a claim and cleared nearby woodland (a 'ley') – the name becoming Yeardsley.

Once a township of the ancient parish of Prestbury, Taxal became a separate parish comprising the townships of Taxal and Yeardsley-cum-Whaley in 1377. The church of St James dates from the reign of Edward I (1272–1307), from which time members of the Downes family of Overton Hall, who held the manor of Taxal, had become church rectors. This family had manorial rights to 'cut turves, get coals and claim waifs and strays'. When the king came hunting, it was a Downes who had the privilege of 'rowsing the game and holding the kings stirrup when he mounted'. At the end of the 13th century, Robert del Downes held Downes and Taxal in fee and inheritance (see Chapter 6). The manor of Taxal passed from the Downes in turn to the Shallcrosses, the Dickensons, the Bowers and finally to the Jodrells. The ancient manor house, Overton Hall, was taken down at the beginning of the 19th century. Taxal moved from Cheshire to Derbyshire in 1936 when the county boundary (then the River Goyt) was moved westwards onto high ground.

GOYTSBRIDGE (SK 014 750)

Together with the names Shawcrosse, Tax Hall and Overton, a small settlement is shown as Goithouses on John Speede's typically undetailed map of 1610,

The curved broken wall of St. John's holding (SK 017 750).

with the River Goyt shown as *Goyt Flud*. On a map of Hartington of 1614, enclosures named as St Johns Holding are shown on the east bank of the river. Focused on the hamlet, they comprise irregularly shaped fields with distinctive curving upper boundaries of drystone walling at the moor's edge. Now truncated downslope by Errwood reservoir, they may have late medieval origins. The settlement, later named as Goytsbridge, at the confluence of Wildmoorstone Brook and the River Goyt, appears to have been established at a ford, with a later packhorse bridge over the Wildmoorstone Brook slightly upstream. The shallow crossing point was on the line of a major medieval through-route across the Goyt Valley. This traditional route declined both in importance and usage with the coming of the turnpike roads of the 18th century. Several small farms once stood on the valley-side shelves. The ruins of Upper Hall, Brownhill and Nook Farms, for example (SK 021 765), are marked on Burdett's 1767 county map. Although Brownhill Farm was first recorded in 1640, given the locations of these farms on the most favourable agricultural land in the valley their origins may well be earlier.

MEERBROOK, NETHER, MIDDLE AND UPPER HULME (SJ 989 608) (SK 00 60)

In the mid-13th century we find mention of a Robert of Meerbrook and by the early 16th century there was evidently a settlement with a chapel. The siting of the settlement was probably determined by access to the upper part of the Meer Brook valley and to the common waste, which lay chiefly on Gun and the Roaches.

During the mid-13th century there were settlements east of Meerbrook village called Nether, Middle and Over Hulme (now Upper Hulme) – the original settlement of Over Hulme probably sited on high ground west of Back Brook where two farms were recorded in the early 16th century. The element 'hulme' in the place-names (including Kettleshulme in Cheshire) has led to suggestions of Scandinavian (or earlier) origins. It may of course be just the dialect issue that is in play here. The earliest settlements in this particular area appear to be Dieulacres Abbey's granges in the upper part of the Meer Brook valley. The sites of several other farmhouses were occupied by the early 16th century. A mill on the nearby Meer Brook is recorded in 1676. In the late 1560s there was a mill on the Back Brook upstream from Hulme Mill, while in the 18th century the mill was known as Dains mill. A hamlet grew up on the lower ground beside the brook in the 19th century after the opening of a silk mill there. Dains Mill stopped working c.1946 following a breach of the dam but a recent development of the site, which includes an overshot waterwheel, suggests a measure of self-sufficiency is planned.

HOLLINSCLOUGH (SK 065 665)

When first recorded in the late 1390s, the settlement was known as *Howelesclough* and was part of Alstonefield manor. In 1497 a lease refers to a 'walk mill' and 'fishing rights' on the upper Dove. A fulling mill, perhaps a mill north-west of the village (Washgate area?), was recorded in 1564. This, together with the name Tenter Hill for south-facing land between the river and Golling Gate, suggests cloth production in this immediate area. The earliest settlements outside the village included one at Moss Carr or Moscure, recorded in Alstonefield manor in the earlier 15th century and a house in 1400 called Winterside, northwest of the village. Dun Cow's Grove, below Edgetop, was recorded as Duncote Greave in 1600. Records from the manor court in 1601 reveal surveyors for the highways. An open field called Town Field was mentioned in 1617. By the early 1630s the village had only three houses and seven cottages.

A nonconformist chapel was built by a hawker, John Lomas, and registered in 1797. In 1840, Sir George Crewe, prompted by the vicar of Longnor, rebuilt a village barn as a church and a school. Families of hawkers, pedlars and button manufacturers are mentioned in the 18th century. Both men and women working as domestic silk weavers are recorded in the mid-1800s. In the 1851 census, when the village had strong connections with Macclesfield, out of a population of 400 there were 37 Hollinsclough people listed as 'silk weaver' and 13 listed as 'button maker'.

A traditional name for a road in or out of a settlement in this area is 'rake'. Hollinsclough has three such rakes: Hollinsclough Rake, Swan Rake and Limer Rake.

WINCLE (SJ 958 660)

By 1357 a bridge had been built over the River Dane at a location recorded c.1190 as *Scliderford* – a slippery ford. Two Cistercian granges, barely one mile apart, were established in the upper Dane Valley on either side of the river at Wincle. Both were involved with the European wool trade. Wincle Grange, founded around 1232 by Ranulf III, the Earl of Chester, was originally constructed from local red sandstone and was a grange to the mother house of Combermere Abbey in south Cheshire on the Welsh border. It is referred to in the original charter of Combermere Abbey and also in documents for the Hundred of Macclesfield relating to the Taxation of Pope Nichloas as follows: '*item habet apuc Wynkhall, in dec de Macclesfild duas caruc terr. El val. Car. Per annum, 10s.*' The grange buildings were considerably altered in 1670 and retain few of their original features today. The nearby grange of Swythamley (see Chapter 7), whose site is probably occupied by Swythamley Hall, had its mother house a mere six miles away at Dieulacres, Leek.

Chapter 6. THE HUNTING FORESTS

INTRODUCTION

By 1079, William I and his closest noblemen had requisitioned 21 hunting areas (about three percent of England), from which time the Norman and Plantagenet monarchs increasingly subjected much of the landscape to 'forest law'. These laws provided the ruling elite with a means of protecting both the game and the landscape for themselves. The word 'forest' in its medieval sense is not a description of the topography of an area. It is a legal term describing land outside (*foris*) the common law and subject to a special code based on the arbitrary legislation of the king. The creation of royal and private forests had the effect of decreasing and restricting the common rights of manorial tenants and provoking natural resentment of these imported laws from Normandy, applied here in special forest courts. There were three categories of forest court. The lowest court met every forty days for 'attaching' (arresting) offenders accused of minor trespasses. The next higher court was the 'swainmote' (practically the same as the attachment court), which met every two to four months. By far the most important of the courts was the dreaded 'eyre', held at intervals of anything up to 35 years, by two or three justices specially appointed to try the most serious cases. The territory under forest law expanded steadily, reaching its widest extent in the reign of Henry II (1154–89).

For offences against the forest law, whether of 'venison' (i.e. trespass to the hurt of the beasts, namely the red, fallow and roe deer and the wild boar) or of 'vert' (i.e. anything of prejudice to trees, plants and undergrowth that gave the animals shelter and food), there were severe punishments available. Intended solely to safeguard hunting, the laws had special reference to poaching, unauthorised turf-cutting and the grazing of sheep and cattle. This latter was necessary to ensure the maintenance of pasture for the deer herds. The 'venison' could be neither legally bought nor sold. It was intended to be given exclusively as a high-status gift and was forbidden meat to the common man upon pain of the harshest penalties.

The Charter of the Forest (1217) followed hard on the heels of King John's Magna Carta (1215) and together they were responsible firstly for preventing the creation of further new forests, and secondly for

Red Deer and Fallow Deer.

enforcing the disafforestation of all additions since the reign of Henry II (d.1189). At a time when half of England was under forest law, the Charter of the Forest (revoked as late as 1971) had a far-reaching impact and was of greater practical importance than Magna Carta itself. It gave the common people more access to the forest's resources and removed the savage penalties of the old forest law. This replacement introduced a system of fines and/or imprisonment for the more serious crimes.

In the Domesday survey of Cheshire there are eight undetailed references to 'in foresta', (forests), of which three are now in Wales. Staffordshire has five references whereas Derbyshire is shown not to have any. However, Derbyshire had a large area that would soon become the Royal Forest of the Peak.

The hunting forests were not depopulated hunting reserves. They contained communities complete with villages, pasture, managed broadleaved woodland and agricultural land (subject to formidable restrictions), and occasionally encircled large towns – the town of Macclesfield (Cheshire) being a good example. Many of these reserves remained in private hands. It was the forest rights and not necessarily the land itself that belonged to the king. Following the Conquest, two large adjoined hunting areas were designated, each sharing the common boundary of the River Goyt. These were Macclesfield Forest and, sometime later, the Royal Forest of the Peak, comprising very thinly populated areas of largely uncultivated moorland and scrub surrounded by wooded valleys and occasional farms and settlements in clearings. A considerable part of the medieval forest of Macclesfield lies within today's South-West Peak, where, by the late 14th century, its management seems to have been directed more towards grazing, timber-felling and rents rather than timber conservation and control.

MACCLESFIELD FOREST

No direct reference was made to the Forest of Macclesfield in the Domesday Record. However, we know from the few surviving charters that the main Anglo-Saxon manors of Adlington and Macclesfield in Cheshire had boundaries with the River Goyt. The Anglo-Saxon elite, who had no separate 'forest law', are known to have practised deer management and hunted the area. They caught wolves in pits, deer in nets and collected wild honey from the woodland. Before the Conquest, Edwin, the last Saxon earl of Mercia, held the manor of Macclesfield.

Hugh D'Avranche, who in 1071 was to become the first of the Norman earls of Chester, controlled the extensive forest and manor of Macclesfield. Better known as Hugh *Lupus* – 'the Wolf' – he was an ambitious nephew of the Conqueror. The earl, in whose name the forest law was enforced, administered all the Cheshire forests.

MALBANK FRITH

Macclesfield Forest was very similar to royal forests and under royal protection 'for their pleasure and recreation'. It originally included an area containing the townships of Fawfieldhead, Heathylee, Hollinsclough and Quarnford, which in the 12th century was known separately as the 'Forest of Alstonefield'. It was detached from Macclesfield Forest following the grant of Leek manor by Ranulph III of Blundeville (1181–1232), Earl of Chester, to Dieulacres Abbey in 1232, but was administered by the earl's foresters. This hunting area east of the River Dane and west of the River Dove is mentioned in Ranulph III's charter for the burgesses of Leek. It was under-tenanted by the Malbank family, lords of Alstonefield manor,

as a separate hunting reserve and became known as Mauban or Malbank Frith (Malbank's private forest) – a name that continued. The Malbanks had rights to hunt boar but there seems to be no evidence for deer management within the Frith. The land may have been used for beef or dairy cattle – a common enough practice at the time.

By the early 15th century, the Beresford family held the office of Forester of Malbon Frith. In the late 16th century the area is described as '4,335 acres of waste', while as late as 1670, Malbon Frith was known to have been stocked with deer.

In the year of his death Ranulph III gave part of his Macclesfield Forest land at Wincle to establish a monastic grange with pasture for a specified number of sheep, cattle, horses and mares (see Chapter 7). In 1237, Macclesfield Forest reverted to the Crown when Henry III annexed the Norman earldom.

At the time of the Domesday survey, the Macclesfield hundred apparently contained very large areas of woodland. The Domesday Book records woodland six leagues by four; in Adlington, a wood eleven leagues by two; in Werneth, woodland three leagues by two; Hofinchel (lost) and Tintwhistle each two leagues by two leagues. A league was a varying measure of travelling-distance by land, usually about three miles. Throughout the Norman period and early Plantagenet years the territories under forest law steadily expanded and included areas of arable and pasture, i.e. neither woodland nor waste. In 1303 a report mentions wolves and a device for catching them. Wolves had gradually decreased in number by the 15th century and were finally exterminated in the reign of Elizabeth I.

FOREST MANAGEMENT AND THE COURTS

The destruction of game had been a crime punishable by blinding, mutilation or even death during the early Norman times. For lesser crimes, large fines were levied but later earls became more concerned to secure an income at the expense of the inhabitants than to prevent the offences. There are no details about the administration of forest law until 1285, when an important court was held at Macclesfield for the pleas of the *hundred*, the *borough* and the *forest* when justices were specially commissioned to enquire into particular forest offences. The forest dwellers seem to have enjoyed customary rights. At the 1285 forest court, the townships of Bosley, Bollington, Adlington, Poynton, Norbury, Heppales, Torkington, Rode and Gawsworth successfully defended their rights to 'cut oaks in their demesne woods without view of the foresters'.

The earl employed a large staff of officials to manage his forest. They are often mentioned in documents: woodwards and verderers to attend the forest courts, agisters to collect money for the pasturing of cattle and swine, regarders (twelve or more knights), who inspected the forest every three years, and kennelmen to look after the dogs. Regarders are named in writs for election between the years 1285 and 1638. In 1347 there were seven under-foresters. Verderers, agisters and woodwards are named between 1347 and 1638. Associated with these forest workers mention is made of 'lodges'. These were probably overnight shacks rather than substantial dwellings. Above them all, and ultimately responsible for staff efficiency, was the justiciar (judge) at Chester. This official often acted as mediator between the commoners and the foresters. Periodically he held a 'regard' where offences were investigated – the most common being illegal hunting and poaching, illegal assarting (i.e. illegal enclosure and clearance of forest land for agricultural purposes), and the similar crime of purpresture, where making a fence or hedge, enlarging a field, building a mill or a fish pond would encroach on the domain of the earl's deer, restricting their movements. Very heavy fines were instituted for this offence.

There were enclaves where the forest law did not apply, including the town of Macclesfield itself, which had a castle and a park associated with fallow deer, these enclosed by means of a palisade. In the 14th century, an area of demesne underwood at Hurdsfield was called *Le Fence*. Higher Fence at SJ 931 738 represents *Le Fence* on the current OS map. The Forest Courts were held at Macclesfield on behalf of the Steward of the Forest, who was answerable to the Earl, as Lord of the Forest. There was a so-called 'halmote' court which met once a month and may have been the court of attachment. A 'court-leet' was held once a year for 'the manor and forest of Macclesfield'. The important forest 'eyre' was held in the town, often at quite lengthy intervals, where the justiciar from Chester appears to have presided. Those who broke forest law could be sentenced for committal to Macclesfield gaol.

THE FORESTERS

The original office of hereditary master-forester of Macclesfield was held in fee by the Davenport family, the grant having apparently been made by the Earl of Chester, Hugh II, between 1153 and 1160, to Richard Davenport who was appointed as 'Supreme Forester of the Earl's Forest of Leek and Macclesfield'. This confirms that at one time the earl's forest extended beyond Cheshire to his manor of Leek (Staffs.). By the late 13th century there were eight or nine subordinate Foresters in fee who performed forest duties and enjoyed privileges granted for answering the king's summons to provide men and arms when necessary. These hereditary foresterships were held by the following: Richard Vernon held Marple and Wybersley; Robert Downes held Taxal and Downes; John Sutton held land in Sutton and Disley; Thomas Worth held 'Ratonfield' (Whitefield and Upton); Robert Champagne held High Lee in Sutton-Downes (Higher Sutton) and Jordan Disley held land in Disley. Roger Stanley's lands were at Stanley in Disley and Adam Sutton also held land at Sutton. If the family line became broken, the office could be passed to others. Prominent families who held foresterships in later centuries include Legh, Savage, Pecton, Sherd, Orby, Venables and Fitton. After the lapse of the earldom, the office of hereditary master-forester seems to have become an honorary one. The foresters had their lodges, from which they administered the forest laws and safeguarded their own interests. Little is known of these lodges but later on it was the Chamber in the Forest that appears to have been a residence of the master-forester himself.

The forest officials were highly skilled in deer management and were charged with maintaining healthy herds by culling weak or diseased animals, preventing any disturbance to the hinds and their fawns during the 'Fence Month' (two weeks either side of Midsummer's Day) and ensuring plentiful supplies of browsewood throughout the winter by careful woodland management. They also trapped predatory wolves in pits.

HUNTING

It is not known how frequently the earls of Chester hunted in the Macclesfield Forest but Edward I did so many times between 1277 and 1284. The King and his court used 'the chamber in the forest in the Langley valley' as a hunting lodge. Large quantities of food to be delivered here are recorded in the accounts. For the privileged few who hunted, forest animals (ground quarry) would generally be pursued on horseback with hounds and killed by bow and arrow; birds of all kinds were hunted with falcons. For the early Norman kings, their barons, bishops and abbots, hunting using mixed packs of specialised expensive hounds was the principal relaxation and sport. Riding skills were deemed a necessary acquisition. The hunts, which could last up to three days, were considerable events controlled by skilled forest officials and 'beaters' provided by the manorial lords. During this period forest law did not cover animals like wolves, hares, otters, foxes, cats and rabbits. By the time of Edward III (1327–77), although red deer and the smaller fallow deer (less hardy and introduced by the Normans) continued to be hunted, roe deer became less highly prized and were struck off the list of 'beasts of the chase'. Deer might be taken by netting or trapped in deep pits by the foresters for the lord's use. Others might be given as prestigious gifts to friends who, from the later medieval period, were stocking private parks and chases created out of depopulated land. Lengths of timber, especially oak, were also considered to be high-status gifts. During the later medieval period few instances are recorded where boar were hunted for sport. They appear to have been controlled by forest officials and then driven by hounds into pits for slaughter before butchery.

RESTRICTIONS AND NECESSITIES

The common forest-dwellers were forbidden to possess greyhounds or coursing dogs. They lived in the midst of temptation, broke the law and took the deer when they could; if caught they were tried and punished. 'Estovers' (necessities) constituted a legal right by villagers to take wood, known as *bote*. They could take *housebote* (i.e. timber for repairing houses etc.), *firebote* (i.e. small timber for warmth or cooking), *haybote* (i.e. lesser timber for fencing, crofts and enclosures) and *hedgebote* for hedging. They could dig peat and turves and cut furze (gorse) and bracken without supervision. In certain areas they might dig sand and gravel and, in later times, marl. They could agist (graze on beechmast and acorns) their pigs in the forest at the time of 'mast' (October and November) on payment of 'pannage' – monetary restitution or payment in kind for the damage done by grubbing

pigs. The forest dwellers could also pasture other animals, chiefly cattle and horses on the commons. They had the customary right to cut timber for bonfires for parish celebrations, wedding feasts etc. and (after 1605) to build bonfires for 'Thanksgiving Day', 5 November.

The existence of the forest system was to prove a serious obstacle to economic development. The main landholders could not improve their estates by enclosing their woodland to deny the deer access. As early as the 13th century it was evident that expansion of agricultural land was becoming a matter of some urgency. The forests swarmed with game that was free to ravage crops and in Macclesfield Forest land could only be enclosed and cultivated on the payment of a large, annual fixed sum.

EDWARD (THE BLACK PRINCE) 1330–76

In 1270, the lordship of Macclesfield was granted to Eleanor (1246–90), wife of Edward I, as dower. In 1285 and 1286, vaccaries (cattle farms) belonging to the Queen are mentioned. She held Macclesfield until her death in 1290.

In 1309, this lordship was gained by Isabella, wife of Edward II, and retained by her until 1347 at which time she transferred it to her grandson, Edward (The Black Prince). As Earl of Chester, he thus became lord of the manor of Macclesfield with overall responsibility for the administration of Macclesfield Forest. His chief forester and riding forester were, respectively, Peter Arderne and Robert Legh. Arderne was succeeded by Sir John Chandos who appointed Peter Legh as his deputy. Macclesfield Forest contained oaks that were often gifted for house repairs, especially by the Black Prince to his loyal supporters.

Although interest in the forest purely as a game reserve was beginning to wane, the Black Prince introduced many oppressive measures in an attempt to increase the forest revenue.

On 2 March 1355 he ordered repairs to the Coombs 'if it could be done at low cost'.

In 1361 there were six areas of demesne pasture in the lordship, namely Macclesfield Park, Handley, Harrop, the vaccary at Midgley, the Coombs and Shutlingslow. In the same year, the prince ordered two lodges to be made in Macclesfield hundred to safeguard the game. A large, shapeless mound in the modern forest below Toot Hill at SJ 9715 7185 is likely to be the ruin of the 18th-century Old Chamber

Farm, perhaps built on the site of the forester's lodge or chamber, a relic of the hunting forest?

Early in March 1362, the Black Prince's officials at Ashford (near Bakewell) were ordered to drive all the prince's 'great beasts' from there to Macclesfield. The cattle drive included a mixture of bulls, cows, bullocks, heifers and oxen. The route taken by this 14th-century drive is not recorded but a suitable route can be surmised. With little in the way of enclosure to impede progress it would be fairly direct, keeping wherever possible to the higher commons and wastes to avoid trampling crops in the open fields. Stream crossings would have provided water for the animals. The drovers would have employed good dogs and perhaps requisitioned secure paddocks at night. During this period both the breeding and rearing of cattle, including oxen, was carried on in a considerable way in Macclesfield Park and at other areas in of forest, which by now was increasingly exploited for its pasture. This again dispels any ideas that forests were solely for hunting.

Early fourteenth-century accounts mention vaccaries (cattle farms) of the manor of Macclesfield that had large demesne pasture at Midgely (on the Cheshire side of the Dane above Gradbach) and at Harrop Park in Rainow. By the late 14th century, however, some of the higher pastures such as those at Harrop, Saltersford and Shutlingslow were being leased out and clearance and assarting of lower land was resulting in the creation of demesne townships. Peasants, who had been freed from labour dues, could now freely buy or sell land, especially after the Black Death. Additional sources of revenue mentioned were the iron forges. Two forges, charged to yield over £17 during the year 1348–9, would have yielded more but 'were in the lords hands because of The Black Death'. Coal mines in the forest were mentioned in 1382 and 1575.

While illegal enclosure for pasture and farms within the forest seems to have continued unabated between the 13th and 15th centuries, enclosure by licence (assart) was frequently granted for private deer parks and 'chases' created by noblemen and manorial lords. To contain the deer within such parks, deep ditches and earth banks topped by a wooden fence or 'pale' were constructed. Felling woodland, enclosing convenient portions or building settlements may have been forbidden by forest law but by the 16th century was often allowed or even encouraged in return for an annual fine – a way of generating revenue for the earl.

THE COOMBS

The word 'coomb' means a valley, from the OE *cumb*. This is an area east of Trentabank Reservoir, unfortunately now obscured by early-20th-century dense conifer planting around the location centred at SJ 968 707. It was an area with banks or enclosures relevant to the management of deer but was never referred to as a 'park'. In 1301–2, expenditure was recorded for 'making an enclosure round the chase of Coombs' and in 1303–4 'for the wages of eight men who had repaired the lord's share of the fence of the Coombs'. By 1347 there was 'a hunting lodge at the Coombs'.

From 1362, the Coombs area was providing an additional source of hay for the Black Prince's cattle enterprises in Macclesfield Park, Harrop Park, Midgely and part of Wildboarclough (see above). As at Harrop and Midgely, holly used as 'browse wood' was cut in the Coombs (see Chapter 10, Local Hollin Sites). It seems that in the late 14th century, some area within the Coombs was enclosed by an embanked boundary hedge that was to be maintained by tenants from the townships around the edge of the forest. This boundary hedge was 315 perches (over a mile) long. In 1638 it was stated that 'the deer took their summer feed in the Coombs and their winter feed in Wildboarclough'.

In 1442 the pastures at Saltersford, Harrop, Tod's Cliff (the location is lost), Wildboarclough, Midgely and Shutlingslow were all leased to the master forester for six years at £16 yearly. By the late 15th century, very large areas of the forest were being used as pasture, from which time it is likely that the forester's main duty was the prevention of illegal grazing. In the 16th century, documents refer to the position of 'governor of the king's servants in the lordship and Forest of Macclesfield'. Various Savages, Mottrams and Cholmondleys held this office.

THE FOREST BOUNDARY –
A PERAMBULATION

Although early evidence with respect to the 'metes and bounds' of the medieval Macclesfield Forest proves quite unsatisfactory, the following fifteen component townships appear in a mize roll of 1406 for the 'Forest de Macclesfield': The Town of Macclefield, Bosley, Sutton-Downes, Marple, Taxal, Tytherington, Sutton, Hurdsfield, Bollington, Pott Shrigley, Disley-Stanley, Rainow, Yeardsley-Walley, Upton and Kettleshulme.

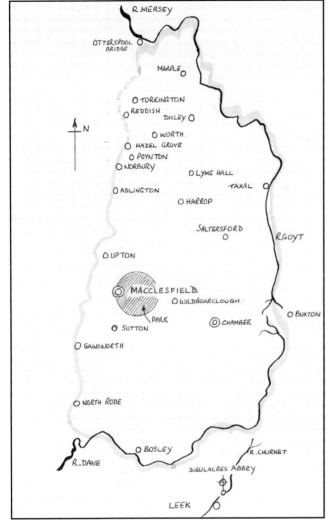

Map: Macclesfield Forest. The 1619 perambulation.

Bridge [near Romiley] and ascending the water of Mersie as far as the water of Guyte [Goyt] and ascending the water of Guyte as far as certain Mosses lying between the water of Guyte and the water of Dane Moss and so on across the Mosses as far as Dane Head and from there descending the water of Dane as far as Crumwell on to Bramhall Hill, and from Bramhall Hill as far as Rode Green [North Rode] and from thence to the church gate as far as the village of Gawsworth, which is all in the forest except the Hall and the Church, and so on from Gawsworth by the direct way before you to a certain hill anciently called Norbury Low, lying near to a house now called Bullock Smithy [Hazel Grove] and on the western side of the aforesaid way; and from Norbury Low in the direct way before you, near the house of Robert Handford, leaving that house within the forest aforesaid, as far as the brook of Bosden, and descending the brook of Bosden, to a corner of a certain meadow called Barlie Meadow and a certain meadow called Reddish Meadow; and from the little bridge aforesaid, in the direct way before you as far as the aforesaid bridge called Otter's Poole.'

From the above description, supported by the townships list, we can deduce the western boundary of the forest by a line from Otterspool Bridge through Offerton Green, Norbury, the line of the present London Road through Hazel Grove, Poynton and Adlington to Prestbury. It then skirted Macclesfield township, continued to Gawsworth, avoiding the precinct of the church, and then passed southwards via North Rode to Bosley. The rivers Mersey, Goyt and Dane bounded the forest to the north, east and south.

Within the forest all the higher hills were open moorland and only the lower slopes and the plains were partly wooded. Such surviving names as Wildboarclough and Wolf Edge are suggestive of the wild and rugged character of this early hunting forest.

In 1403 John Stanley, a confidant of Richard II, succeeded to the office of Master Forester. In the reign of Edward IV (1461–83), Thomas Stanley was granted the stewardship of the town of Macclesfield and two years later he assumed the office of Master Forester,

No mention was made of the future townships of Wildboarclough, Macclesfield Forest or Wincle.

At the time of the 17th-century boundary perambulation (see below) the following townships are known to have been within the jurisdiction of both the hundred and the forest of Macclesfield with the boundary passing through them: Macclesfield, Adlington, Butley, Gawsworth, Poynton, Prestbury, North Rode, Norbury, Heppales and Torkington.

The first boundary description that can be accurately dated is that extracted from the 17th Court Roll of James I in 1619, by which time the area of the forest had decreased. The account relates to the perambulation of the once extensive Forest of Macclesfield. '. . . begins at a certain bridge now called Otterspool Bridge, anciently called Rohehound granted by Richard III for his allegiance and forces during the decisive Battle of Bosworth Field. Henry VII created his successor Thomas Stanley, Earl of Derby and Constable of England. However, in 1661, both offices together with the forest lands reverted to the Earl of Chester.

RIGHTS AND PRIVILEGES

In 1533 a plea by Richard Done, the master-forester of the nearby Forest of Mara (Delamere), Cheshire, describes the rights and privileges he claimed.

'. . . and clayme to have the latter pannage in the saide forest, and claymeth to have windfalen wood, cropes of trees cutt down with axxes, crabstock, and stubb, in the demesne wood of the said forest: halph the bark of all fallen okes . . . and claymeth to have of every beast, as oxen, kine, bulls, bullocks and goats taken, and strangers beasts, betwixt Mychellmas and Martlemas, an halphpenny. And claymeth to have all sparhawks, marlens, and hobbys, found within the said forest. And claymeth to have all swarmes of bees. And claymeth to have the right shoulder of everie deer taken; and claymeth if any stroken deer be found dead in the sayd forest, that he should cause the hornes and the taw sides of the said deer to be sent to the castell of Chester, and the foresters to have the residue of the same. He also claymeth to have weiffes found in the bailywick, and claymeth to have all pelfe in his office, except that the lord earl of Chester ought to have, and claymeth to have, all hounds and greyhounds, to take foxes, heires, cattes, weesel, and other vermin in the forest.'

Additional to these rights and privileges (but not mentioned in the plea above) was the entitlement of master-foresters to 'the fishing, hawks and eagles in the forest'. They could have holly for their own beasts inside their own bounds where they were free to take whatever they needed from the woods for any enclosure, building and fuel. They could have foggage (pasture stubble) when the lord sold foggage and were entitled during the time of pannage (acorn and beechmast foraging) to pannage for their own use and for their men's pigs.

In 1652 Sir William Brereton purchased the forfeited stewardship of Macclesfield Forest. Part of the contract for the forest included 'that messuage or lodge called the Chamber'. This may have been the forester's residence (see above), possibly a chamber

where the Forest Courts were held anciently before they transferred to the town of Macclesfield. A 'forest chamber' shown on Saxton's map of 1577 may have been the Black Prince's lodge. A 'new chamber' or hunting lodge was mentioned in a survey of 1610 as 'somewhere near the Coombs'. An 'old chamber' is shown on Burdett's 1777 Cheshire map, on the one-inch OS map of 1842 and on the Tithe Award map of 1848. The actual site (or sites) is lost.

Over centuries, more and more enclaves of disafforested land had limited the forest area and restricted the grazing of forest animals. The areas of common land had increased, the deer herds dwindled and hunting them ceased to be important. Peasants took rabbits from the warren, game for the pot and, despite the possible consequences, poached the deer. Following the Restoration in 1660, the Forest Court was declared redundant when it was realised that settlers now occupied half of the forest. This increased settlement was vital if the land was to support the growing population. The great Forest of Macclesfield then survived only as an administrative area and has now shrunk to today's hill-country parishes of Macclesfield Forest and Wildboarclough.

THE ROYAL FOREST OF THE PEAK

INTRODUCTION

Abutting the medieval Macclesfield Forest to the west and sharing the common boundary of the River Goyt was the extensive Royal Forest of the Peak, a royal demesne and hunting reserve of three wards: Longdendale, Hopedale and Campagna or Champayne – which included much open grazing land. A considerable portion of the Forest had been part of the royal manor of Hope in Saxon times and may therefore have previously been used for hunting. In 1068, William Peverel 'held the Royal manor of Hope and adjacent lands for the king' (William I). In conjunction with this grant came numerous lordships in Derbyshire, Nottinghamshire and other regions, which were together known as 'the Honour of Peverel'.

THE FOREST BOUNDARY

The bounds of the forest, as set out in the Forest Pleas held in 1286, are given as follows in modern English translation: 'The metes and bounds of the forest of the Peak begin on the south of the New Place of Goyt, and thence by the River Goyt as far as the River Etherow; and so by the River Etherow to Langley Croft at Longdenhead; thence by a certain footpath to the head of Derwent; and from the head of Derwent to a place called Mythomstede [Mytham Bridge]; and from Mythomstede to the River Bradwell; and from the River Bradwell as far as a certain place called Hucklow; and from Hucklow to the great dell of Hazelbache [at Eyam]; and from that dell as far as Little Hucklow; and from Little Hucklow to the brook of Tideswell, and so to the River Wye; and from the Wye ascending up to Buxton, and so on to the New Place of Goyt.' These limits of the Peak Forest remained to its close the same as they were in the 13th century.

Like Macclesfield Forest, the Royal Forest of the Peak had its own forest laws. Its administrative centre and prison for offenders against these laws was Peveril Castle, built on the site of a former stronghold and occupying a position of remarkable strength above the small town of Castleton. The outmoded defences were strengthened with a stone keep in about 1176 by Henry II following his seizure of the estate of the poisoner of Ranulf, Earl of Chester – a

descendant of William Peverel. At the centre of the forest, there was a foresters' hall at the present village of Peak Forest. The forest courts were held at Castleton, Bowden (Capellam de Frith 1241/Chapel-en-le-Frith), Tideswell and Wormhill. The forest remained in the hands of the Crown until 1372, when it was transferred to the Duchy of Lancaster and thence returned to the Crown by absorption in the following century. The forest gradually became encroached upon and colonised. A final attempt was made in 1579 to save what little remained of the depleted forest. A fence was built to contain an area around the chamber at Peak Forest, the present parish – but by the second half of the 17th century the forest had effectively ceased to exist. A 13th-century chapel built in the western part of the forest gave rise to the settlement name of Chapel-en-le-Frith.

FOREST PENALTIES

The severity of forest law is often referred to, but to judge from the records the punishments inflicted for offences against vert and venison were very lenient. In many histories we read of the cruelty meted out to desperate offenders; of death, maiming or blinding for killing a deer. Scrutiny of the ancient Rolls of the Forest has revealed the surprising leniency of the penalties. No case of capital punishment is recorded and most of the offenders were let off with moderate fines on a pro-rata basis. These fines were little more than disguised licences. Only in the worst cases, where violence had been used against the king's officers, was imprisonment ordered.

In the Royal Forest of the Peak, the forest laws seem to have quietly fallen into contempt. After the reign of Edward I, the kings of England took little interest in it and the various inhabitants and forest officers encroached upon the king's land at their pleasure, killed his deer and cut down his woods at will for building, fencing and fuel so that, by the end of the 15th century, little remained in the king's hands. Finally, in Charles II's reign, the hunting forest was officially disafforested.

Map: Probable boundaries of the Royal Forest of the Peak in the 11th Century.

Chapter 7. REFORMED MONASTICISM

INTRODUCTION

Of the refounded monastic orders that appeared within a century of the Conquest, the most influential was undoubtedly the Cistercian. Centrally controlled from France, these 'White Monks' set a standard of austerity that perhaps best illustrates the nature of their restless but pious generation. Removing themselves wherever possible from a distressing world, they sought solitude to establish self-sufficient economies, representing themselves as heroic settlers on unproductive land – 'to make fruitful that which is barren.' This was the ideal but was rarely followed.

DIEULACRES, LEEK (SJ 985 578)

In 1147, a Cistercian colony founded by Robert Pincerna, butler to Ranulph II, Earl of Chester, was built on the banks of the River Dee at Poulton in Cheshire. To guarantee the salvation of their souls it was customary in the medieval period for the wealthy owners of estates to assign a portion of the estate itself (usually poor land) to a religious foundation. This group of monks seem to have been subsequently persuaded by Ranulph III, Earl of Chester, to move and resettle an alternative site. In 1214 they took possession of part of Ranulph's large estate in North Staffordshire to which, the story goes; the earl's wife gave the name *Deux encres* (Fr.: 'May God grant it increase'). Ranulph, as patron, may have fixed the name as *Deulencres* when he laid the Abbey foundation stone c.1220. Perched on a nearby hill was the little town of Leek, its church founded in 1042. As lord of the manor of Leek, the Earl had seen the town developing and in 1232 he transferred the lordship of both the forest and the manor of Leek, with its Wednesday market (from 1207) and eight-day annual fair, to the Abbot. The abbey was also granted land at Wetwood and mills at Leek and Hulme. Cistercian estate management, like the rest of medieval society, was intimately bound up with lordship. They held courts for their tenants in the same style as other lords, collected rents from their tenants and demanded tolls from the market traders. Houses were acquired in the town where wool could be stored and sales negotiated. The monks acted as middlemen in the wool trade, buying up fleeces from their neighbours and putting them up for sale with their own produce.

The abbey of Dieulacres was built on the banks of the River Churnet, the moorlands of North Staffordshire being ideal for colonisation by monks whose rules required that they settle in remote areas. The sheltered site had hill pasture for sheep, a fertile valley with a good stream (the Churnet) and existing parcels of already cultivated land where fishponds could be built to keep fish alive for food. The Cistercians were very competent water engineers so water was piped to latrines, wash-places, brewhouses, kitchens, the bakehouse and the infirmary etc. The Abbot of Dieulacres in 1293 was known to be very keen on hunting and a 'grant of free warren' gave the monks rights to hunt other animals, i.e. badger, wildcat, marten, fox, partridge, pheasant, rabbit, squirrel and hare. The hare was known as the 'principal beast of the warren'. In 1430, a bridge over the Churnet at Bridge End, Leek, on the Macclesfield A523 road, was called Coneygreave Bridge suggesting a nearby rabbit (coney) warren. This may be the warren documented for Leek Frith in the same year.

Because their valley was prone to flooding, the monks built a paved causeway across the floodplain of the Churnet to maintain year-round access from the Abbey to the town of Leek. It can be followed today as the short stretch of road from Abbey Green to Broads Bridge. Called the 'Surey' or 'Sury' at the 1724 Quarter Sessions, the maintenance of this causeway 'from the end of Surrey Pavement to Gun Gate', part of a very important road, was judged to be the responsibility of the people living in 'the village of Surrey in the Parish of Leek'. This may have been a small settlement on raised ground near the Abbey Inn. The extension of this route to the north was referred to in 1230 as the 'Trusseway', a name suggesting packhorse use. From Abbey Green it climbs the deep hollow-way from Fould (SJ 977 587) to Gun Side.

The monks designated blocks of land under exclusive Abbey ownership called 'granges'. Existing village communities are likely to have been completely relocated if the monks wished, for example, to convert arable to pasture, with the populace used as estate workers. Grange land was cleared and drained and, to maximise efficiency, each grange was limited to about 300 to 400 acres. In the early years, the resident labour force of these granges consisted of illiterate lay brothers. Later the lay brothers were phased out, when, rather than farming 'in-house', many granges were actually let to tenants.

THE LOCAL GRANGES

While there are no monastic 'mother houses' in the Peak District, grange names are common. Some are post-medieval farms that took the name to suggest a long ancestry but others were monastic farms founded in the economic expansion of the 12th to early 14th centuries. Some are still farms today, occasionally retaining parts of their typically large and curving 'bank and ditch' field boundaries which have survived for 800 years to define the limits of monastic land. The siting of such granges in the northern and western hills naturally encouraged the monks' involvement with the wool trade.

Outlying granges of the 'mother house' of Dieulacres were set up at **New Grange** (1291) at the confluence of the Churnet and Meer Brook (now under the waters of Tittesworth Reservoir at SJ 993 601), **Swythamley** (SJ 973 646), **Fairborough** (SJ 958 609), three granges at **Foker** recorded in the 1330s (SJ 97 58), and **Wetwood** (1291), possibly on the east side of Gun near Lower Wetwood, plus two near **Heaton** (Rushton Spencer). The post-Dissolution tenant Thomas Vygers held a house in 1542 called **Foker Grange** (SJ 985 575). It is entirely possible that both **Roche Grange**, recorded in 1246 (SJ 992 633), and the nearby large outcrop of The Roaches acquired their names from the Norman French-speaking monks of the abbey, *rocher* (Fr.) meaning rock or crag. Between the granges and their abbey, the monks would have constructed and maintained roads.

Each of these granges or farming units would be growing crops for their own use. These would include barley for bread and brewing, and oats for oatcakes, porridge and as fodder for horses. The Abbey also held considerable pasture rights for cattle at Morridge – as did other abbeys. This seems to have resulted in frequent disputes.

By the 14th century, however, sheep farming had become the most important agricultural activity at the granges. Sheep would provide milk for cheese, wool for monks' habits, tallow for candles and skins for parchment. The main source of the abbey's wealth was high-quality wool, purchased under contract a year in advance by Florentine merchants and supplied to the European wool trade as a cash-crop for the parent institution – one of the most lucrative businesses in the Middle Ages. Indeed, the Cistercians' skilful exploitation of their lands, which proved to be ideal for sheep pasturing, resulted in the order becoming England's leading producer of wool at a time when the wool trade was the source of half the nation's wealth. By 1347 the Black Prince, who as patron of the abbey had extended his protection 'against annoyance', was buying Dieulacres wool. Fine-quality wool was sometimes assured by housing the sheep throughout harsh winters (11 November to Easter) in long sheepcotes. Such sheep farms were known as 'burcaries'.

Surviving records for the Cistercian monasteries show that they moved their wool to distant markets and ports by packhorse and/or cart. The long hauls from the abbeys of Vale Royal and Combermere in Cheshire and Dieulacres Abbey in Staffordshire to London, or from the inland port of Torksey on the River Trent to Italy via the east coast port of Boston and, later, Hull, suggests such journeys were not unduly difficult. To the west of the region was the port of Chester, but as this was never a 'staple' port, it was an illegal outlet for the export of such commodities as wool or lead.

The first reference to the fulling of cloth in England occurs in monastic documents of 1125. The actual *mechanical* fulling and scouring of woven wool using wooden 'stocks' or hammers lifted and released by waterwheel shafts – perhaps perfected by the monks – occurs in the early 13th century. From this time the export of wool as raw material dramatically reduces (see Chapter 14). In 1567 there was a building called the Woolhouse at Abbey Green in Leek. There was certainly a fulling mill at Abbey Green in 1677. 'Waulk Mill Pool', recorded in the early 16th century as formerly belonging to Dieulacres Abbey, may have been associated with a fulling mill in Leek manor mentioned in 1548. Some Cistercian abbeys had ships to export their wool. Thus, wine could be imported and grain obtained during times of local shortage.

There is, then, little doubt that the monks of Dieulacres had both the resources and the manpower to construct artificial watercourses and to use waterwheels to perform several different functions. While most of the remaining structures and remnants at known water-powered mill sites in the study area are likely to be less than 300 years old, some along the rivers Dane, Churnet and their tributaries probably occupy ancient sites associated with the medieval monastic granges. As bread was both a vital part of a monk's diet and essential to celebrate the Mass, small water-powered mills were built for the abbeys and granges, often sited within or close to the precinct. A mill (probably a corn mill) at Hulme belonging to the abbey and still in use at the Dissolution may have stood on Back Brook at Upper Hulme. There is also evidence that many religious houses used water power to crush oak bark to make tannin for leather-working, and to power bellows for smelting and forging iron. Monastic ironworking is mentioned in Domesday and although no such documentation exists for Dieulacres Abbey, iron would have been in demand for ploughs, horseshoes, nails, hinges, etc.

A worsening climate and localised outbreaks of bubonic plague, including the Black Death of the 1340s that came on the heels of the 1315–22 famine, were common until the mid-17th century. Although these outbreaks had a direct impact in the Peak District, some depopulation was probably the result of people moving to better lowland areas, with others forced off the land where landlords had abandoned labour-intensive arable cultivation and increased their sheep flocks. Surviving accounts from the years between 1370 and 1380 reveal that during this time the *major* landowners were gradually extricating themselves from sheep farming and were leasing their demesne land to smaller, independent producers. Thereafter, during a gradual demise of serfdom, monastic agricultural focus was to change to cattle rearing and records show Dieulacres Abbey to have controlled a large herd at Swythamley. By 1535, most of the abbey's land had been leased to tenants.

The enormous prosperity resulting from their overseas wool trade would seem to sit rather uncomfortably with the Cistercian ideals of piety and simplicity and attracted the attention of several monarchs long before Henry VIII dispossessed the monasteries. Their order was eventually to become a byword for decadence and avarice. Many of these institutions failed to move with the times in which the staff had grown used to a secure and comfortable life.

DISSOLUTION (1536–40)

At the time of Henry VIII's 1534 Act of Supremacy, the Abbot of Dieulacres was maintaining an armed band of thugs to oppress the local people. His hunting rights covered a wide area north from Leek to the county boundary and besides the normal officials on the estates there was a 'forester of the Forest of Leek'.

Meanwhile, the abbey's sheep-rearing activities had completely declined and the much-publicised self-indulgence by the monks had gained them a further unfortunate reputation. The abbey's debts stood at £172, at which time the community consisted of the abbot and 12 other monks, with 30 servants, 8 'lauders and poor bede women' and 19 lay brothers.

In 1538, Dr Thomas Legh, a Royal Commissioner, took possession of Dieulacres Abbey and the abbot and monks were pensioned off. This great church, which had been enlarged and rebuilt in the 14th century, was stripped of its contents in a matter of days. The six bells and the church plate were sold, 175 tons of lead valued at £720 was removed from the roof and the windows were torn out, reducing the abbey to a windy ruin. Part of the roof may have gone to Gawsworth Church, Cheshire. In the same year, nearby Wincle Grange surrendered to the crown. With the Dissolution, *all* monastic property and land passed to the crown for resale, often at knockdown prices, thus securing loyalty to the new order.

During the middle ages, towns maintained their own roads, but elsewhere the liability for road repairs rested with the lord of the manor or monastic houses. With the Dissolution, although this latter contribution ceased, liability was passed to the new owners of monastic land who pushed up land prices and rents. This was followed by a prolonged period of gradual land enclosure and private improvement schemes, which took place either by agreement on individual farms, or were imposed by large estates.

DIEULACRES ABBEY TODAY

Immediately west of the abbey site today, and in private ownership, is Abbey Farm. It is timber-framed on a sandstone course and near to where the scant remains of the monastery are marked by the foundations of the crossing piers and south transept. In 1614, the farm was the home of Thomas Rudyard, lord of Leek manor. It is uncertain whether any part of the present fabric dates from before the 17th century. The abbey site had been easy prey for ready-cut stone since the Dissolution and when the remains were again uncovered in 1818, much of the revealed stone was used in the erection of outbuildings for the farm. Recent archaeological resistivity surveys show that there are good remains surviving below the ground. There are also significant earthworks defining the areas of the precinct.

PART THREE
EARLY COMMUNICATIONS

Chapter 8. MEDIEVAL ROADS AND TRAVEL

INTRODUCTION

To the medieval traveller the countryside would have looked very different. The South-West Peak was an open landscape of moorland with craggy ridges, small areas of ploughed earth for growing crops, with common pasture on higher land – a patchwork of grass and woodland. There would have been few stone walls or hedges – even the open fields around the few settlements only had banks at their edge dividing them from the commons beyond. Barns and dwellings would be made of timber, clay and thatch. The long 'enclosures' walls were yet to be built; there were few major routes across the area and perhaps just the very occasional stone marker, manor house or church to act as a landmark. Crossing this thinly populated and perhaps unfamiliar region in foul weather, it would have been all too easy for strangers to lose 'the way'.

Experienced traders, however, would be making lengthy cross-country journeys often by the most direct route across any dryer uplands. Parts of these routes, usually bypassing any settlements, can still be seen as parallel hollow-ways running sometimes for many kilometres. In the South-West Peak, the major (perhaps medieval) through-routes are limited to the drover's 'Great Road' from Congleton to Nottingham (see below), the Manchester to Derby (via Buxton) Roman road mapped by Ogilby in 1675 (see Chapter 18) and the Saltways from Cheshire to Chesterfield and Sheffield (see Chapter 9).

These routes that had evolved from habitual lines of travel would have formed integrated networks but it is sometimes difficult to see where they were leading. Some may have originally come into use in pre-Roman, Roman, Saxon or Medieval times and if they remained in use during any or all of these previous periods, evidence needs to be confirmed from any surviving historical records, boundary lines on maps, old river crossings or guideposts and by place-names.

Detailed documentary evidence for use of a specific ancient route is quite rare; evidence for post-medieval use is sometimes easier to obtain. Where routes bypassed cultivated land and are not ploughed out or otherwise destroyed, fieldwork might reveal the physical evidence of fording and bridging points and the confused remnants of raised causeways, terracing or braided hollow-ways, some adjacent to a later road. Although the drier months of the year might afford the carriage of heavy or bulky goods in wagons, there were only two regular means of travelling: either on foot or on horseback. The majority of goods were carried on single packhorses or trains of animals. The alterative was by droving large numbers of livestock that required wider lanes with sections of pasture for the animals to graze whilst on the move. These droving routes provided connections with the great markets and larger centres of population.

LONG-DISTANCE TRADE AND TRAVEL

Although relatively few individuals needed to travel very far, it was important for the whole economy that both people and produce were able to when required. For goods there were two alternatives: they could travel by water or by road. Overland carriage of bulky and weighty goods of low value across the region was, until the arrival of the railways, far more expensive than the carriage of such goods by water in other regions. The landlocked Peak District did not have this option as the rivers were obstructed by low bridges, weirs or fish traps and were therefore not navigable. For the most part, these rivers were simply too shallow and often ran north–south, which was seldom the direction required. High value textiles, particularly woollen cloth, could be taken to inland fairs and markets by packhorse – this trade being able to provide a door-to-door service and to absorb the greater transport costs. Minerals such as lead and many heavy manufactured goods were taken laboriously overland and exported via eastern sea ports or the nearest inland river ports, chiefly Doncaster, Bawtry and Torksey.

It is hard to accept the 'total quagmire' view of medieval roads in Britain. If you used a road regularly then you made sure you kept it in working order. Because some new towns were not on any existing routes, adequate new routes would have certainly been needed to serve these towns as well as any areas of settlement in between.

In 1285, the Statute of Winchester placed the responsibility of highway maintenance upon the manors and enforced it by Common Law. If a route was much used, it became a substantial track with two important provisos. The first was that if the road was obstructed or became 'foundrous' in wet weather, then the traveller had the right to diverge, even if that entailed trampling crops. The second proviso was that if the road had to climb a hill or bank, causing multiple tracks to develop (hollow-ways), the traveller was able to choose the easiest route available.

Although routes in this book might be described as 'from' and 'to', many of course continued onward *through* the given destinations.

ROYAL TRAVELLERS

Prior to the Tudor period, kings with their retinue and baggage train comprising from ten to twenty carts and wagons, containing on occasion a considerable entourage, seem to have been constantly on the move. In a single half-year, King Edward I (1272 -1307), for example, moved his residence seventy-five times. There were castles, palaces, manors and religious houses in every English county and there are surprisingly few recorded complaints about the road conditions at any season of the year. This suggests that such long-distance routes were either used infrequently, and therefore quite adequate for their time, or that nobility and the royal household took the prevailing conditions for granted. It is possible that the monarchs travelled lighter, men on horseback being better able to negotiate roads that proved difficult for lumbering wagons. Royal itineraries can often be compiled from letters, charters the kings were granting and from their household accounts. By searching these itineraries for place-names and looking at any

surviving crude maps it is possible to reconstruct the general direction of these routes, but not necessarily all the 'roads' used.

In 1157, King Henry II received the conquered Scottish King Malcolm IV at Peveril Castle. The routes of their arrival are not known, but both left for Chester, probably via Whaley Bridge (Horwich?). King John (1199–1216) appears not to have remained anywhere for more than a month throughout his entire reign. On 8 September 1235, King Henry III was in Chesterfield. On 11 September he was at Castleton and by 14 September he had arrived in Lichfield. The routes are not known.

Between 20 and 22 August 1275, King Edward I, the last of the Plantagenet monarchs to hunt regularly, spent three days in Tideswell hunting in the Royal Forest. He managed to travel, on average, 32km a day when on the move. Three weeks later, Roger Lestrange, Bailiff of the Forest, was ordered to send all venison in the king's larder at 'Tydeswell' to Westminster. The king, meanwhile, was travelling from Ashbourne to Macclesfield, probably via Chapel-en-le Frith. In 1290, Edward I returned to Tideswell from Macclesfield via 'Weyl' (Whaley) and departed to Chesterfield via Ashford (in-the-Water).

On 2 September 1382, Henry Plantagenet (later Henry IV), aged 18, visited Tideswell and purchased a 'grey hound' from Benedict Tatton for 20 shillings.

PORTWAYS

Many early roads or routes were given names indicating the type of traffic using them, e.g. 'Saltway' and 'Portway'. A 'portway', or portage road, for example, was a track for carrying and transportation to and from markets and fairs. '*The* Portway', generally considered to have been a specific long-distance route from Bakewell through Wirksworth to Nottingham, is still exercising the minds of historians both amateur and professional. It is inevitably controversial but certainly less time-consuming to conjecture the course of previous tracks on the basis of the reoccurrence of the common location 'portway' from a few place-names on a large-scale map. Any number of these 'portways' crossing the Peak District could be contrived to fit together into such a route and perhaps become erroneously called 'The Portway'. A similarly lengthy portway has been surmised between Chesterfield and Wirksworth.

DROVE ROADS

As towns grew and populations increased, the neighbouring countryside became unable to satisfy the demand for meat. Cattle-droving then became increasingly important and the drovers so numerous that by the 16th century they had to be controlled by statute. It was enacted that every drover had to satisfy certain requirements with regard to his maturity, marital status and reliability.

Nationally, large groups of animals were driven from Scotland and Wales towards the rich pastures of central England. From here the herds were moved to the capital and other great market centres. This animal-droving, well-established by the medieval period, only reached its peak as the railways arrived in the mid-19th century and then swiftly declined, although the driving of sheep still went on after the railways had taken over most of the cattle trade. Driven at a steady pace by drovers and dogs, cattle were moved in manageable herds, the sheep in larger flocks. Where possible, the drovers would avoid taking the herds through any towns, keeping instead to the extensive commons and drier uplands. To avoid paying tolls on the turnpike roads, as these had become widespread by the early 18th century, the drover would make detours across any unenclosed land.

For the duration of the drove the feet of cattle were shod, each hoof needing a pair of small iron shoes. Pigs (frequently muzzled) might be fitted with leather boots but were only driven comparatively short distances – perhaps six miles a day. Huge flocks of turkeys and geese were driven to markets. At the start of the drive, the geese were made to walk through tar and then sand to provide protection.

Surviving physical evidence for drovers' routes is usually limited to unenclosed moorland and commons. Place-names and field names will often support such evidence.

'THE GREAT ROAD'

There is certainly one major droving route across the South-West Peak. This is the well-affirmed 'Great Road' to the east from Congleton, in Cheshire, to Nottingham. Passing north of Leek and over the southern slopes of Gun Hill, this 'Great Road' descends past Oxhay Farm to Meerbrook (SJ 990 608) and Upper Hulme. The herds would begin their long, slow climb past Hurdlow Farm, above which hollow-way evidence first becomes available within a small piece of enclosed woodland (SK 021 607). Across the semi-improved 'open access' pasture east of the parish boundary wall, the drover's route to the 'Mermaid' (SK 037 605) is again revealed as parallel lines of hollow-ways, in places 100m wide. It is recorded that the final stretch of the climb was causewayed with stone slabs. Formerly Blakemere House, the 'Mermaid' was at one time on a major crossing of old routes where fairs were held for the sale of livestock. Although a

Part of the 'Great Road' east of Herbage Barn.

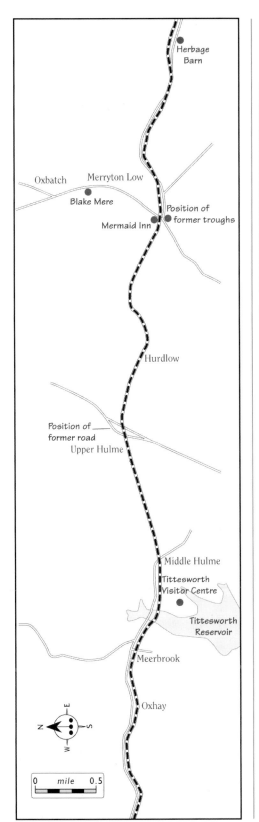

Map: 'The Great Road' between Congleton and Nottingham.

The Mermaid Inn from Blake Mere.

variety of water troughs once existed opposite the inn, large herds could be watered at nearby Blake Mere (SK 040 613) where an area of nearby moorland is called Oxbatch. Passing either side of nearby Merryton Low, the blanket peat can still be found deeply cut by hooves and wheels. These tracks predating the nearby enclosures and walls attest to a route of some importance and probably great antiquity. The divided route converges again and crosses rough pasture towards Herbage Barn (SK 057 603). From here a lesser branch runs across Swallow Moss, heading for Brund Mill and Pilsbury. The 'Great Road', meanwhile, continues eastwards over Revidge (Rough Edge) and then in a deep hollow-way north of Warslow to Hayesgate (SK 099 596). From here it heads towards Hulme End and over the River Dove to Hartington and Winster (SK 242 605).

Distinctive *local* droving routes existed. Using broad ridges across the upland commons where possible, livestock was driven between winter and summer grazing and to nearby local markets for onward sale or as 'meat on the hoof'.

By the 15th century, because the revenue from cattle and sheep had rapidly increased, the upland communities of the South-West Peak, for example, were finding it more economical to export surplus livestock and import grain, which had not increased proportionally in price. This advantageous trade and the time saved from labour-intensive agriculture, encouraged the growth of a diversity of small industrial developments where goods produced generated further traffic in a variety of raw materials and finished products.

HOLLOW-WAYS AND LOCAL TRAVEL

Many surviving hollow-ways were only local cattle tracks to streams or between summer and winter pasture. Others may have been frequently used ways to turf cuts, springs or woodland. It is all too easy to join a number of such individual hollow-ways together and then mistakenly identify them as one significant route. Many such hollow-ways are often short, disjointed and perhaps of no great age. Some of the upland hollow-ways have cut through the peat

Hollow-way worn down to bedrock (Chapel Gate).

and shales to either gritstone bedrock, or to original subsoil which now supports much paler vegetation. This is very apparent on aerial photographs. Some may have been created when winter fuel was brought down on sledges or light carts from the communal turf cuts and may have doubled as cattle tracks to the upland grazing. Sections of pre-turnpike 'coal roads' and 'lime roads', and shown as such on 19th-century maps, are often to be found surviving as hollow-ways isolated by subsequent improvement and enclosure. Rough tracks on the limestone area with their thin overlying soils were less susceptible to erosion so that hollow-ways here are much less obvious.

To connect the remote settlements and farms of the South-West Peak both with each other and with the local manorial centres and markets, intricate travel routes would have evolved. Most were dictated by the area's topography and climate, by external demand for any natural resources and by the needs of its few residents. Many old tracks are obliterated but occasionally, in a certain light, it is possible to detect their ghosts beneath today's landscape. A faint track previously described as 'part of an old drove road' might upon investigation lead to the moss-covered footings of a small group of buildings robbed of their stone – and no further. Enquiries made of local people will often confirm suspicions that the 'drove road' was merely an isolated and abandoned 18th-century farm track and that historical accuracy is not always the sole province of the historian.

A surprising aspect of some routes is that pack-horse carriers sometimes seem to have scorned easy gradients for more direct ones, even if the way was uncomfortably steep. Some route decisions were perhaps made according to the season, the local weather or because of the inconvenience of enclosure walls – it was, after all, the horse doing the work, not the carrier! The deep hollow-way crossing the steep Terret (SK 035 717) seems a strange route choice to carry coal from the nearby mines to the Grin limekilns, when an almost level alternative across the nearby saddle at Axe Edge may have been easier and quicker. It is of course possible that the Axe Edge saddle was used for full panniers, with the steep Terret way used for returning 'empties' (see maps).

PILGRIM AND CHURCH ROUTES

The Peak District was incorporated into the diocese of Lichfield at some time during the 8th century and it is from this time onwards that we find 'pilgrim' routes to visit shrines; although in an age more pious than ours, these tracks were never used solely for pilgrimages. A few tracks used primarily for local access to the parish churches were known as 'churchgates' or 'kirkgates', where in many parts of England, particularly in the more remote areas, the establishment of churches was delayed because the population pattern was dispersed rather than nucleated. Because only the parish church had the right of christening, marriage and burial, these 'churchgates' could became quite prominent tracks.

Markets and Fairs

The inhabitants of the hamlets and scattered farmsteads of the South-West Peak would all have been familiar with their nearby market towns of Macclesfield, Leek, Chapel-en-le-Frith, Longnor and perhaps Hartington. The markets had become established by charter and regulated by laws as early as the 13th century, for buying and selling livestock and other produce. Weekly markets with one or more annual fairs were often located at the junctions between contrasting landscape areas where differing types of farming took place and where good roads and bridging points were available. Since there were few shops as we know them, except perhaps at the market centres, the weekly village or town market would have been the busy focus of retail trade and 'market day' a major event in people's lives. As there were few areas of settlement further from a market than seven to ten miles, this distance afforded manageable return travel for people prepared to walk or ride during the hours of daylight, to buy or sell.

CAUSEYS

The Middle English word *causie-wei* (causey way) was a corruption of the old Norman French *caucie* meaning (1) a raised track, or (2) an ancient paved highway such as an old Roman military road. From this no doubt the modern English word causeway evolved. The word is still used in local speech where 'causeyed track' or a 'causey edge' means a slightly raised pavement across soft surfaces of moorland or woodland, or terraced into the sides of hills where deep grooves might form. In attempts to create some stability in the bottoms of existing hollow-ways, lines

of gritstone slabs were a cheap and useful method sometimes employed by the parishes on a local and limited basis to prevent further wear and tear. Old causeys can still be discovered – sometimes a single line laid down for packhorses, or a double line for carts that often served as a major highway. Many were the result of private initiative by both lords and freeholders to slab the way across their land. Often worn and overgrown, they are perhaps the commonest surviving feature of the packhorse era. They are impossible to date; they could have been laid down at any time from the medieval period to the 19th century. The destruction of the (now stabilised) southern stretches of the modern Pennine Way by 20th-century walkers shows how once the surface vegetation of a moorland track has been worn away, peat erosion quickly follows.

Across many eroded moorland paths and heavily used hillside tracks and ridges in the Peak District today, flagstones from derelict textile mill sites in Lancashire are being flown in by helicopter to create new slabbed or 'causeyed' paths, this time for the comfort and convenience of modern-day walkers by encouraging them to keep to the path and prevent further erosion.

LOCAL CAUSEYED PATHS

Recently slabbed paths reminiscent of those created during the packhorse era can be found crossing some eroded uplands of the South-West Peak. These include the public footpath from Macclesfield Forest edge to the summit of Shutlingslow (SJ 976 696) and 3km of the nearby county boundary across the bare peat of the public footpath between Shining Tor and Pym Chair in the upper Goyt Valley.

In the Dean Valley east of Kerridge Hill, Rainow, a continuous stone-slabbed footpath (SK 945 768) can be followed for a kilometre across the fields between Sugar Lane and Waulkmill Farm. Ensuring dry feet for the employees of the various water-powered textile mills once situated on the lower reaches of the River Dean, these unique paths are either the result of private initiative by mill owners or, more likely, were created piecemeal by the workers. Such paths are particularly numerous in the Ingersley Vale/Kerridge Hill area, partly no doubt because the stone was so readily available. Although parts of some are overgrown, they make a considerable contribution to the character of the area.

Slabbed path and Shining Tor.

A MEDIEVAL RIDGEWAY?

A Macclesfield Forest 'medieval ridgeway' that would join the Roman road from Buxton to Manchester was suggested in the classic publication *Peakland Roads and Trackways* by AE Dodd and EM Dodd. This theoretical route is therefore worthy of some consideration and examination.

From Langley village (SJ 941 715), follow Clarke Lane, passing Higher Ridgegate Farm in a tarmacked hollow-way rising steeply below the large rectangular earthwork currently scheduled as a medieval deer enclosure on Toot Hill. Ridgegate continues to the tiny hamlet of Macclesfield Forest (SJ 974 721) to be joined by a walled stony track from Walker Barn, now called Charity Lane but previously known as 'The Ditch', Dirty Gate or Chapel Lane. The combined route then drops steeply down Oven House Lane to Bottom-of-the-Oven. The described route turned north to Torgate Farm (Torgate: the way to, or near, the Tors), supposedly leading up along the ridge composed of a series of Tors: Shining Tor (SJ 995 737), The Tors, Cats Tor and Pym Chair. After crossing The Street at Pym Chair, the ridgeway was said to continue northwards past Windgather Rocks to Black Hill before descending to join the ancient Derby–Buxton–Manchester highway (see Chapter 3, Roman Roads).

At the foot of Oven House Lane ('Oven' does not imply baking here; it is a name meaning deep valley), fieldwork reveals the obvious route continuation over the stream, rising eastwards beyond Bottom-of-the-Oven Farm as a single deep hollow-way. However, this quickly curves southwards to follow the Clough Brook down into Wildboarclough – probably a local route down the valley before the existing road was constructed.

Despite a meticulous search, no evidence can be found today of even a hint of a route to either Torgate Farm (SJ 987 724) or up the steep southern aspect of Shining Tor to gain 'The Tors' ridge. The ridgeway described suggests unfamiliarity with the waterlogged nature of the deep peat and the degree of exposure experienced here on all but the finest of days (See 'Causeys' above). This ridge, although appreciated by modern leisure walkers, is the first major obstruction encountered by the prevailing westerly winds rushing in across the Cheshire plain. From Macclesfield, to access the Buxton to Manchester Roman road, the Saltway via Rainow and Saltersford was perhaps the most practical way (See Chapter 9, Salt and Saltways), or the upper Goyt Valley would be crossed to Buxton as described below.

BETWEEN MACCLESFIELD AND BUXTON

There is certainly good hollow-way evidence for pre-turnpike horse routes over high ground between Macclesfield and Buxton. From Walker Barn (SJ 956 737), a horse route shadows the A537 as far as

Braided hollow-way east of Torgate Farm.

Hollow-way on the Macclesfield route west of Errwood car park.

Turnshawflat, at which point it forks right for 2km on the line of the 1759 turnpike to Buxton. It is joined north of Greenways Farm at SJ 978 731 by the Ankers Knowl route from Lamaload. Leaving the metalled road, the combined route plunges down a wide hollow-way to Brookhouse Farm, before climbing past spring-fed troughs at SJ 982 728 and descending as a tree-lined track to the Tor Brook. Crossing lower Long Clough as a spread of minor hollow-ways, the braids converge at the junction of the A537 and the older turnpike at the foot of Stake Clough (SJ 998 726). (A further hollow-way route ascending Wildboarclough to join this highway can be seen in rough pasture above the Clough Brook at SJ 992 724.)

Torgate Farm might perhaps be considered as a fulcrum for these steep and tiring routes. It is located below the high moors on improved pasture close to a number of streams and wells. The substantial farm may have been a resting place for packmen and their horses.

Continuing up Stake Clough, 200m beyond Stake Farm we have two divergent routes:

(1) Across Stake Side the route appears reduced to one or two shallow hollow-ways following, and mostly hidden by, a long north–south drystone wall along the ridge above Shooters Clough. However, these cut under the wall at SK 004 740 and curve gently north-east, braiding across the broad pasture towards the River Goyt – one particular branch south of the car park being particularly deep. The more obvious hollow-ways are easily found, centred on SK 009 747 above the present Errwood Car Park, below which the widening of the steep-sided valley here would have provided the packmen with a convenient shallow fording point and, by the 18th century, a horse bridge upstream. This location was a primary focus for major west–east packhorse traffic and was perhaps a reason for the establishment of the tiny hamlet of Goytsbridge (SK 014 750). From Goytsbridge hamlet, the detailed route towards Buxton and Fairfield is described in Chapter 9.

(2) Following a ruined west–east wall, a hollow-way, initially with shallow braids at SK 001 729, drops eastwards steeply down Stake Side, before crossing Stake Clough and Deep Clough towards the ruins of Goytsclough Mill and Goytsclough

Farm, beyond which it becomes briefly obliterated by 20th-century forestry. Fording the River Goyt, now with a modern bridge at SK 016 729, the route comprises two main branches, initially with considerable braiding, heading up Berry Clough. The north-eastern route fades away into heather and cannot be followed. The long 1804 Hartington Enclosures wall blocks the eastern route, still a deep hollow-way as it crossed the ridgetop. Continuing through Burbage Edge Plantation, it deepens and braids down rough pasture towards early 19th-century quarrying for construction of the long-disused C&HPR railtrack at SK 033 728. Beyond this point the route towards Shay Lodge and the town has been obliterated.

Seventeenth-century estate maps reveal that the area now covered by the town of Buxton was occupied by the two small villages of Buxton and Fairfield, with a scattering of individual farmsteads quite typical of the adjoining parishes of Hartington Upper Quarter and Fernilee. Although these two complimentary routes over the upper Goyt were perhaps dictated by either seasonal or local commercial considerations, one or the other may have provided the packmen with a convenient onward bypass around agricultural land (some of it already enclosed) onto higher ground, avoiding both the villages and the Wye gorge.

THE ERRWOOD HALL TRACK

At Stake Clough, the Macclesfield to Buxton traditional route is reduced to one deep, rising hollow-way. Beyond Stake Farm, this coincides with a more modern level cart track, following the long enclosure wall (See (1) above) along the ridge for the next kilometre, at which point the track descends sharply through this wall on a series of 'hairpin' terraces to follow the Shooters Clough stream to Castedge and Errwood Hall. The Grimshaw family constructed this track in the 1830s. It provided direct access from the Macclesfield to Buxton turnpike, near to the Cat and Fiddle Inn, to their Castedge mines and their residence Errwood Hall, where it facilitated both building and plantation management.

BETWEEN LEEK AND MACCLESFIELD

A well-documented medieval highway between Leek and Macclesfield, and no doubt part of a much longer route, leads across the 'Surey Pavement' to Abbey Green and is then etched deeply into the fields above Fould (SJ 977 587), where in c.1230 it was recorded as the 'Trusseway'. Still in places a bridleway, it climbs to the western flank of Gun Hill, where in 1724 it was known as 'Gun Gate'. Here it joins the tarmac road leading to Eleven Lane Ends but leaves it after 400m to follow the line of a public footpath down

The Cleulow Cross mound.

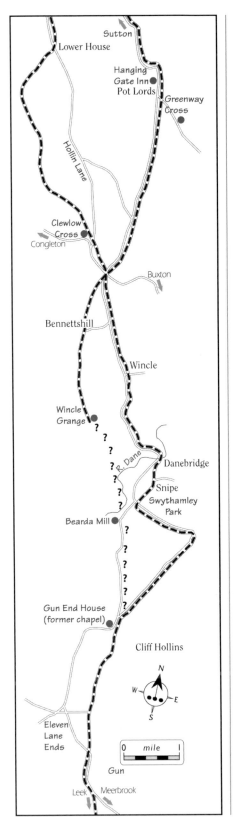

Map: The traditional route between Leek and Macclesfield.

to Gun End. The exact route from here is somewhat less certain. It has been suggested that travellers to Wincle Grange may have dropped very steeply down alongside the tributary stream past Bearda (originally Beardholme), to ford the Dane at its confluence (SJ 962 644) before climbing directly to, and then perhaps beyond the grange, across Bennettshill. Alternatively and perhaps more likely, traffic would have taken an easier way around Swythamley Park (SJ 97 65) to Snipe Cottage to ford or make a bridge crossing of the river at nearby Danebridge. The current road forming the southern boundary of the Swythamley estate was in place by 1831 and was perhaps cut to provide access for the Danebridge cotton mill.

From Danebridge, the present deeply hollowed tarmacked road climbing out of the Dane valley through Wincle up to the A54 probably represents most of the old route. Irrespective of which Dane crossing was used when climbing northwards out of the Dane valley, travellers would have looked for the large mound and Anglo-Saxon cross at Cleulow. A short hollowway below the west of the mound drops across Hollin Lane as a firm track, initially across improved pasture. Sections of this route, now a bridleway, follow the Rossen Brook as far as Lowerhouse (SJ 939 697). Here it rejoins Hollin Lane, leading to Sutton Lane Ends and Macclesfield. This medieval road was still in use in the 18th century.

By keeping east of Cleulow Cross, a high, well-drained ridgeway with open views would have been used in wet weather. Joining the medieval 'Greenway' (see below) above Pot Lords, the combined route to Macclesfield descends in a deep curve around the Hanging Gate pub (SJ 953 696) to follow (a) along Ridge Hill, passing Manor Farm down to Sutton, or (b) down to Meg Lane, past Drove Hey to Langley Hall and across The Hollins.

'GREENWAY CROSS' –A highway marker (SJ 9460 6923)

By the roadside on a recognised major east–west medieval route above Higher Sutton, Macclesfield, is a standing stone with perhaps prehistoric origins. It has been 'Christianised' with half-relief simple crosses on two faces and is known locally as 'The Greenway Cross' – the name reappearing as Greenway Bridge over the nearby Oaken Clough stream. Parts of such routes, close-cropped and manured by the passing animals, were known locally as 'greenways'. Although time and continuing agricultural enclosure and road improvement schemes have erased much evidence of their existence, the word 'greenway' survives as a farm or a road name here and there as an interesting reminder.

This particular 'greenway' can still be followed eastwards from Macclesfield to Higher Sutton and beyond. Above the Hanging Gate pub it is joined by a ridgeway, part of a medieval route from Leek. At this point (SJ 952 695), the fork to the left is the 'Greenway'. Below Greenway Bridge the route follows part of a parish boundary above the Highmoor Brook, passing Lower Nabbs Farm to continue as an old tree-lined lane. It then climbs briefly to join the A54 at Allgreave before following the minor road east via Midgeleygate to cross the River Dane near Manor Farm, Quarnford (SK 002 663), north-east of Gradbach.

Following the Flash Brook upstream, the route was joined beyond the road junction (SK 005 663) by a similar horseway dropping in from the north. This was the old route from Brand Side (SK 045 688) across the head of the River Manifold and through Flash. Today, the old route is represented by the steep minor road from Flash village.

Still following the Flash Brook, the 'Greenway' continued to Flash Bottom; an important junction for horse routes north–south and east–west. Once more assuming the character of a packhorse way, it rises steeply over the northern shoulder of the Ann Roach ridge. Although briefly cut by boggy and broken ground as it passes above Adders Green (Edders Grenehed 1562), a 150m remnant of the horseway can still be found aiming resolutely for Morridge Top. This is overlain and effectively severed by a bank and ditch boundary at SK 0260 6535 from where any continuance of the route to the east is now obliterated by pasture improvement on the southern flanks of Roundhill.

Crossing today's A53 and going east from Morridge Top, the horse way continues as a track, crossing the stream at the head of Pyeclough. Here, a hollowway route perhaps from Gib Torr, beyond the ridge, joins it. The combined route, initially confined by enclosure walls, rises to become faint hollow-ways across improved pasture before descending (SK 046 644) to Merril Grove Farm (Merley Greve 1406). From this point, the minor road (a mid-18th-century

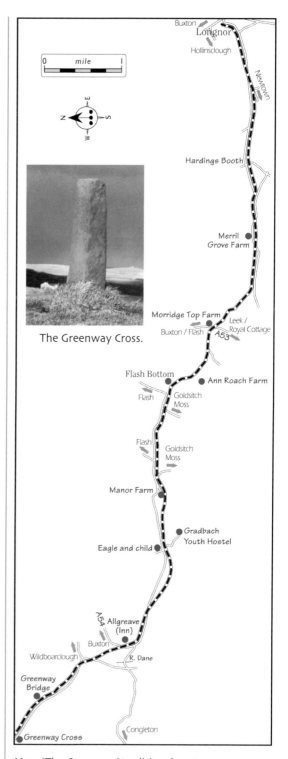

The Greenway Cross.

Map: 'The Greenway' traditional route.

Traditional route to Flash Bottom
from Ann Roach Ridge.

Braided hollow-way above Merril Grove Farm.

turnpike) then shadows the route east to Hardings Booth (Hardingsboth 1327), Longnor, Crowdecote, Monyash and Bakewell, to pick up a way to Chesterfield and perhaps further. By the 13th century some of these settlements had weekly markets and although it is most likely that salt from the Cheshire 'wiches' was carried along this route, there is little in the way of place-name evidence to support the theory.

Sometime before 1840, Sir George Crewe built a new, straight, cart-width road between Flash Bottom and Flash village and at the same time improved the old horse route between Flash Bottom and Manor Farm to a similar standard.

BETWEEN LEEK AND BUXTON

Before the construction of the present Leek to Buxton turnpike (now the A53) in the mid-18th century, travellers through or from Leek, heading north-east towards Chapel-en-le-Frith or the small settlements of Buxton and Fairfield, would have crossed the Churnet by Broads Bridge on the causeway to Abbey Green. From here the route would pass New Grange (now under the waters of Tittesworth Reservoir) to Meerbrook. Some of the pasture east of Meerbrook reveals remnants of this route on the steeper slopes. Following today's public footpath it passes Windygates, climbing to the very obvious gap between The

Deep hollow-way between The
Roaches and Hen Cloud.

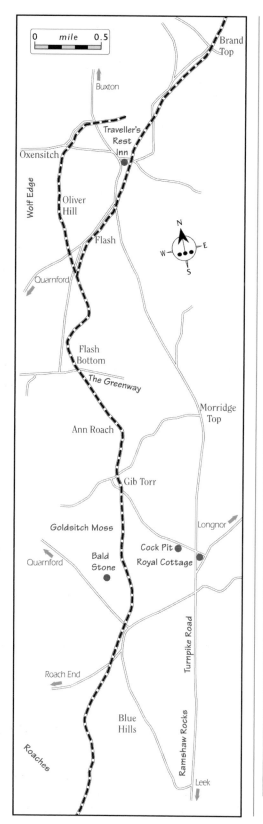

Map: The traditional route between Leek and Buxton.

Roaches and Hen Cloud where the hollow-ways have been almost erased by pasture improvement. Beyond the gap, the main hollow-way, clearly pre-dating the nearby enclosures, becomes deeply cut through bracken and heather, indicating a pre-turnpike route of some importance. Running over Goldsitch Moss, the route continued to Adders Green, Flash Bottom, up the south-facing slopes of the infant Flash Brook and north over the west side of Oliver Hill (SK 024 676). By 1749, however, Bowen's map shows the route realigned and running north-east through Flash village from where the old track descends behind the Travellers Rest towards Dove Head and Brand Top, passing Thirkelow Rocks to disappear in an area of quarrying and limeburning south of Buxton. Through the village of Flash, the earlier sunken packhorse route with gritstone marker-posts can be followed northwards between Wolf Edge and Oliver Hill.

Traditional route between Wolf Edge and Oliver Hill.

Chapter 9. SALT AND SALTWAYS

INTRODUCTION

From prehistoric times, spring tides allowed seawater brine to enter large evaporating pools (salterns) along the seashore; the liquid evaporated during the summer whilst in the autumn the crust of salt and earth was collected. This was roasted on an open fire to prepare the salt for the next stage when it was put in solution in large pans made from clay supported over a fire. The water was then boiled off and the salt collected and packed in moulds to solidify for transportation. The salt trade was vigorous even in Roman times, when part of a soldier's pay was his rations or *salarium* (Latin, *salis*) of salt, from which we get 'salary'. At Middlewich and Nantwich, archaeology has shown the industrial scale of Roman salt production.

In the past salt was so important that it was taxed and controlled by governments; the taxation was not repealed in England until 1825. Lack of salt would cause great hardship. It was essential for the preservation of meat, fish, dairy produce and also in the making of other staples such as bread, where salt will control the action of the yeast. It is a bulky commodity, difficult to transport, but has been produced industrially from the earliest times. In the 17th century, for example, it was estimated that up to a quarter of the volume of the salt would evaporate before reaching its intended market. Early salt traders would have used carts for local journeys and boats, wagons or strings of packhorses on longer trips.

To preserve meat for winter, salt was of basic importance. Although better breeds of livestock were eventually developed, earlier breeds became thin in the autumn from the poor grazing of the stubble fields and upland commons and many were butchered and salted in anticipation of winter fodder becoming scarce. Most survivors would be breeding stock kept on short rations until spring. The preservation of fish, to be successful, had to be done within a day or two of the fish being caught. Drovers used the attraction of animals for salt to control the lead cows while driving herds to market. The drover would hold salt in his hand and allow the animal to taste it. It would then follow him to get more of the salt.

Salt was also used in the preparation of hides for the leather industry, to fix dyes for the early textile industry, for glazing ceramics, for soap-making and to heal wounds – and increasingly by all for the kitchen. It was a very high-value mineral, carried overland for centuries to the market towns of England, often by packhorses along regular routes, the carrier being known as the 'salter'. The considerable cost of transporting salt – or any other goods by this method – would make it uneconomical to return with empty panniers. Various other commodities were therefore carried on the return journey, this being known as 'back carriage'.

THE REGIONAL SALT TRADE

Not all salt came from coastal salterns. The salt transported across the Peak District was mostly obtained from large, deep underground sources derived from dried-up seas of the Triassic period at Nantwich, Middlewich and Northwich in Cheshire.

These three locations with the OE suffix *wic* (-wich), meaning a salt works, are all to be found in the Domesday survey. The most important was Nantwich, *Nametwihc* in 1194. In the Domesday survey, it had, amongst others, 'a brinepit and eight demesne salthouses belonging to the king and Earl Edwin'.

This inland salt was exploited from natural brine springs or pumped from the deep beds until the mining of the salt beds began after 1670. The brine was boiled in lead pans over wood-fuelled furnaces or, later, in iron pans over coal furnaces. It was transported in a variety of containers over long distances.

A round trip by packhorse from the large Cheshire deposits into Nottinghamshire, Lancashire, Cumbria, Derbyshire and Yorkshire – even as far as Doncaster – was reckoned at between five to nine days. To carry salt from the Cheshire 'wiches' to destinations sometimes quite near the east coast may seem strange, but rock salt was considered far superior to sea salt, particularly for meat preservation and in butter and cheese making. Inland bulk cargoes gradually moved to the canals and then to the railways.

THE MAJOR SALTWAY ACROSS THE UPPER GOYT

It is always dubious to name a route after one particular type of user; only rarely was any route used for a single purpose. 'Saltways' therefore were packhorse

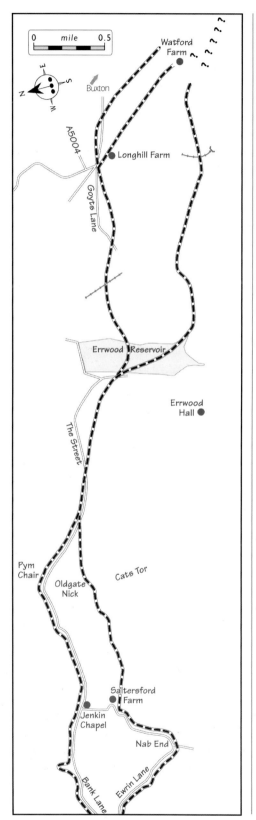

Map: The Saltway across the Upper Goyt.

ways and no different from the 'ways' used by other traders, although those routes used for salt can be followed from place-names supported by local tradition. The place-names contain the word 'salt' or more commonly 'salter': Saltersford, Saltersbridge, Salters Lane, Saltersgate, Saltersley, Saltergate Lane, etc (see map p.67).

In the upper Goyt Valley a sturdy farm located west of The Tors ridge has a stone in its west-facing wall bearing the date 1593. The building, mentioned in a document from 1452, is called Saltersford Hall (SJ 9841 7628), making it almost certain that the nearby west–east hollow-way that pierces the gritstone barrier of the ridge, leaving a sharp notch at Oldgate Nick, was part of an ancient route to the east from Chester and the Cheshire salt deposits via Macclesfield and Rainow to Chesterfield. The Old Norse *gata* 'road' and the Old/Middle English *gate*, meaning 'entrance, opening or gate' were still common parlance during the medieval period. The word *nick* meant a cut or notch in a ridge, breaking the skyline when seen from a valley and used by the packmaster to guide his train through the hills.

Saltersford Hall Farm below the Oldgate Nick.

'The Corkscrew'(see below).

Leaving Macclesfield through Rainow, the way branched eastwards roughly along the line of Ginclough, where a number of faint hollow-ways running west–east are still evident across today's improved pasture. Seasonal considerations may have determined the choice to ford the Todd Brook by two alternative routes:

1) Up Waggonshaw Brow (SJ 974 763) and down the Nab hillside. The deeply eroded solitary hollow-way has become the tarmacked Ewrin Lane that takes the easy way around Nab End to ford the Todd Brook below Saltersford Hall.

2) Past the site of an ancient marker or cross (SJ 9715 7655) along Bank Lane, to descend the deep hairpin bends of 'The Corkscrew' to ford the Todd Brook at Burton (SJ 979 768) then climb past the Jenkin Chapel. The highest part of Bank Lane has spring-fed horse troughs that would be gratefully used by traffic labouring up the Nab in the opposite direction.

The Saltway across the Upper Goyt.

After fording the Todd Brook, these two routes can be picked up again: Route (1), which climbs to Saltersford Hall where the packman and his horses might overnight before continuing through the Oldgate Nick; or Route (2), which climbs from the Jenkin Chapel up the steep road to Pym Chair (SJ 995 767). This winding tarmacked road appears to have been dug down to bedrock in places at some time in its history, with the waste piled high at the roadsides – presumably parish work on the King's Highway. These two alternative routes, barely half a kilometre apart, came together to form the Street, funnelling down to the key fording and bridging points across the River Goyt at the now submerged hamlet of Goytsbridge (SK 013 749).

Imagine a train of packhorses with panniers of valuable salt, coaxed and bullied by a team of packmen, climbing through the 'Oldgate Nick' onto Withenleach Moor before dropping down the braided hollow-ways of The Street to ford or bridge the River Goyt. From here the packmaster might then look for

The Saltway dropping down to Nithen end, Buxton

the driest climb, swirling eastwards up the hollow-ways, sometimes in a swathe 200m wide, either side of Goyts Lane to its junction with today's A5004 at SK 032 752. Here, part of the route is briefly severed by the spoil heaps of a mid-19th-century trial railway cutting at Longhill Farm (see Chapter 20). Two or three braids continue to Brookfield (SK 040 751) before curving downhill to follow the Wye tributary towards Nithen End (SK 049 739), while the remainder of the multiple route spills down the opposite bank of the stream.

From the River Goyt crossing, an alternative route continued up the northern bank of Wildmoorstone Brook to become concentrated in a single deep hollow-way at the ridge above Beet Wood (SK 036 741). From here the route followed down the northern tributary of the Wye. Passing east through Buxton and Fairfield, the line of this Saltway is now known in some detail. It crossed Great Rocks Dale to Wormhill then Monks Dale to Heatheydale Ward and the Saltersford at Tideswell Townend. It continued over Cressbrook Dale to Longstone Moor, Deep Rake and Bramley Lane to Stanton Ford across the River Derwent, then through Curbar Gap and across Big Moor to Saltergate, Chesterfield.

OTHER SALTWAYS

A more northerly Saltway left Macclesfield as before on the present B5470 road but took short-cuts west of Harrop House Farm and across Charles Head to Slater's Green Farm (formerly Salter's Green), Kettleshulme. From here the Saltway ran to Green Head past Taxal Church to ford the River Goyt further downstream. The place-name Salters Knowl then indicates the way forward to Chapel-en-le-Frith, over Peaslow to Sparrowpit and down the Winnats into Castleton, Hope and Bamford where there is a Saltergate. At Brough we encounter Salters Barn and Saltersgate Lane en route to Sheffield over Stanage Edge.

The most southerly Saltway across the South-West Peak follows part of a well-documented long-distance route from the Cheshire 'wiches', via Congleton and north of Leek up to 'The Mermaid' on Morridge. This was 'The Great Road' described under 'Drove Roads' in the previous chapter. A lawsuit of 1749 refers to this part of the route as being 'used by packhorses who carry salt out of Cheshire into Derbyshire and Nottinghamshire' and mentions a stone causeway up the steep ascent of Morridge.

Map: Saltways across the South West Peak.

From 'The Mermaid' a route to the east probably followed the parish boundary over Lumb Edge and Swallow Moss. From here the line is preserved as a metalled road to New Road (SK 090 612); it then becomes a footpath to Brund Mill where two divergent routes to Chesterfield, one with the place-names 'salter', are recorded. From Brund Mill the route to the north-east forded the Dove at Pilsbury and continued via Parsley Hay and Bakewell. The alternative to the east followed through Sheen, Hartington, Pikehall (shown on Ogilby's 1675 map) and Winster, to Salter's Lane, Matlock and Salter's Lane, Ashover.

In addition to the Cheshire 'wiches' as producers of salt, mention should be made of Droitwich (Hereford and Worcester), which during the Roman and Anglo-Saxon periods was just as important, and of Whitchurch, Shropshire, where between the 13th and 18th centuries salt was manufactured from somewhat weak brine springs.

SALT TAXES AND EXCISE DUTY

The first reference to salt taxes in England is in the 11th-century Domesday survey when revenue on the number of boilings by the individual salthouses was imposed. This tax, which was heavy, together with 'tolls' levied on salt transportation from the Cheshire 'wiches' was paid to the King and the Earl of Chester. The tolls, already well established by the Saxon period, are shown in the Domesday record for the Northwich Hundred as being 'between one half-penny and two pennies' for a packhorse load. Along with spirits, spices and (after the medieval period) tobacco, salt was a valuable item often smuggled to avoid the tax. For centuries it had been transported in the panniers of packhorses across the region, each horse carrying about 2cwt (100kg) of salt. There were heavy penalties for fraud and tax evasion. This particular tax ceased in 1825.

The very first Excise Duty issued by Parliament was on beer. The second was on salt, imposed in 1643. An Act of Parliament that taxed salt at the point of manufacture was passed in 1694 and was initially intended to provide money for the wars of William III. All salt works were registered and Excise Officers had powers of entry and search under an Act of 1702. Fraud and corruption were rife and smuggling using the packhorse train was widespread. Salt duty appears and disappears under various monarchs during which time, despite vigilant Excise men, it was systematically stolen for sale by robbery and intrigue and remained so until the duty was finally abolished.

Chapter 10. PACKMEN AND PACKHORSE WAYS

For centuries, if we exclude river transport and the sea, the packhorse (or mule), using traditional informal routes and any narrow, poorly maintained local road, was the general means of transporting merchandise for long distances overland until the completion of the turnpike system by the early 19th century. To avoid paying turnpike road tolls, some traders continued to use the remote routes, but with much of the land increasingly subjected to enclosure, followed by the introduction of the canals and then the railways, it is generally agreed that packhorse traffic was in *gradual* decline from about 1750. Readers will perhaps understand that such a long period of reliance on the horse for carrying has created uneasy difficulties when trying to straitjacket packhorse travel and carrying information into historical subject/time slots that are impossible to apply.

THE PACKMAN AND HIS HORSES

A name given to regional packmen or carriers was that of 'jagger'. A jagger seems simply to have been any packhorse man who travelled with a load, or *jag*. Many packmen became independent businessmen and would buy and sell as they travelled. With either a single horse or a string of horses, they formed the most familiar sight on the early highways and became a very valuable part of the rural economy. The name jagger is still perpetuated in the Peak District where Jaggers Bridge, Jaggers Clough, Jaggers Lane, etc. are found in many parts of the region.

The Galloway or Galloway-cross seems to have been the favourite breed of packhorse. Indeed, the name Galloway or the slang term 'Galley' still exists in historic packhorse country such as Wildboarclough and at Three Shires Head where the names *Gallowlands*, *Galleywood* and *Galloway Knowl* can be found on 19th-century maps.

From south-west Scotland, the Fell Galloway, like other packhorses, was, and still is, a medium-sized animal of around 14 hands, often described as neither a horse nor a pony but somewhere in between. Galloways are elegant, compliant, surefooted and strong. Smaller horses were avoided because many routes lay along narrow tracks where heather, bushes or projecting rocks might damage the carried goods. Too tall a horse would be tiresome to load and unload during the journey. The horse may or may not have been shod. This would depend greatly on the demands made upon it, including the size of the load and the difficulty of the terrain, where working the animal continuously on wet ground or stony roads would cause the horny casing of the hoof to wear away rapidly or crack. To prevent damage and assist the horse, horseshoes seem to have been used whenever necessary – such decisions being taken by the packmen, who were usually skilled in horse management. The skills of the many local blacksmiths who would provide this service for the packmen were essential not only to the many riders and packhorse carriers but also to the everyday life and work of the rural communities these travellers passed through.

A simple truth about horses is that, if ill-treated or neglected, then they will not work, and so they were often treated better than men. Horses cost money, whereas in industrial contexts, at least another man could be sent on if an employee was sick. Depending on the terrain and the type of load, a nine-hour day walking at around 3mph for a packhorse would be ample, after which it would be ready for a good meal and rest. A string of fifty Galloways on a long-distance route would need eight or nine mounted packmen to look after them, not least because they and the loads carried were valuable and vulnerable to attacks by robbers. For certain winter journeys, part of the carried load might be feed for the horses. Goods were carried in two panniers or baskets of varying sizes, depending on the commodity, hung onto a well-padded wooden frame packsaddle and finely balanced and secured. The saddles varied in design – some had horns or crosstrees that fitted into the holes in the back of the pannier. The horses were muzzled to prevent them grazing en route, whilst regular stopping places, particularly on steep inclines, would have wells and spring-fed drinking troughs. Some troughs still survive, with the one above Gradbach Mill being a fine example – although stream crossings were plentiful and might commonly have been used. These pack trains were made up of horses that knew the route and would work nose to tail along it. Riding with the pack train or walking in groups for safety might be a variety of other travellers including merchants, itinerant tinkers and farmers going to market. These large groups of people and animals were to

Horse troughs above Gradbach Mill.

become a very frequent cause of delay and quarrelling on the early turnpike roads.

Duplicate packhorse routes sometimes survive, providing convincing evidence of seasonal variation with more direct lines taken in summer and longer routes in winter, avoiding any soft and marshy areas and flooded river crossings. Braided or duplicate hollow-ways up steep and tiring slopes may have been deliberately used as 'one-way systems' either by custom or tacit agreement between packmen. The mayhem caused by two pack trains walking in opposite directions in the bottom of a steep and difficult hollow-way is easy to imagine. Horses may be herd animals but such an artificial social encounter for them would have been a disaster. It was therefore necessary to warn other approaching pack trains, especially during fog or the sudden onset of darkness. The leading horse, usually a 'bell mare', would have a special collar from which were suspended a few larger harness bells that rang loudly as she went along. A primary reason for these bells, however, was to advertise the coming of the pack train to customers and generate some excitement and anticipation.

An enormous variety of goods were carried to ports, markets and the great regional fairs. Really heavy and valuable items, such as grindstones and millstones from the quarries on the eastern side of the Peak District for example, would have been transported slowly and carefully in robust, oxen-drawn wagons – although Daniel Defoe describes how he saw millstones encased in timber being transported by using them as wheels with a wooden axle. However, the majority of long-distance goods were carried by the pack trains: yarn and woven textiles; tools, utensils, books and luxury goods; hides, fleeces, salt, tar, treacle, cheeses and whole salmon using 'stage' packhorses; corn for the mills to be distributed by licensed 'badgers'; lead, copper and iron ores and their smelted metals; charcoal for smelting and forge work; chert *to* the Potteries and pottery *from* the Potteries; limestone and coal to the limekilns; lime for mortar and agriculture; calamine for brass-making; while tobacco was carried from Liverpool eastwards to the industrial centres – the list seems endless. This carrying of materials and the return with back-carriage grew significantly but it is not always clear from business accounts whether wheeled transport or packhorses were being used, perhaps for part of the journey. Hops, together with barley and malt produced in Nottinghamshire and Derbyshire for brewing, appear to have been very popular commodities for back-carriage. Because there were no common breweries before the 18th century, brewing was undertaken both by the housewife and the innkeeper.

Throughout their history, pack trains can never have had an easy passage. Although preferring to stick to high ground and avoid wet valley routes, there were still difficult river crossings to be made. Robbers, atrocious weather and the post-medieval increase in traffic added to their problems. During the 18th and early 19th centuries, government Enclosures Acts had involved the building of miles of walls to enclose former common land for agricultural improvement, while Turnpike Acts of the same period were imposing uncompromising road construction which often cut right across any traditional packhorse routes.

CARRYING

A packhorse would carry a load of about two hundredweight (cwt). It would therefore require ten such horses to transport a ton (20 cwt = 1 ton). This weight was the customary load for a local carrier's two-wheeled cart pulled by one horse on a fairly level route – although they often pulled more. In hilly country, perhaps even three horses would be required to pull such a load; the charge for carriage using extra horses being calculated accordingly.

Four-wheeled wagons, used less frequently than two-wheelers, would carry bulky goods not sold by weight. Their carrying capacity has not been recorded (see Chapter 19, Freight Carriers). Local families frequently combined farming with other occupations as a supplement to the inadequate incomes from their smallholdings. Men, using a small cart and a farm horse, often undertook short-distance carrying as extra work, particularly before and after the harvest when the roads were normally dry and firm. Clearly, as the turnpike road system was developing it was necessary to have some knowledge of the preferred routes and then decide which transport method would be the most cost-effective. The development and proliferation of carts and wagons able to carry considerable loads over the easier gradients of the new turnpike roads was to put the packhorse out of business on many routes.

To get a feel for the increase in commerce between the Tudor period and the present, consider today's 36-ton truck delivering a load from Manchester to London in half a day. More than 300 horses would have been needed to carry the same load and would have taken two weeks to deliver it.

BADGERS AND SWAILERS; PEDLARS AND TINKERS

There were also other packmen, often the only suppliers of goods and services to people living in the countryside before shops began in the 17th century. The 'badger' or badge-man was initially a licensed beggar who was required by an Act of 1561 to wear a badge. Later, these became grain or corn middlemen, gradually becoming general dealers, buying and selling not only cereals but also flour, poultry and dairy produce. Buying in one market and selling in another was called 'badging'. 'Swailers' were also dealers in articles shown on their licences, which at various times included cloth, tobacco, salt, oatmeal, malt, butter, cheese and eggs – but by the middle of the 18th century, the terms 'badger' and 'swailer' had become interchangeable. Many of these itinerants evaded the licensing system altogether and carried

on their businesses outside the law. 'Pedlars', 'hucksters', 'hawkers', 'chapmen' and others, both women and men, were travelling retailers who either advertised their wares by proclaiming them in the street or offered them to customers over their thresholds as petty bargains. The goods were carried in small carts, in baskets on ponies or donkeys, or they often walked and carried the packs on their backs. These often solitary carriers would buy a variety of small commodities from craftsmen and shopkeepers or at fairs and markets to sell on cheaply. Typical items carried might be pottery, brushes, simple toys, trinkets, thread, ribbons, ballads, buttons and small fashionable garments and dress material. The 'tinker' was the itinerant mender of pots and pans and a retailer of cheap metalware. These travellers were all welcome retailers of gossip in thinly settled areas where all attempts to put into effect a licensing system, or to prohibit such activities, were destined to fail.

FORDS AND BRIDGES

Crossings of the relatively narrow rivers of the Peak District, where depth and flow were low enough to permit wading, we know as fords. These were well chosen, often at points imposed by the shape of the land where the bed of the river could be paved with flat stones. Sometimes the word 'ford' is found in early settlement place-names, e.g. Ashford-in-the-Water and Quarnford – the names perhaps being in existence long before they were written down. Where the river was not easily forded and when bridges were subsequently built at or near these crossings, some settlements took their names from bridges, for example Danebridge and Goytsbridge. Often fords remained in use even when a bridge was built; retained because the original bridge was insufficiently wide for certain types of traffic, or as a measure to reduce wear and tear and thus maintenance costs on the structure. However, because of the hilly nature of the land, many such bridges have usually replaced fords directly. Near to some horse bridges in the South-West Peak it is still possible to identify the line of the approach to a former ford.

From medieval times bridges, fords and causeways attracted more attention than roads – church records often refer to them. Obligatory church repairs and those carried out by other groups with traditional responsibilities often disappeared, so that unless bridges were either badly damaged or washed away by flood, repairs became badly neglected. Special grants of 'pontage' could be applied for when it was found that no person, persons or organisation could be held responsible for the repairs to a bridge. A further source of revenue for bridge maintenance was, of course, the right to exact tolls on people passing over *or under* bridges.

The building of firm causeways and arched bridges over wider streams and rivers had begun before the Norman Conquest, many built or financed by the monastic houses, sometimes as works of piety to relieve the suffering of travellers. The early-14th-century bridge spanning the flood plain of the River Wye in Bakewell, for example, has five low arches, each pier having strongly projecting cutwaters with pedestrian refuges above. The original width of this bridge provides evidence that during the medieval period wheeled traffic was using Pennine routes. Widened in the 19th century, this bridge is still a remarkably elegant example of the medieval bridge-builders' skill.

Despite the 1531 Statute of Bridges that had given JPs the power to levy a county rate towards bridge maintenance and to appoint surveyors, the sudden withdrawal of monastic funding at the time of the Dissolution was to have a detrimental effect on the upkeep of the transport system. Parish constables were made responsible for the maintenance of small bridges, perhaps with some assistance from the county, while during the late 17th and 18th centuries, county authorities obliged JPs to spend money in widening, repairing or rebuilding any county bridges that by this time, as wagons got heavier, were stone replacements.

Many of the remaining so-called 'packhorse' bridges of single or multi-arch, mortared-stone construction, found deep in the hills of the Peak District, may be dated from documentary sources to the period between 1660 and about 1760; that is, between the middle of the Stuart and the middle of the Georgian periods. In less desolate areas wooden bridges were replaced by new stone ones capable of taking heavier wheeled traffic on the many routes that were improved in the second half of the 18th century – many of course associated with the turnpike system.

Because of the steep and awkward terrain of the Peak District, the packhorse transport system here was late in being slowly but inevitably curtailed by the canals and by wheeled vehicles on turnpike roads. Since it is unlikely that new *remote* horse bridges

would be built after the opening stages of the turnpike period, and as the packtrains were increasingly using the turnpikes, a construction date for such bridges before c.1760 seems appropriate.

If we assume the erratic behaviour of draught animals and the likely width and manoeuvrability of simple wains and carts before the 18th century, when bridges were described as either 'horse bridges or 'cart bridges', then a cart bridge cannot be less than 6ft wide. A horse (or bridle) bridge can therefore be defined as being 6ft wide or less and built before 1760, constructed where steep banks or a swollen river would make the usual crossing hazardous.

A few horse bridges and some that do not entirely meet these criteria can be found in the South-West Peak, surviving on the upper reaches of streams and rivers on redundant routes. A few have been widened to carry farm carts and, later, tractor traffic, or in some cases have been dismantled, strengthened and rebuilt nearby on modern road crossings. At redundant crossings, abutments of destroyed bridges and/or the ruins of paved fords, where cattle and heavy horses were usually diverted, sometimes exist, although some have been buried, removed or washed away. The local bridges vary from simple stone beams having a slight natural arch, such as those spanning the infant River Dove north-west of Hollinsclough, to the fine arched bridges widened or reconstructed during the turnpike era and now strengthened to carry modern traffic. Typical horse bridges have either very low or non-existent parapets. They are often steeply humped in the middle, following the curve of the arch. Constructed during a period of highway

Stone beam bridge, Knotbury.

Foot bridge over the Harrop Brook, Pott Shrigley.

improvement in response to increasing clamour from the traders who used them, they were built to protect goods from the damage that might be incurred if packhorses panicked when a stream was forded – not necessarily a swollen stream, as one reduced to a trickle could prove just as problematic. For a variety of reasons and in certain situations, it can be unwise to ride or drive a horse through flowing water. If the animal is sticky and uncomfortable, for example, the desire to roll, rid itself of its load and cool down often becomes irresistible when it finds itself splashing through water. Such an occurrence would have been disastrous for a packhorse train as once one animal had succumbed to temptation it would probably have been imitated by others.

OTHER LOCAL HORSE ROUTES

The area around the parish of Quarnford in particular has many classic packhorse routes that can be easily recognised and followed, with certain sections now designated as public bridleways, enriching the landscape once again in their historic role. Just north of Gib Tor (SK 022 649), the old routes between Leek and Buxton are joined by a hollowed east–west packhorse route (some of it now tarmacked) from Washgate, Tenterhill, Golling Gate, via the Dun Cow's Grove ford, over the broad ridge south of Daffodil Farm to Adders Green Farm.

From the Goldsitch Moss Colliery (centred SK 008 640) a braided horse route follows the southern bank of the Black Brook before climbing the northern slopes of Roach End to cross the saddle towards Roche Grange, Meerbrook and Leek.

The areas of Brand, Colshaw, Howe Green and Thirkelow on the upper reaches of the River Dove are criss-crossed by a maze of old walled lanes and hollow-ways, some leading north-west towards Axe Edge and the Goyt Valley, others towards High Edge and beyond but now cut off by an extensively quarried area south of Harpur Hill and Buxton.

From Clough House Farm in Wildboarclough a packhorse route climbs up Cumberland Clough past the long-abandoned Danethorne coal mine. From here the track leads onto the moors, joining the Danebower Hollow cart-track between the Cat and Fiddle and the mines and quarries at Danebower below Dane Head. The Danebower Hollow track was built by a John Murray c.1780. It pre-dates the Congleton and Buxton turnpike of 1789 but post-dates the 1759 Macclesfield and Buxton turnpike. Horse routes followed the Dane to join with several others converging at Panniers Pool. The routes encircling Blackclough, Orchard and Knotbury can be followed around Turn Edge and Cut Thorn, upstream over Axe Edge and down to three old Dane crossing points in Quarnford parish: (1) Gradbach, (2) Panniers Pool and (3) Birchenbooth, an ancient settlement no longer existing east of Knar at SK 006 677. Birchenbooth, where there were two Dane crossings, may have been more important at one time than Panniers

Pool. The grassed-over ruined footings of a number of small buildings can be found here. A further centre of packhorse activity was by the stream at 'bottom of the flash' or Flash Bottom, where major east–west and north–south packhorse routes cross. A farm here may well have provided food and accommodation for packmen (see Chapter 8).

SOME LOCAL PACKHORSE BRIDGES

GOYTS BRIDGE (SK 0140 7320)

Known as Goyts Bridge, the horse bridge below Goytsclough Quarry in the upper Goyt Valley was moved into its present position in the 1960s by Stockport Corporation Water Works when the Errwood reservoir was built, thus saving this classic horse bridge for posterity. Its earlier position was over the Wildmoorstone Brook at the now drowned hamlet of Goytsbridge. A larger, later road bridge at the hamlet, still intact and revealed during periods of drought, has a roadway 8ft 6in wide spanning the River Goyt. The two bridges were only 100m apart at a position where there were adjacent buildings dated 1762. The resited bridge with its winged walls has a span of 12ft and is 41in wide between 20in high parapets.

WASHGATE BRIDGE (SK 0524 6740)

Surely a most remarkable horse bridge – perfectly proportioned, untouched by wheeled traffic and as functional as when first constructed – has to be the Washgate Bridge and its ford north-west of Hollinsclough on the River Dove. It is the focus of several rakes and paths that can all be followed on the 1:25,000 OS map. This lovely bridge has a span of 24ft; the width is 55in between 10in high parapets.

The setting was superb but the bridge has been overwhelmed in recent years by a rash of threatening, mature sycamore trees. Up to the early 20th century, local farmers would choose a warm day and gather their flocks of sheep by the bridge. A temporary dam would be constructed where the men, standing waist-deep in the water, could thoroughly wash the fleeces prior to shearing. This farming practice is no longer carried out in rivers.

Immediately west of the bridge are the south-west-facing slopes of Tenterhill, the old name and position

suggesting loosely-woven woollen fabric, washed in the Dove below before being stretched across timber frames on small metal tenterhooks, to bleach after fulling or stabilise after dyeing (see Chapter 14, Woollen Cloth Fulling).

The substantial ruins of Washgate Farm, beyond the barn on the lane to Leycote, may have been the site of an early textile mill, or provided a refuge for pack teams. This whole area still retains these walled and often steep, paved packhorse lanes known locally as 'rakes' where tragically, the ongoing passage of high-revving powerful motorcycles, 'quads' and other 'off-road' vehicles has wantonly destroyed the waterstops and beautifully constructed stone pitching. Despite enjoying the convenience of these lanes themselves, the people of the area must be bitterly disappointed to find that the CROW (Countryside & Rights of Way) Act (2000) has so far provided so little protection for their heritage.

HOPPING BRIDGE (SK 0630 6688)

A little over 1km downstream from the Washgate Bridge is the old paved ford below Hopping Farm, a Dove crossing for various old packhorse routes from Longnor into Cheshire, or via Fough Farm and Booth (where it crosses the way from Washgate) to the coal mines and limekilns west of Buxton.

In the late 19th century, Hollinsclough Parish Council built a stone bridge by the ford. The regular 15ft arch holds the 50in wide tarmacked footway high above the river. The 18in high parapets of Hopping Bridge have cement-rendered coping stones.

QUARNFORD BRIDGE (SK 0010 6640)

In common with many other horse bridges in the study area, Quarnford Bridge straddles two counties, in this case Cheshire and Staffordshire. In these situations, the cost of repairs to the bridges was therefore shared.

THREE SHIRES HEAD OR THREE SHIRE HEADS

By 1200, England had been divided into units of administration called counties. The headwaters of the rivers Goyt, Dane and Dove all rise on Axe Edge Moor, providing a convenient convergence point for the county boundaries of Cheshire, Derbyshire and Staffordshire. Before the expansion of Derbyshire

Panniers Pool bridge.

westwards in 1936, these boundaries had probably remained fairly constant although the actual point of convergence was frequently in dispute. Today, the three boundaries converge at Panniers Pool (SK 0093 6853). The first documentation of this convergence point as '*The Three Sheres*' is found in the Bateman (ii) Hartington manuscript, Ref. 1532-33 (Chatsworth House). At Panniers Pool, horse traffic would have used the small, narrow Galleywood Bridge over the Dane but carts were obliged to ford the river. By the pool below, men and horses would have rested and taken refreshment while others might encamp overnight.

The 'Boundaries of the manor or lordship of Warneford' (Quarnford) claimed by Sir John Savage in a boundary dispute of c.1564 mentions the 'Three Meerstones at Gamon Greenhead' (see Chapter 1) but also mentions '*the three sheres at the Dane hed*' – a position some 3km from Panniers Pool.

On Speede's Derbyshire map (1552–1629) the '*Three Shire Stones*' depicted near Dane Head, and still existing there in the early 19th century, will have been county boundary markers but there is no evidence

for three conspicuous stones either at that position or near to Panniers Pool today. With the exception of the dispute map of 1804 (see below), map makers (or copiers) from the 16th century through to the first OS map of 1840 have all shown the convergence to be either Cheeks Hill *or* nearby Dane Head. However, from here on, the map position reverted to Panniers Pool.

• Saxton's Derbyshire map 1577 – '*The Three Stone Mere*' – Dane Head

• Earl of Derby/John Harpur 1673 – '*The Head of the Dane where 3 Shires Meet*'

• Plot's Staffordshire map c.1680 – '*The Three Shire Heads*' – Dane Head

• Bowen's Staffordshire map 1759 – '*Three Shire Head or Stones*' – Dane Head

• Yates map 1775 [Meer Stones at Flash Bar] & '*3 Counties meeting*' – Cheeks Hill

• Burdett's Cheshire map 1777 – '*Three Shire Heads*' – Cheeks Hill

- Enclosures Dispute map 1804 –
'*Three Shire Heads at Panniers Pool*'

- OS 1840 1inch [3 Meer Stones/ Flash Bar]
& '*3 Counties meeting*' – Cheeks Hill

- OS 1883 1:10,000 shows three counties
meeting – Panniers Pool

- OS 1975 1:10,000 – '*Three Shire Heads*'
– Panniers Pool

- OS 1979 1: 25,000 – '*Three Shire Heads*'
– Panniers Pool

- OS Current 1:10,000 – '*Three Shires Head*'
– Panniers Pool

In 1836, tenants and occupants of the Chatsworth Estate (with vested interests) raised subscriptions and widened the Panniers Pool bridge to take cart traffic. Two distinct arches can be seen underneath tied with iron bolts. The combined width is 8ft between 20in parapets that are held together with iron staples. The 'Three Shire Heads' shown near this position on today's 1:25,000 OS maps are surely the three 400m bulky 'heads' of land that dominate the horse bridge below. It is an atmospheric and popular picnic spot; a place to imagine journeys measured by the pace of a pack train or the lines of plodding horses and carts laden with coal from the nearby mines.

The 'commons' in this particular area were subjects of protracted boundary disputes between powerful landowners and brought into focus by the mineral wealth. This was eventually resolved with the drawing of a formal boundary between the counties, with two arbitrary straight lines meeting at a point at the northern end of Orchard Common. This artificial triangular wedge of rough grazing, pointing accusingly into Derbyshire from Cheeks Hill at SK 026 699, must have been approved by the commissioners as a suitable boundary when they surveyed for the 1804 Hartington Enclosures. It is now defined by a drystone wall.

The Firestone Brook, flowing down through Orchard Common to its confluence with the Dane at Panniers Pool, is only 1km from the head of the River Dove and would have provided a shorter and more obvious natural boundary line to separate the counties of Derbyshire and Staffordshire – but was ignored. The Cheeks Hill boundary point is still affirmed by local people whose great-grandparents knew it as '*Threysha Yeds*' (Three Shire Heads).

LOCAL HOLLIN SITES

Prior to the significant improvements in farming that were to follow, agricultural writers of the 18th century had commented on the use as fodder of leaves and twigs of a variety of trees such as elm and ash, but, particularly in the north-west of England and the southern Pennines, of hollin (holly). Being an evergreen, hollin was especially useful as winter fodder for livestock and deer when snow covered the ground or when hay was running short – which happened most years. Unlike the modern decorative garden hollies, wild holly (commonly growing throughout the area) is at its most prickly at or near the browse level of domestic stock or deer. Above this height, where the leaves are much rounder, it was gathered as 'browse wood', often from parts of woodland managed as hollin plantations or 'haggs' where the trees might be pollarded above browse level. Hollin was also grown in hedges for the same reason.

There is a good survival of holly trees in Harrop, where, in the 14th century, there was a park surrounded by a palisade. In the severe winter of 1363–4, a man was paid to crop hollin in Harrop for 25 days. Earlier, in 1358–9, at Midgley, four men were paid for a day to cut hollin.

In areas of considerable packhorse activity or cattle droving, some farms near to these routes became resting places offering hospitality to the packman or drover and providing paddocks or fodder for the animals. Many such farms have the name 'hollin' and it has been suggested that these may have displayed a branch of holly to indicate their availability and willingness to provide such services. Hollin place-names can include the spellings – hollen(s) and holling(s), no doubt derived from the OE *hollegn*. Modern 'holly' place-names are ignored.

A typical hollin farmstead usually stands alone, facing onto pasture or a group of little paddocks near to a 'greenway' or a packhorse route. Generous water troughs, a large pond, a stream or a number of wells are often found alongside access tracks, making it easy to water many animals simultaneously. Packhorses would need to be unloaded at night and turned loose to graze and rest, the packs being taken under cover for security. Stock drives, on the other hand, would perhaps only cover five or six miles for a daily journey with grazing en route. At known hollin farmsteads, the drover might find social contact and a bed for the night where a paddock might be available for his animals. These farms, usually substantial groups of buildings and the highest settlements before the open moor, are often sited close to township boundaries. Many have architectural features indicating considerable status in the past.

Although packhorse traffic was declining in the late 18th century, small-scale local stock droving was not greatly affected until the railway age. If we consider over how long a period these hollin-names might have been in meaningful use, we find 'hollin' as a place-name pre-dating the Norman Conquest, but this does not of itself prove the site to have been a resting place and the names may derive from local natural abundance. Such sites *may* have been resting places throughout the medieval period but many more emerge in the 16th century. Modern maps of the study area reveal a number of examples, with older detailed maps showing many that include 'hollins' as field names.

Hollin-names found locally, often on old areas of common, close to, or part of, tracks used by packmen and drovers include: Hollinset Farm, Hollinhall, Burntoak Hollins, Hollinhey, Spire Hollins Farm, Hollins Farm, Stick Hollins and The Hollins (a range of low hills between Langley and Macclesfield). Hollin Lane, now a minor road between Sutton Lane Ends and Cleulow Cross, follows the line of an ancient route. Spire Hollins may be the shape of mature wild holly trees, grown in a conical shape with a point or spire at the top.

Inns, providing not only accommodation for packmen and drovers but also drink and conviviality, perhaps coexisted for a long period but eventually replaced the 'hollin' farmstead. Such inns would display the name and sign of 'The Holly Tree' or 'The Holly Bush'.

GUIDESTOOPS

Spaced along many known regional post-medieval routes as waymarkers, often at cross roads, are pillar-like stones standing from three to over five feet high. They are inscribed with colloquially spelt nearby towns, some having three-fingered pointing hands indicating their direction. Other stones without pointing hands require the traveller to be familiar with the accepted convention when facing such a stone. To travel to the town written on any side directly facing the traveller, he or she must turn right and walk only in that direction to the required destination. The

stones may have the initials of road commissioners or the broad arrow of a later surveyor's benchmark and are known as guidestoops. Many of these gritstone markers use 'road' more frequently than 'way' on their inscriptions. Some are dated whilst others are not. Guidestoops would have been a very welcome sight to the increasing numbers of travellers making difficult journeys on the pre-turnpike roads where wheeled traffic over the hills and moors was a rarity.

Some were set up to comply with a Parliamentary Act of 1697 which authorised JPs to order the erection of guide posts or stoops where route-crossings were remote from towns and villages. The order met with little response and by 1703 very few stoops were in position. In 1705, the Derbyshire JPs acted with firmness, finally making them compulsory at track junctions. Guidestoops were required to display the names of the nearest *market towns* but perhaps for a variety of reasons this was not always complied with. Records show that, as late as 1737, seven additional stoops were erected, suggesting that a further order had been imposed.

In parts of the region where the traveller had opportunities to ask the way if in doubt, then these

Guidestoop.

76

The Wildmoor Stone?

way surveyors were simply instructed by their JPs to 'erect or fix a stone *or post*'. In the last two decades, a number of stone guidestoops have been unearthed and re-erected at or near their original sites. Some were buried to confuse enemy spies in World War II! Unfortunately a few of those unearthed have been re-oriented incorrectly.

Many plain, isolated gritstone waymarkers can still be found by old routes in much of the region. Probably once painted with limewash, they might be considered the forerunners of the later milestones and of today's metal and plastic route signs. Some were perhaps uprooted to serve as gateposts as rough tracks gave way to new turnpiked roads. A few have merely fallen over, while others have been incorporated into drystone walls or are lost amongst encroaching vegetation. To hide traditional rights of way, some of these prominent markers may have been buried.

It is interesting to find that the 1842 OS map of the upper Goyt Valley shows a Wildmoor Stone at the head of the Wildmoorstone Brook. At the nearby railway tunnel north entrance, the old horse routes climb alongside the public path eastwards and converge at the ridge, where a guide stone or cross would have silhouetted well. A large, pink gritstone post with a pointed top has been broken in two and utilised to form a step-over stile in a nearby derelict wall. Perhaps this is the Wildmoor Stone? Below the rail tunnel, at SK 0270 7435, a large, atypical rounded boulder, perhaps a glacial erratic, sits in the hollow-ways near the confluence of the Wildmoorstone Brook and its tributary stream from Burbage Edge. This may be an even better contender for the Wildmoor Stone.

markers were perhaps considered unnecessary. Although strangely absent around most of the South-West Peak, where real travel difficulties might have been encountered on the bleak western moors, wooden stoops, which will have disappeared after 300 years, may have been erected. The parish high-

Chapter 11. FRUSTRATION AND CHANGE

ROADS AND TRAFFIC

The increasing amounts of traffic provoked the Tudor administration to publish the Highways Act of 1555. This had taken the task of road maintenance from the manors and transferred it to the local parish inhabitants who were responsible to JPs at the county quarter sessions for the upkeep of roads and tracks within their boundaries. Under the terms of this Act, owners of carts, wagons, oxen and horses were obliged to send them for use and every householder was required to repair the roads for four and later, under a further Highways Act, six days a year under two elected, unpaid 'highway surveyors', usually local farmers. The result was a mass of local repairs that restricted some of the worst decay but consisted mainly of inefficient and unsuccessful bodging operations like filling holes with rubble. Despite the imposition of fines for evasion of this statute labour, most roads deteriorated further as they became more heavily used. Unfortunately, the well-intentioned Act had failed to specify standards of highway maintenance on roads used in the most part by travellers from a distance. By the late 17th century, the crude methods of construction and repair performed by resentful farmers and perhaps landless cottagers proved inadequate to cope with the increased amount of traffic generated by the rapid growth of the economy. The 1555 Act was to remain in force until highway boards were constituted three centuries later. The packhorse train was still the only certain way to move most goods across the hills, but for local transport, crude sledges and wheeled wagons had long been in use where tracks and weather permitted.

Elizabethan and Stuart travellers often had to rely on the experience of local guides and on printed chronicles. Traffic on any main routeway both before and during the early turnpike era would have been slow and mixed. Because of the relatively poor road surfaces, wheeled vehicles were restricted where the horseman and the packhorse train predominated. Such roads became churned up by hooves and then rutted by primitive heavy coaches and stage wagons, often becoming impassable in poor weather. In open, unfenced country, travellers left a bad road and walked or rode at the sides but as enclosure of the land increased, both travellers and drovers found that their choice of routes was restricted to those roads and lanes authorised by the landowners. As traffic became concentrated in these narrow defined tracks, the situations worsened. Vehicles might be caught by floods, bogged down or overturned. Frost, ice and snow created cracks and holes, often resulting in such vehicles becoming buried in snow, sometimes for days.

SLEDS, WAINS, WAGONS AND CARTS

The use of heavy horse-drawn railed sleds with curved oak runners was, until the beginning of the 20th century, very common in the hillier parts of the Peak District where a variety of farm produce such as hay, corn, oats and especially turves of peat cut from the moor were transported by this method. Peat use as a fuel declined in the 19th century when the new turnpike roads and the railways allowed cheap coal to be imported.

In hilly areas such as Kerridge Ridge, Rainow, sledges carrying quarried stone were used within living memory and have gouged sinuous routes down the hillside. Graded inclines to be found at a few of the smaller local drift mines were perhaps constructed for sledges to move coal as far as the nearest good road for transfer to wheeled vehicles.

While the construction and names of the wheeled vehicles utilized during the medieval period is somewhat vague and surviving examples probably nonexistent, we do know that if the ground was not too difficult, heavy and bulky goods were transported in simple robust wooden vehicles called *wains*, although in some cases their use might be restricted to the drier months, thus avoiding the muddy or frozen ruts of the winter. These vehicles would be used to carry dressed stone, road stone, slates, ironstone, coal, dung, wine and beer in barrels, timber, lead and a whole variety of bulky and weighty goods. Quarry access roads were of course used by such vehicles to draw blocks of stone and thousands of stone slates. Information from manorial court rolls and estate papers confirm such vehicle use across the region well before the 17th century, with carrying being most profitable where roads were passable both in winter and summer and where demand for carriage and back-carriage was regular and substantial.

By the Tudor period, a heavy four-wheeled vehicle and a more common two-wheeler seem to have both been knows as wains, even though some inventories show ownership of both wains *and* carts. The term wain gradually dropped out of common usage during the early-modern era when the small vehicle became the horse-drawn two-wheeled cart. The heavy wain used for the haulage of bulky goods became the wagon, or stage-wagon, with broad wheels and, eventually, a pivoting front axle.

CROSSING THE MOORS

Apart from a few isolated farms sheltering in side valleys, the high moorland of the region has remained largely unoccupied. Here, the grits and shales are overlain by varying thicknesses of spongy peat with saturated mosses marked by nodding cotton sedge and cut by streams in deep gullies. A network of packhorse routes avoiding the worst of these areas had evolved but little detailed guidance was available to ordinary travellers on how to cross the Peak District and how to avoid the many treacherous bogs. Until the arrival of the 18th-century road builders, most travellers would be forced to make lengthy detours indicated by grass, bilberry and heather at the very edges of the moors – sometimes in thick mist. The condition of these horse routes in the winter and the amount of traffic using them can only be guessed at. We do know that the dreadful climate of the 'Little Ice Age' (14th to 18th centuries) was at its worst during the latter half of the 17th century when the savage winters would surely have made the routes impassable at times. Most people could not afford to keep a horse and often had to travel on foot. Travellers' records from this period tell of horses and men perishing in the snowdrifts and local guides unwilling to provide their services.

Travel across the high ground of the South-West Peak was not entirely limited to the drovers and the packhorse carriers. There are a few old hollow-ways still to be found that have been widened and stabilised with stone to support sleds or carts. These usually lead to abandoned quarries, old peat cuts and early coal workings. Some of these wider hollow-ways are now V-shaped where soil erosion has altered their profiles. One such example can be found north of Cisterns Clough (SK 038 704) on the A53, climbing onto Axe Edge moor towards the 542m spot-height shown on the OS maps. The 1804 Hartington Enclosure Award indicates that this road from Hartington via Earl Sterndale and High Edge was an improved road known as the 'coal road' that had succeeded a much earlier route along which coal was being moved prior to enclosure. As with other parts of the traditional network, routes like this survive only where the Enclosure Commissioners and Turnpike Trusts ignored them, or when they fell into disuse on land unfit for improvement.

Winter walkers on the Macclesfield to Buxton route.

THE FIRST TOLL ROADS

In 1603, the crown passed to the first Stuart monarch, James I, and after the failed 'Gunpowder Plot' there followed a period of intolerance and superstition. Meanwhile, all were coping with outbreaks of the Plague. Under Charles I in 1625, the kingdom was beset by long-standing social problems. There were many beggars and vagrants and eventually Civil War. The Peak District fell under Parliamentary control and although many local men were bribed or pressed to fight and to tolerate unpopular Decrees under Cromwell, farming and the wool trade continued to occupy most families. Lingering remnants of medieval rough justice were still being played out. Murderers were burned at the stake and market-day floggings of men and women were common (but not in the study area).

By this time there were commercial and industrial arguments in favour of better inland transport and a realisation that radical government intervention was long overdue. The first Parliamentary Act allowing the levy of tolls to provide money for the repair of a road was passed in 1663. Part of the Great North Road was chosen for the experiment but the expectations of the legislators were not realised and over forty years would pass before the experiment was repeated. This Act of 1706 was to be the first of many and created a Turnpike Trust that included local landowners and other prominent people as trustees charged with ensuring that the intentions of the Act were carried out (see Chapter 18). Letters had been carried by the post-horse system since the time of Henry VIII, and in 1548 the postage rate was fixed at one penny per mile. Although Mary, Queen of Scots was said to have occupied the first horse-drawn coach seen in Derbyshire, around 1570, travel for most people in the South-West Peak remained difficult and frustrating.

TOWARDS ENGINEERING

Rural craftsmen worked in wood, metal or other materials and the refinement of the products of their skills is often of very localised significance. Foremost amongst a host of skilled woodworkers were the wagon-builders who constructed the sturdy vehicles used on the farm and in the wider countryside. Associated with wagon-making was the craft of the wheelwright, who often worked on his own and supplied wooden wheels as required. Shrinking a red-hot iron tyre onto the wheel would be performed with the co-operation of the blacksmith. The village smiths were remarkable metalworkers. They were the indispensable odd-job man of the rural community, shoeing horses, making chains, nails, hinges and latches, making and repairing the essential tools of the farmer, constructing wrought-iron gates and a variety of decorative work in designs to suit most pockets, often with great skill. Some of the wood and metal trades that began as rural crafts would move by degrees into

the nearby villages and towns, their traditions combining to create the millwright – part blacksmith, part carpenter, part odd-job man, who was called upon to do new work. These were the beginnings of engineering – part of a continuum of remarkable inventiveness.

AGRICULTURAL CHANGE AND INDUSTRIAL DEVELOPMENT

The early post-medieval period is distinct from the medieval because of a gradual change from a feudal to a capitalist society. Industry had become truly industrial, with manufacturing starting to be organised on a national basis. However, despite the popularity of the restoration of the monarchy in 1660, these were still difficult times. Although the comparatively well-off were beginning to rebuild their village houses in stone, throughout the reigns of Charles II, James II and William and Mary many of the rural poor were facing hardships created by enclosure schemes, either by agreement on individual farms or imposed by improving landowners. The resulting increases in poverty were not relieved until the mid-18th century when industrialisation in the shape of revolutionary technical developments, linked to agriculture, textiles and the extractive industries, provided a new and much-needed source of livelihood. Industrialisation, of course, was instigated for the benefit of the rich and led to terrible conditions for the urban workforce that were far worse than those in the countryside.

Mineral mines, previously abandoned due to flooding where drainage soughs and water-driven pumps had proved ineffective, were to find an alternative method of removing water from their workings. One year after George I became king, a robust, early Newcomen-type steam-powered pumping engine was installed in the Yatestoop lead mine at Winster, Derbyshire. The year was 1715. Although these early steam engines were incapable of pumping mines much below the water table, they could be used in conjunction with the earlier drainage methods. Successive improvements in steam engine design then kept pace with the extension of deep mining techniques, so that by the late 19th century, the problem of flooding in such mines was effectively solved.

Chapter 12. THE REMOTE NONCONFORMIST CHAPELS

THE CHURCH OF ST JOHN, SALTERSFORD (SJ 984 766)

At a crossroads on the saltway from Cheshire, near the head of the Todd Brook valley, stands the tiny remote Jenkin Chapel in an area known locally as Burton. It was built using local gritstone 'by voluntary contributions from John Slack of Saltersford Hall and others' in 1733 and has contemporary gravestones. The architectural style is definitely vernacular; like a sturdy farmhouse with rows of Georgian windows on either side. In the centre of the south wall is a chimney stack. Typical of the simple qualities of Nonconformity and enthusiasm for religious dissent (but only by some) that survived and revived at this time, the chapel still serves the farming community of the area, some of whose ancestors no doubt actually helped with its construction. Its interior is plain, compact and has the original oak box pews and tall pulpit. On the nave floor are grave slabs of the Turner family (see below) who, for much of the 18th century, were packhorse carriers from nearby Saltersford Hall. The chapel has an outside flight of steps leading to a gallery and bell tower that was added in 1754–5. Below the dedication stone on the tower, a further carved stone now eroded or defaced long ago, reveals '. . . At John Slacks expense in 1739 made sacred for ye Worship of Almighty God'. On completion, the chapel was dedicated to St John the Baptist – a saint frequently associated with the pre-Christian traditions that came before him. The building was not consecrated for more than sixty years, at which time the Bishops of Chester insisted that the building become a chapel to Prestbury and be rededicated to St John the Evangelist; the modern sign outside the chapel fudges the issue – which 'St John' isn't specified.

The chapel is popularly thought to have been built to replace an old cross shown in a 14th-century document as 'Jankyncros'. Evidence for any 'Jenkin' or 'Jankyn' (perhaps a diminutive of John), or for the accurate position of any such cross, seems unobtainable although the chapel site itself or the nearby rounded summit of Fox Hill would seem an ideal spot for a simple cross intended as a boundary marker or a guide on what was a major route. It is of course entirely possible that the term 'cross' meant nothing more than an indication of a place where many paths or tracks crossed – and still do.

Opposite the chapel was Burton School, giving education to 30 or 40 valley children. The fact that the school, perhaps built by public subscription, existed well before the 1870 Education Act is revealed by its inclusion on the one-inch OS map of 1840. Falling into disuse in the late 19th century, it was finally demolished about 1920 when some of the stone was used to build a tiny privy for use by the chapel.

This upland area, known more generally as Saltersford, is one of three townships that make up the parish of Rainow. It is roughly on the county borders of Cheshire and Derbyshire where the wide valley of the Todd Brook, now used for grazing, has probably experienced a diversity of agriculture from medieval times.

A curious roadside stone (SJ 978 759), recently replaced on the old hollowed packhorse route (now Ewrin Lane) below Buxter Stoops Farm, has an inscription which on one side reads: 'Here John Turner was cast away in a heavy snow storm in the

Jenkin Chapel, Saltersford.

night in or about the year 1755.' The grim inscription on the reverse reads: 'The print of a woman's shoe was found by his side in the snow were [sic] he lay dead.' John Turner was a local carrier – a packman who lived less than half a mile away – so why had he perished so close to home? The inscription on the original stone at the same location gave the date as 1735.

The Ewrin Lane Stone.

A similar stone can be found between Whaley Bridge and Disley on the 1724 Buxton to Manchester turnpike high on Longside Common, although the inscription is more concise. The stone commemorates the murder of William Wood of Eyam, who, returning from Manchester having sold his wool, was attacked and robbed by three men and died near the spot now occupied by the stone. Wood's assailants were subsequently brought to justice. These and other roadside stones of a similar nature were perhaps erected as a warning to travellers. They are known locally as 'murder stones'!

THE CHURCH OF ST STEPHEN, MACCLESFIELD FOREST (SJ 974 721)

Wildboarclough civil parish touches on the lofty hamlet of Macclesfield Forest, where for generations the valley communities, including those of Wild-boarclough, would have had stiff climbs to attend both school and chapel. Newly built as a chapel to

the ecclesiastical parish of Prestbury in 1673, at the junction of packhorse routes from Macclesfield, the tiny chapel of St Stephen is architecturally similar to the Jenkin Chapel at Saltersford. The register dates from the year 1759 and reveals the tragedies of local people who had died after being lost on the nearby moors.

Although rebuilt in 1834 and renovated in 1906, it remains a low simple building with an equally simple bell tower. Before the provision of seating, those attending chapel would have stood for the entire service on a thick layer of locally gathered rushes to insulate their feet from the cold mud or stone floor. Despite the provision of pews, a Rushbearing Service, held on the nearest Sunday to 12 August, is still retained to commemorate the important feasts such as Easter, Whitsun and the church's patronal festival when the old rushes would have been swept out and fresh ones carried in.

At Rushbearing, the exterior of the chapel is decorated with plaited rushes interwoven with flowers. The service is normal evensong but a special Rushbearing Hymn, composed at the beginning of the 20th century by a former vicar, is sung and the sermon relayed by PA to the churchyard.

The Church of St Stephen, Macclesfield Forest.

PART FOUR
INDUSTRY

Chapter 13. POWER FOR INDUSTRY

WATER POWER, THE HISTORY AND TECHNOLOGY

By the 17th century, Britain had a consumer society catered for by an astonishing variety of crafts, small industries and industrial centres with a network of rough and ready cart tracks and packhorse routes connecting them. For centuries the main sources of power had been animals, wind and water. The steady growth of the application of wind and water power was to reach a high pitch of refinement by the 19th century, at which time they were gradually replaced by the steam engine.

In the 18th century, when water power was applied to textile spinning machinery, the size of the machines meant that textile production moved out from the home into purpose-built factories. This transition, or 'industrial revolution', refers to that time when Britain was gradually transformed from an agricultural society into one that became increasingly industrial. The term 'Industrial Revolution' disguises general trends and overemphasises those periods when change became particularly rapid. There are those who would argue that the industrial revolution is still under way and that the term is a poor but useful piece of historical shorthand. Nevertheless, it was a unique period in our history when astonishing inventiveness went hand-in-hand with shrewd business acumen.

Even though the Peak District was landlocked and the packhorse trails amongst the most difficult, these industries flourished and many firm and level tracks were built to more readily access the quarries, limekilns, mines and water-powered mills. Although advantageous in the long term, industrialisation was by no means a blessing to all those who lived through it. The eventual and perhaps surprising willingness of the growing workforce to readily adapt to technical innovation perhaps encapsulates the social history of the period.

The waterwheel, rotating in a vertical plane on a horizontal axis, was introduced into Britain by the Romans and seems generally to have been of the undershot type. The first historical reference to a waterwheel in Britain occurs in an Anglo-Saxon charter dated AD 762 but the archaeological evidence for such mills in this period is slim and often conflicting.

By the late 11th century, watermills were a common feature in both town and country in most parts of England. Depending on how its many references to 'half a mill' or 'one sixth of a mill' are counted, the Domesday Book records somewhere between 5,600 and 6,100 mills. Over the whole of England, this means that on average there was one mill for every thirty to forty households. It is apparent that a mill's value depended upon two factors: its proximity to a centre of population and the size of watercourse upon which it was built. Assuming most were water-driven, no evidence is provided to suggest that such waterwheels drove more than a single set of millstones and the term 'mill', therefore, probably described one milling unit comprising a waterwheel and a single pair of stones, one fixed and one driven to grind a variety of grains. The mills are recorded under the manors they served but exact locations, or information other than the ownership and value, are withheld. The large number of mills implies that there must have been skilled craftsmen, millwrights who were capable of setting out watercourses and building wheels and machinery. A few mills are referred to as 'winter mills' as these did not have adequate water to operate during the drier summer months. In subsequent medieval sources there is often little evidence to determine whether such wheels rotated in a horizontal or a vertical plane. Although Domesday fails to reveal *any* mills within the study area, one is recorded at nearby Macclesfield.

Few waterwheels were driven directly from large rivers, most being fed by a more readily controlled flow of water taken off the main course of a tributary stream. A natural rock step, or a weir or dam built of timber or stone across the stream, provided a fall and a means of diverting some of the natural flow into an artificial channel known as a leat or headrace. Millponds or reservoirs were dug, usually sited close above the mills they supplied, allowing water to be stored until required for use.

For hundreds of years, alongside various rivers and tributaries, water-driven wooden wheels would have been employed with locally quarried millstones to grind the seeds of cereal crops into flour and animal feed. Dual-purpose mills, where corn milling and cloth fulling, for example, were carried out under one roof, were more common after about 1350. All these structures were probably small horizontal or vertical-wheeled mills primarily serving local demand for oats, barley and other grain products to sustain the people and their animals, including the grinding of malt for brewing. Favourable land was usually given over to arable for root crops and cereals, especially oats in the South-West Peak where coarse oat bead and oatcakes were the staple.

In the Medieval period, watermills were usually located with good access from well-used roads and sometimes where a number of roads or tracks met. These mills were built by, and for the benefit of, the lord not the tenants, who were obliged to keep the mill's watercourses clear of undergrowth and silt as part of their manorial duties. The system by which the tenants were compelled to have their grain milled at the lord's mill and pay a percentage of their grain in toll was, for the lord, an important and regular source of income. The miller also took his toll, a payment in kind. For those who refused this service, fines were imposed. No doubt domestic quern stones were manufactured and covertly used for the grinding of grain despite the manorial rules.

POST-MEDIEVAL TECHNOLOGY

Because of land-ownership changes after the Dissolution, gradual improvements in standards of living and a rise in population after the 16th century, increasing pressure was put upon natural resources – particularly on the use of land and watercourses. More trades adopted power-driven machinery to meet both a growing demand and to increase the range and quality of production. There was considerable rebuilding

or enlarging of mills in the 17th century, often overshadowed by the technical achievements of the 18th century. Millers, no longer merely manorial tenants or servants, were able to improve both the performance of their mills and the variety of their products.

BASIC WATERWHEEL PRINCIPLES

The **Horizontal** wheel forming the earliest form of watermill has a simple mechanism without the need to transfer power through a right angle, which with wooden gearing is not always very efficient. Their size, however, is limited by the weight of the millstones that have to be carried in a substantial structure above the water.

An **Undershot** wheel, the most common of early vertical waterwheels, produced relatively small amounts of power. Running water, either from the river or from a headrace or water channel, pushed the wheel's paddles from below.

An **Overshot** wheel, located off the river in a headrace, required a constant supply of water falling into the wheel's buckets from above. The weight of the falling water into the buckets turned the wheel, using its energy more efficiently. Buckets were better suited than paddles for this purpose.

Breastshot wheels relied upon both the impulse and weight of water to turn them. With this system, the water fell onto the wheel near its midpoint, at about the level of the axle.

In the latter half of the 18th century, cast-iron shafts appeared, allowing larger wheels to be built, while wrought-iron buckets were introduced in 1780. During this period the **High Breastshot** wheel design was favoured, where water filled the wheel's buckets from above the level of the axle shaft, with gravity turning the wheel. By 1800 some waterwheels were constructed entirely from iron, which allowed them to be larger, more powerful, more easily assembled from prefabricated components and longer-lasting.

Power was transferred from the wheel axle via a series of gears along the vertical and horizontal transmission shafts, linking up with the machinery to be driven by leather belting. Advances in transmission systems allowed power to be carried over greater distances within buildings, enabling larger factories to be built.

LOCAL APPLICATIONS

In addition to the milling of cereals, water power in the South-West Peak has been applied to numerous local industries. It has been used in the fulling of woven wool, in papermaking, grinding coal for dyeing, and to power saws for cutting stone and wood. It has been used to power bellows for forging and probably for smelting iron. At a remote site in the upper Goyt Valley, using a series of water-driven edge-running stones, the constituent ingredients of gunpowder were ground together to produce the finished product. Waterwheels were used to power simple pumps to remove water from the local coal mines and for smoothing the surfaces of gritstone paving slabs. They have been used in the modern period for grinding barytes for the paint industry. Waterwheels have provided power for the spinning and weaving of textiles, but by the late 18th century, the increasing numbers of dams, reservoirs and leats upstream often interrupted water flow.

THE STEAM ENGINES

The 18th-century industrialists displayed a steadily increasing demand for more mechanical power. The energy obtained from 'natural' sources of power, i.e. animals, wind and water, had been redirected for human use but the development of efficient steam engines was to unlock power from such unlikely materials as coal and mineral oil. An urgent need for such a machine had appeared in coal mines, where the perpetual struggle against flooding put a severe operational limit on the depth to which shafts could be sunk. What was needed was an efficient pumping apparatus to replace the outmoded waterwheels and bucket chains.

After the successful introduction of Newcomen's 'atmospheric' steam-powered beam engine in the second decade of the 18th century, the improvement and efficiency of these new power sources became the concern of millwrights and engineers, including James Brindley, John Smeaton and, in particular, James Watt. Before 1800 an average steam engine was capable of producing no more than 18hp (13.5kW), which was within the capacity of the waterwheel. Waterwheels therefore continued to be an efficient power source, particularly after the use of cast iron for gearing and shafting replaced the mainly wooden machinery of the 18th century. The waterwheels themselves could now be made larger and more efficient using prefabricated iron plates and iron buckets. A more precisely engineered and robust steam engine came from Boulton and Watt in the period of their famous partnership from 1775 to 1800.

The **reciprocating action** of such early beam engines was ideal for pumping coal mine workings but their consumption of fuel (freely available coal) occasionally inhibited their pumping use because of cost, in other industries. Nevertheless, the double-acting beam engine became a popular way of transmitting power from the piston to the main drive until the middle of the 19th century.

Continuous **rotary motion** was to depend solely on the waterwheel until the 1780s, from which time the application of a crank to the beam engine and James Watt's parallel motion, which gave a positive connection between the piston rod and the beam, was to have the greatest industrial significance. It enabled what had previously been a pumping machine, using simple reciprocating action, to become the means of turning the wheels of all sorts of industrial processes. From 1800 onwards the variations in types of configurations of steam engines became so great that it becomes impossible to find any general acceptable categories under which they may be described.

From hereon, the combination of double-acting cylinders, parallel motion, governor, separate condenser and crank were to assure the continuing success of the rotary steam engine. During this period Richard Trevithick produced a more compact and efficient **rotary** engine called the 'Cornish Engine' and eventually constructed his first experimental steam locomotive.

Because it was believed that a **horizontal cylinder** would wear unevenly, the early engine builders stuck firmly to the principle of keeping their engines vertical. The experience of locomotive builders such as Trevithick and then Robert Stephenson, who had switched to diagonal and then horizontal cylinders, convinced steam engineers generally that this could be both a convenient and efficient arrangement. By the second half of the 19th century, horizontal steam engines had become the normal configuration.

Smaller engines for winding, housed in single-storey buildings, were also developed in the early 1800s (see Chapter 20), while in the late 19th and early 20th century, horizontal steam winding engines were employed during the final phases of coal extraction from the Cisterns Clough, Axe Edge and upper Dane collieries.

Early corn mills and fulling mills using water power had coexisted quite happily but the proliferation of bleach works, dyers, print works, paper mills, breweries, etc. who all sought clean water, often found their supplies fouled by their neighbours upstream. A further disadvantage of water-powered sites was that they suffered from variations in the water supply, flooding was a risk and drought was also common. This early dependency on waterwheels at remote rural sites meant that the transportation of raw materials and finished products could be both lengthy and expensive. With the arrival of the rotary steam engines and the adoption of the flywheel to give a smooth movement to drive, for example, the machinery in the textile mills, industry became liberated from such locations. By the 1830s, the more efficient coal-fired steam engines were producing 75% of the textile industry's power where steam could be adapted to suit the changing technology more effectively. From this time, many of the riverside mills of the South-West Peak became uncompetitive and workers slowly drifted away to find similar work in the towns on the edge of the plain, to Leek, Congleton, Macclesfield, Bollington, Whaley Bridge and New Mills.

Gradbach mill during conversion to a youth hostel in c.1983. Note the wheel pit at this end, (formerly housing a high breast wheel) and the stone chimney pots. CLM Porter photo

Chapter 14. THE MAIN INDUSTRIAL PROCESSES

THE MILLING OF GRAIN

Prehistoric hand-operated querns discovered in the South-West Peak would have been replaced by the introduction of primitive watermills. Possible sites have been suggested for such water-powered corn mills but no positive evidence has ever been found. The arrangement of waterwheel, shafts and millstones was known as the 'mill', rather than the building in which it was contained as is the case today.

In a corn mill with a horizontal wheel the drive is direct, with both the waterwheel and the upper millstone mounted on the same shaft. Where a vertical wheel was used, simple gearing was constructed to turn the vertical rotation of the waterwheel into the horizontal motion required by the millstones. In order to control the milling process by raising or lowering the top millstone, the miller could vary the rate of feed of the grain between the stones; a necessary measure taken to grind a range of different grains. This rough configuration of machinery was used to mill various types of grain to produce flour and meal from time immemorial right up to the middle of the 18th century. By this time, the introduction of an improved system of gearing allowed a number of pairs of millstones to be arranged around, and driven by, a central spurwheel which was itself driven by a bevel gear from the single waterwheel. By the 19th century, bevel-gearing was capable of driving multiple pairs of millstones in a straight line from a horizontal line-shaft parallel to the wheelshaft.

CLOTH PRODUCTION

The development of cloth production for clothing was a very necessary skill devised by prehistoric communities in Britain if they were to survive the vagaries of the climate. The two central processes in the production of textiles are spinning and weaving. Wool from sheep was available and flax was grown and it is possible that nettles were also used to provide fibres. Hemp was probably introduced in the Roman period.

LOCAL CLOTH PRODUCTION

Clear documentary and physical evidence from earlier periods for much local domestic manufacturing is, at present, scarce. There exists, however, the somewhat limited occupational evidence of late-14th-century 'court rolls of the manor and forest of Macclesfield' that suggests part-time textile/agricultural workers concentrated in the township of Rainow. Manufacture of woollens is probably the oldest of the cloth industries that had moved to those hillier regions, which offered more suitable sites for water-driven fulling mills. Domestic spinning wheels and simple weaving looms would have been in common use long before they were recorded at Macclesfield in the 16th century. Here, woollen cloth produced by farmer/weavers was sold in the weekly market. The woollen industry was to gradually become localised and concentrated in Yorkshire.

By the 18th century, although the *spinning* process had undergone mechanical improvements and domestic framework *knitting* was widespread, the conversion of domestic *weaving* to mechanical power was a difficult engineering task. It was not perfected until the early-19th-century improvements in machine construction.

Button Making

There is early-18th-century documentation of a local textile-related cottage industry of button making in 'silk, mohair and twist' in the villages of, for example, Flash and Hollinsclough where parish registers, inventories, directories and census returns reveal button-makers – men, women and children – right through to the mid-19th century. Similar evidence is available at the start of the 18th century when merchants from Macclesfield and Leek would 'put out and take in the buttons' from the surrounding villages. Round moulds of wood and bone, sometimes coloured with natural dyes, formed the basis of buttons of various sizes. The buttons were often padded and embroidered with a combination of silk and linen thread, horsehair, ox hair and mohair. Members of many families might find full or part-time employment in both silk button-making and in many of the preparatory and finishing processes associated with textiles, including dyeing.

WOOLLEN CLOTH FULLING

'Fulling' is an ancient process where loosely woven woollen cloth was cleaned of oil, grease and dirt and then beaten so that the fibres would shrink and mat together into the smooth texture of 'broadcloth'. Bolts of this cloth were trodden or walked on in a trough of 'fuller's earth' and water or sometimes stale urine, these acting as de-greasing agents. Fuller's earth is naturally occurring clay with a high magnesium oxide content that has the advantage of readily soaking up water. Its export was forbidden. This 'walking the cloth' produced the name of 'walk mill', 'tucking mill' or 'gig mill' for fulling mills. The personal surname of Walker is now considered to have originated from this activity.

By the 13th century, mechanical 'fulling stocks' had appeared, where cams on the rotating shaft of a waterwheel would move heavy vertical stampers or timber hammers (stocks) that would fall onto the material being processed. The lengths of woollen cloth which shrank were then washed in a soapy solution formed from the soapwort plant, before being gently shaped, stretched and hooked on racks, or tenter frames, for bleaching (if necessary) in the sun and rain or by immersion in sour milk. The fibres could then be teased out using the heads of teasel plants. By the 14th century, the export of English broadcloth (fulled, undyed cloth) had begun to replace the export of wool as the major source of the nation's commercial prosperity. The home woollen cloth manufacturing industry grew and was to eventually consume all the wool produced. This very early water-powered industry was spread throughout the countryside rather than being concentrated in towns.

FLAX SPINNING

Flax is a fibrous native plant cultivated in the British Isles since prehistory. Crops were sown in spring and harvested after about three months. The plant was pulled from the ground by hand, dried, de-seeded by threshing and then 'retted' (see below). The manufactured fabric is called linen because linseed is the seed of flax. The processes of linen manufacture closely resemble those of cotton but the initial preparation was more complex. Before mechanisation and the setting-up of spinning mills, flax was grown and processed by many householders on farms on the Staffordshire side of the Peak District to produce their own supplies of yarn, often in sufficient quantities to make all the linen needed for their own clothing and domestic use. Yarn was made from the fibres contained in the plant stalk, which had to be prepared for spinning. The preparatory processes of retting (decomposition in water), followed by the removal of the woody stems by 'scutching' or beating, broke up the flax into a fibrous mass from which a skein could be drawn. The fibre bundles were combed to straighten the long fibres called 'line' and to isolate the short fibres called 'tow'. Spinning of flax was similar to that for cotton with line used for fine yarn and tow making a somewhat coarser thread for cord and twine.

By the mid-18th century, British linen producers could still not satisfy the home market demand for cloth and, as with the silk industry, they suffered severely from the competition with cotton, which was cheaper to produce, lighter to wear and easier to launder. (See Chapt. 15)

SILK THROWING

Around 4,000 years ago only the Chinese were making silk and by a secret method. From these origins the secrets slowly spread throughout Europe and by the 17th century silk was becoming a luxury commodity amongst the well-to-do classes. Attempts to breed silk worms in England had proved unsuccessful but a silk industry organised on the domestic system, with weavers using hand-operated wooden looms and inferior grades of silk provided by merchants, first became established in London. Throwing is the process by which raw silk is wound from the skein, twisted, doubled and twisted again.

THE LOCAL SILK INDUSTRY

From its early-18th-century development in Derby, the mechanisation of the various preparatory processes of throwing, winding and dyeing of the silk filaments in water-powered mills spread, amongst other places, to Macclesfield. In 1744, Charles Roe installed the new silk-throwing machinery in a mill at Park Green, Macclesfield, powered by the River Bollin. In 1755 similar machinery appears in a mill at Congleton.

To supplement their incomes from agriculture, many home-workers in cottages and farms wove this silk thread to make ribbons, hatbands, fringes, squares, garters, kerchiefs, stockings, shawls and covering for buttons. The thread was delivered and finished work taken back to the town merchants through the hills by packhorse and, later, along the turnpike roads. Superior quality silk was sent initially to such places as Norwich and Manchester to be woven but by the 1790s the water-powered mills in Macclesfield, Congleton and Leek had begun their own broadloom weaving, the industry developing further during the Napoleonic wars.

In 1824, the high import duties on raw silk were abolished to concentrate resources on throwing rather than weaving. Only power-driven weaving looms then remained commercially viable and home weaving went into swift decline. However, the tradition of a cottage silk industry persisted for a long time in the rural Staffordshire Moorlands area. For instance, in Hollinsclough as late as 1851 there were 33 local people out of a total population of 400 listed as 'weavers' – 32 of them silk weavers. But in the Gollingates/Tenterhill area, close to Washgate, the figures are even more startling: there were 19 silk weavers listed in only 13 houses, suggesting the late survival of a tight community of hand weavers. Even today, many village houses still have wedge-shaped holes above their fireplaces into which the shafts of their 'homework' looms, taking up most of their 'house-room' space, were once embedded.

In time, silk mills powered by coal-burning rotary steam engines were built, gradually liberating this mechanised industry from remote riverside sites. Faster-running machinery was introduced, the hours of work were lengthened and wages fell. Not surprisingly, working conditions deteriorated and in 1844 the minimum age for children working in these mills was fixed at nine years. Eventually, cotton proved a cheaper substitute and many silk mills made the transition. Some silk weaving remained in Macclesfield, Leek and Congleton as a result of a new demand for silk stockings in the 1930s and for parachutes for the Ministry of Supply following the outbreak of war in 1939. Rayon, developed in the early 20th century, became increasingly used as an alternative to silk and in 1939 the American company Dupont invented nylon. By 1971, all the area's silk-spinning mills had closed and today, power-loom weaving of scarves, ties, ribbon and handkerchiefs only occurs on a very modest scale in Macclesfield at the Paradise Mill museum.

COTTON SPINNING AND WEAVING

The growth of the British colonies in what is now the southern United States, where cotton had been so successfully introduced, combined with the popula-tion growth of Britain's large industrial towns, was to create a thriving home market for a cheap, general-purpose textile. The shirts, shifts, sheets and underwear of rich and poor alike had once been made of wool or linen produced and woven locally, but by the 1760s cotton manufacture was booming. Cotton could be laundered more easily than wool or linen, thus giving improved hygiene. Enterprising initiative and technological ingenuity was to bring about the transformation of the small-scale domestic cotton industry into what would become a fully mechanised factory-based system.

The siting of cotton mills when the industry first became mechanised in the 1760s was, as with the silk industry, determined by the availability of water power. The process of spinning the short staples of raw cotton into a continuous thread required a preliminary sequence of operations using various machines arranged sequentially until the fibres became yarn that could be woven. Machine cotton-spinning using a 'waterframe' was a technology employed by many spinners contemporary with Richard Arkwright at Cromford, Derbyshire, who has been credited with the development of machine cotton-spinning. However, much-needed improvements in spinning fine thread were finally realised in 1799 with the appearance of Crompton's spinning 'mule'. Liverpool proved the ideal port through which to import the raw cotton. The cotton yarn produced in the region found ready markets in Manchester and Glasgow.

THE LOCAL COTTON INDUSTRY

The water-powered mills, in east Cheshire in particular, were either newly built for cotton, or converted to cotton from silk spinning and weaving. The damp Pennine air, by helping the fibres to cling together, reduced the strain placed on them by the machinery. Coal and soft acidic water (essential for bleaching, dyeing and printing) were plentiful and the ease with which they could be obtained encouraged the introduction of steam power. Weaving, however, remained a handicraft practised by many small agricultural communities until they were jolted into the industrial age by the capital and vision of the cotton 'barons'. By the early 19th century, the steam-powered (or steam-assisted) cotton mills had arrived. Any that have survived can be identified by their tall chimney stacks for steam-engine furnaces, ponds and sluices for waterwheels and distinctive saw-toothed glass roofs to illuminate the looms on the weaving floors. The hill villages of Rainow and Kettleshulme are typical examples of where, despite the arrival of rotary steam engines fuelled from local coal, the focus for the expanding cotton industry had, by the 1830s, migrated towards the South Lancashire coalfield. It became highly concentrated in the towns around Stockport and Manchester, where labour was cheap, roads and canals had proliferated and the railways were just arriving. The decline of the cotton industry in the South-West Peak was almost as rapid as its furious initial growth.

FUSTIAN CUTTING

All different types of fustian fabrics are constructed or cut in the same manner. A basic woven cloth had extra wefts sewn in it as it was made. The cloth was stiffened with lime and stretched on frames, along which the fustian cutters would take a long sharp knife-like instrument and walk the length of the cloth, cutting the weft loops so that they formed a pile. Velveteen and corduroy were both made this way. Towards the end of the 19th century, velvet dealers, who were usually masters of the trade, would set up mills where they would employ people to cut fustian for them. The mills were often long dark places; the workers provided their own lighting and walked many miles in one day. The more you cut, the more you were paid. The process became automated in the 1920s.

CLOTH AND CARPET PRINTING

Printing a pattern on fabric and carpet used to involve the manual pressing down of carved wooden blocks covered in dye; separate blocks being used for each colour. This operation had to be repeated along the length and width of the cloth. This laborious way of printing, however, became mechanised by using rotary copper-covered cylinders engraved with the pattern, instead of the blocks. As the cylinders rotated at speed, the cloth (or carpet) was fed through the machine, which imparted the coloured pattern.

IRON PRODUCTION

INTRODUCTION

The extraction of metallic minerals from the ores in which they occur and their working into useful metal implements was to liberate early people from the restriction of a technology based on wood, stone and fire. The various metallic ores were roughly cleaned, washed and crushed prior to smelting. To begin with, smelting furnaces were little more than partially enclosed charcoal fires built on hilltops or exposed positions. This would give the maximum blast of natural wind to create high temperatures – some of these sites survive as 'bole hills'. Iron began to replace bronze as the most useful metal for tools and weapons in the first millennium BC and became an increasingly important commodity from medieval times, being used in building, agriculture and arms. Because of its ability to unite with other elements, iron can take many forms, but it is possible to divide it into three major groups: wrought iron, cast iron and steel. Today, steel is by far the most important. Cast iron is still produced but the oldest, wrought iron, is practically non-existent.

INDUSTRIAL IRON SMELTING

The early iron industry was essentially a rural process, carried on in heavily wooded countryside by fast-running streams. In the high temperature of a charcoal furnace, oxygen in iron oxides combines with charcoal to form carbon monoxide and carbon dioxide. These escape from the smelting-hearth leaving a 'bloom'. This putty-like mass of red-hot iron and slag can be taken from the furnace (the bloomery) and hammered, helping to consolidate the iron and drive off some of the slag. As most ores are impure, it was necessary to use a flux such as limestone to remove the accompanying rock, as slag. The output of such a bloomery using hand or foot bellows was very small – perhaps just a batch of a few kilograms of metal a day.

Though the actual power output of medieval waterwheels was generally low and the water supply must often have been intermittent or unreliable, where both a good site and adequate sources of ore and coppiced timber were available, water power might be adopted more enthusiastically. By the late 16th century bellows could be worked by cams projecting from the extended wheelshaft – a similar technology to that applied to the mechanical fulling of woollen cloth. These improvements constituted the charcoal-based 'blast furnace' and turned iron smelting into a continuous process where, if necessary, the furnace could remain 'in blast' day and night, for months at a time, to produce a number of batches of iron a day. Other factors governing the choice of furnace sites in this phase of the industry were the proximity of markets and of convenient sources of ironstone. It was often cheaper to carry the ore to the fuel rather than vice versa because of the bulk involved. The sites of water-powered blast furnaces can sometimes be located by surviving ponds and the earthworks of dams.

Limestone, charcoal and roasted iron ore would be stored, and once the furnace was 'blown-in' it would operate 24 hours per day, seven days per week. The amount of iron produced was far greater than by the old bloomery method. Because water power was only used at a furnace for driving the bellows, such furnaces could be sited on fairly small streams. The nature of this process required constant supervision, thereby dictating that some sort of shift system was forced on the workers.

The molten iron was traditionally allowed to run off into shapes moulded in sand. This was the rather brittle product, cast (or pig) iron. By further processing this cast iron by **forging** (see below), it could be made into *wrought* iron – that is, iron capable of being worked by further hammering and shaping.

FORGING

From very early times, people who smelted iron in bloomeries were quite capable of forging iron (in a primitive way) by reheating and hammering the little blooms into such things as spearheads, knives or other tools. However, the development of the blast furnace brought about the specialization of forging and steel-making, where larger quantities of cast iron were further refined and consolidated by reheating and hammering in a charcoal-fired hearth called a 'finery'. This produced superior metal that could finally be forged to the quality or the shape required.

Because forges were also operated by water power and needed charcoal for their operation, some were situated a little way from the bloomeries so as not to clash in their need for power and raw materials. Charcoal was a particularly clean fuel, preventing contamination of the iron, so that until the early 18th century, smelting and forging remained completely dependent upon adequate supplies of charcoal from woodland.

Mineral fuels

As forests were cut down and more ironworks were established, the supply and production of charcoal came increasingly under pressure. Coal was both tried and used from the early 17th century but, because of the impurities it imparted to the metal, met with little approval. Coke, a clean and far superior fuel, was first used in a furnace leased in 1709 by Abraham Darby at Coalbrookdale, Shropshire, and by the 1730s had brought about a significant change to the iron industry. It had freed the industry from dependence on charcoal and the shrinking forests that produced it.

LOCAL IRON SMELTING

A type of iron ore important for industrial purposes occurs locally in strata associated with the coal measures. Lumps of iron pyrites or 'brasses' were found in the shale during coal mining at, for example, the late-19th-century Axe Edge colliery. Another type of iron frequently occurring as separate bluish nodules (giving the name 'kidney iron') of a high grade was also to be found locally. Although ironstone could be mined by opencast methods or in fairly shallow bell-pits, it is not known where it may have been mined locally in sufficient quantity to support the bloomery site described below.

Downstream of Gradbach Mill, the Black Brook joins the River Dane. Around the confluence at SJ 991 658, iron slag containing pieces of charcoal fuel can be found both in the rivers and on their banks. Pieces of this slag are obvious on the surface of the nearby public footpaths. The slag, together with charcoal fragments found in adjacent large grassed-over mounds, indicates smelting hearths here at some time. Parts of the woodland on both banks of the Black Brook have been managed to produce ready supplies of wood for charcoal. Level charcoal-kiln platforms and associated terraced tracks, one of which leads directly to a slag mound near the bottom of the valley, have been cut into the steep wooded hillsides. On the north bank of the brook are ancient stools of coppiced oak. That existing on the south bank represents fairly recent planting rather than a survival of ancient woodland.

At, or near this site, the river may have created power for bellows but, as yet, no evidence for this has come to light. Many medieval metalworking sites have been found where water power was not used. Undoubtedly the cost of digging leats and ponds

A charcoal kiln platform, Gradbach Wood.

Below the stream confluence Burdett's 1777 Cheshire map shows a forge south of Wharnford Bridge.

and of building and maintaining waterwheels was an important consideration.

At the confluence, the Black Brook can be crossed by a modern footbridge at the site of an earlier bridge long known as Caster's Bridge. In the *Macclesfield Times* in 1935, Walter Smith, a well-known local antiquarian, describes his investigations of the Caster's Bridge area. 'I went up to look at the place again. I called at Gradbach Farm, next to the Mill House. An old man, the late Mr Matthew Downes, answered my call. Did he know anything of an old forge near the bridge, I asked. Yes, he thought there had been something of the sort. He volunteered to go down to the spot with me. About a dozen yards from the bridge on the Gradbach side he showed me a small mound. When he first knew it (when he was young) it 'wur just greaced o'er' : he meant it was thinly covered with grass. The mound must have been considerably higher then, for Mr Downes told me that he had shifted tons of slag from the top if it. He had repaired the footpath with the refuse, and out of the footpath with his stick he poked a piece of iron slag some inches wide. From the blowholes within, and the runnings and protuberances on the surface of this piece of ore one could see that it was once molten metal that had bubbled and boiled in the fierce heat of the furnace.'

By 1806, Excise returns for Charcoal Iron-Furnaces

Caster's Bridge.

reveal that only eleven remained in all England. In 1811 Farey writes, 'Quarnford near Wincle Chapel was a place where I have observed the Slag and remains of old Bloomeries and Charcoal Furnaces.' While the location is rather vague, four years later, in 1815, he writes, 'Iron is now made in and near to Derbyshire only in tall Furnaces, heated with Coke of Pit-Coal and blown by cylinder Bellows worked by Steam-Engines.'

Documentation for iron production at the precise location by the River Dane/Black Brook confluence has yet to be found and field investigations, although encouraging, are as yet incomplete. The simple smelting areas and associated charcoal kiln platforms at Gradbach constitute the only iron-production woodland site so far identified in the South-West Peak. Sites with surface evidence of this nature are common in areas such as Cumbria and North Wales and are often medieval in date. Whether that at Caster's Bridge is if similar date or later is currently not known.

THE FORGE AT QUARNFORD

Accounts for the manor of Macclesfield in the 13th and 14th centuries mention demesne pasture at (with other nearby locations) 'Midgeley by the River Dane'. Within the terms of a lease two forges are mentioned, charged to yield over £17 in the year 1348–9, 'that would have yielded more but were in the lords hands because of the Black Death'.

In a lease document drawn up for Sir Henry Harpur of Calke to George Goodwin, James Slack and John Wheeldon, dated 1765, mention is made of a 'forge new erected by Slack in or near Quarnford'. Burdett's Cheshire map of 1777 shows a 'forge' marked just to the south of 'Wharnford Bridge'. This is likely be a forge approximately 1km east of Caster's Bridge at, or close to, the car park (SJ 998 662) near the 16th-century Quarnford Farm (later, Manor Farm), where smiths would have worked the iron into nails, tenter-hooks and a whole variety of agricultural and domestic tools and fittings.

CHARCOAL BURNING

Roasting lengths of timber out of contact with air produces charcoal. Arguably the first true chemical process, the production of charcoal (the destructive distillation of wood) is one of the oldest crafts; its uses can be traced back in Britain at least 4,000 years, where it became the smelting fuel of the bronze and iron ages. The by-products of its manufacture, the tarry liquors, were used for caulking wooden ships. The charring of wooden piles and posts to preserve them from rot and water damage was known in the first century AD.

TRADITIONAL FOREST KILNS

More efficient and faster-burning than a simple pit-kiln or clamp, the forest kiln was built on a slope, the hearth or floor being levelled by the charcoal burner who chose the site carefully to use the kiln to its maximum advantage. Although the necessary uniform combustion depended on the control of air rising through the kiln, as barriers to any prevailing strong winds latticed wood hurdles, piles of bracken or sacking were used as windbreaks. A shelter or hut was built close to the site, with its door facing the kiln, and the charcoal burners would live in this for the duration of the burn(s). Timber was cut into usable lengths and left to dry for at least six months before being finally stacked in a wide uniform circle on the kiln platform. A central chimney was created and employed as a flue around which the stack was built, the construction being kept as a circular curving mound upon which was placed fine earth, grass, straw and bracken. A space was left around the bottom edge to admit some air until the burn was established.

Glowing embers from a previous burn were shovelled down the kiln chimney. After three or more hours, when the kiln was well alight, the chimney was closed, the bottom sealed and carbonisation was now in progress. During the burn the kiln gradually subsided and the burners had to be ready to repair the earth surface, thereby preventing excess air from entering and spoiling their work. When the burn was completed, two or three buckets of water were poured in and the surface earth replaced. This was repeated on several occasions, the kiln left to cool for at least a day or until it was completely cold, at which time the charcoal was taken out and the by-product tars and liquors collected (see also the section above on Local Iron Smelting).

For the simple production of charcoal rather than its by-products, hardwoods are preferred and British practice used beech, oak, hornbeam, hazel and ash. These are examples of native species that will send up new growth, either from a stool or from suckers when cut down to ground level. The charcoal burner's life revolved around the kiln. It had to be watched around the clock as any carelessness in maintaining the earth cover would result in the loss of some two weeks' work. Families of charcoal burners operating in specific areas carried on the craft and it was not unusual for one family to operate several sites with women and children helping and carrying food to the burners. Other, perhaps more settled families, hired labourers for the season.

Burning was mostly seasonal from April until November, the burners turning to woodcutting during the winter when the sap content of the trees was at its lowest. The families of burners generally lived in turf-covered huts on-site. An opening was left for access facing the kilns, while at the rear end of the hut there would be a fireplace. All charcoal was originally made in the forest and carried from there to the place of use. Because the charcoal made by these methods represented a huge saving in both bulk and weight, it was more economical to carry charcoal rather than wood.

In some areas the number of working charcoal burners had been considerable. In four of Edward I's demesne woods in the Forest of Dean in 1282, no fewer than nine hundred people were employed. In 1414 Henry V ordered willow charcoal for gunpowder, but its use was still relatively small and the quality probably doubtful. Several centuries were to pass before proper production control for gunpowder was established (see Chapter 15, Fernilee Powder Mills).

By the late 16th century there was prohibition on the felling of mature trees for charcoal, resulting in an expansion of coppicing as a sustainable alternative. Because the prohibition was largely ignored, by the early years of the 17th century the charcoal shortage became acute. This was to lead to improved kiln design, and by the early years of the 18th century, the slow adoption by the iron industry of the efficient blast furnace using coke – although even as late as 1788 only two-thirds of the blast furnaces in Britain were using coke. In addition to the blast furnaces, forges in this period were demanding substantial quantities of charcoal and it was reported that in Sussex alone, one hundred and forty forges *each* used over five tons of charcoal every week. When manufacture began to be concentrated in larger units on an industrial basis, charcoal kilns began to move out of the forest, from which time cast-iron charcoal retorts make their appearance.

PAPER MAKING

Paper is perhaps one of the most important inventions of the last two millennia. Its manufacture in China was known long before such procedures were understood in the West where, well into the medieval period, clerks were still using parchment or vellum prepared from animal skins. Caxton printed on imported paper when he established his press at Westminster in 1477. There is no evidence at all of paper making in England until 1495.

A ready supply of swiftly running water was essential in the making of paper. This provided power for the pulping machinery and clean water for mixing with the shredded raw material – often plant fibres. By the close of the medieval period the increasing demand for books and the invention of printing with movable type had ensured the development of good quality paper made from rag pulp and employing water power. Paper making long remained a small-scale manufacturing process, with each operator and perhaps his family collecting their own rags to produce pulp that could be sieved from suspension in water vats. From these, fibrous layers were peeled off to be pressed and dried – better quality papers being dipped into size before final drying. By the beginning of the 19th century, European wars had curtailed the necessary importation of rags to satisfy the British paper industry where people had long been encouraged to preserve their cotton and linen rags and sell or exchange them with the rag-and-bone collectors. Paper making first became established in the South-West Peak around the end of the 17th century where waterwheels were used in the early part of the process to turn cams fixed to wheelshaft extensions, to lift and release 'stamps' or hammers that would pulp the rags. Paper making was an industry that could make use of an established fulling mill site, where the fulling stocks (see above) were readily adapted for pounding the rags (See also Chapt.15).

By the early 18th century, the water power of such mills was used to drive a device known as a rag engine or 'hollander'. This was a vessel (invented in Holland c.1660) containing a roller encircled with sharp spikes to cut and macerate rags into pulp. At the same time, the pressing process became mechanised. Fine linen and cotton rags were used for white writing paper and printing paper while poorer-quality rags and canvas were used for the more common coarse brown and blue papers produced by the local mills for wrapping and packing.

By the mid-18th century, there was still no satisfactory method of bleaching pulp, so only white rags could be used to produce white paper. Bleaching using chlorine appeared by the end of the century, but this caused the paper to deteriorate quickly.

By 1850, paper making by these small mills had become uneconomical as a continuous paper-making process had been introduced into Britain, with straw and then wood pulp substituted for rags as the industry's chief raw material and steam-heated rollers used for drying. Throughout the 18th and 19th centuries, a complicated tax structure plagued the manufacture of paper, often resulting in excise men paying very close attention to these businesses.

CUT STONE

Stone has been cut locally using vertical banks of iron saw blades and then ground to give an even surface and thickness. Both these processes could be powered using waterwheels driving machinery by cranks (see Chapter 15, Directory of Mills).

A number of water-powered flint mills in nearby North Staffordshire were built to serve the pottery industry that developed there from the 17th century. The mills worked on the principle of a circular grinding pan into which batches of calcined flint were put with water, to be swept around with loose blocks of chert. The sweep arms or runners were connected to a vertical shaft. The base of the shaft was also made of chert and, as the arms rotated, the flint was worn down with water to form a slurry. When the grinding was finished, the slurry was run off and the water evaporated, usually in kilns, leaving the finely ground flint to be used by potters for making glazes.

GUNPOWDER

Gunpowder was made in England using imported ingredients from the 14th century onwards, much of it made in arsenals by hand with pestle and mortar, but by the end of the 16th century, several water-driven powder mills were operating to provide gunpowder for military use. Although there is evidence of blasting with gunpowder in Peak District mines and quarries as early as the 17th century, industrial production only spread to Derbyshire early in the 19th century with the establishment of water-driven powder mills at Fernilee in the upper Goyt Valley. These were licensed in 1801.

Gunpowder is a mixture of saltpetre (potassium nitrate), charcoal and sulphur, usually in the proportions of 75:15:10 although this could vary. During periods of hostility with producers in Europe and until mineral sources of nitrate became available from South America, crude saltpetre in Britain was recovered by the noxious process of boiling the organic waste from human latrines and from shippons and stables, some with purpose-built channelling to troughs for collection. Sulphur would have been imported from the volcanic deposits of Sicily where a considerable trade developed.

Charcoal, which was the inconsistent factor, involved the selection of the wood and control of the burning process in sealed retorts. Saltpetre crystals could be used straight from the refinery but the charcoal and sulphur were pulverised under edge-runner stones powered by the river. The powdered ingredients were each sieved to ensure uniformity and to remove any gritty particles that might cause an explosion during manufacture, before being weighed out in the required proportions. The ingredients were then mechanically crushed together by a further series of edge-runner stones, a process known as 'incorporating'. The finished gunpowder was then dried using coal-burning stoves. Fumes and dangerous sparks were carried by underground flues to be discharged through chimney stacks standing at a safe distance (see Chapter 15, Fernilee Powder Mills).

Chapter 15. DIRECTORY OF LOCAL MILLS

Some of the following text is based on studies of the use of water power on the River Dane produced as a book, Driven by the Dane, *by Tony Bonson (2003), and from a themed walks booklet 'The Industrial Revolution in East Cheshire' by George Longden (1988) (see Bibliography).*

WINCLE

THE BEARDA MILLS (SJ 963 642)

At Bearda, 1km south of Danebridge, high above the River Dane there are two mill sites from different historical periods powered from mill pools fed by tributary streams of the river. The two sites today are interconnected. Of the Victorian Bearda Saw Mill, little remains apart from the wheel pit and three iron gears used to transfer power from the wheel into the sawmill. The large, recently restored mill pool allows water to flow through a headrace pipe above the wheel pit, while the adjacent sluice takes overflow down the flume to the river. Water power was used in northern Europe from late medieval times to drive mills for sawing deal and planks using reciprocating saws mounted in vertical frames driven by cranks, the action of which imitated the manual sawing of timber in pits. The circular saw did not appear in England until the late 18th century and by the 1820s, although there were wind-powered sawmills, there were still very few water-powered circular-saw mills.

The wheel at the much earlier Bearda Corn Mill was powered from a pool formed from the dammed stream to the south and another steam flowing down from Swythamley Park. There are records of a mill at Bearda associated with Dieulacres Abbey in the early 1500s and suggestions that the mill may have been built in the 14th century. Other references to a mill at Beardholme, Beardhulme or Beardall (the same place) occur in sale documents from the 17th century. A mill symbol appears about this position on Yates's map of Staffordshire of 1775. All the mill owners of the 19th century are known. The mill, built of local stone, has been converted into a dwelling where the current owner has installed a new high-breastshot waterwheel in its original position. Near the new wheel can be seen an old composite millstone, probably a French 'burr'. Blocks of French stone were imported into England, from which millstones were built up, backed with plaster of Paris and bound with iron hoops.

FOLLY MILL (SJ 971 664)

On the Cheshire bank of the Clough Brook, just above its confluence with the River Dane at Allgreave in a steep-sided and wooded valley, is the isolated ruin of a former paper mill known as Folly Mill or Grove Mill. A Mr Abraham Day of Allmeadows Farm, Wincle, may have built the first mill on this site, possibly between 1780 and 1790. It must be strongly emphasised that the whole site is now in a very dangerous state and can only be accessed from the cliff-top path down steps below the ruined workers' cottages. Near the confluence, a wide zig-zag track once gave access to the mill but the lower portion has been washed away at some time by one of the notorious 'bores' of the Clough Brook. The present mill ruin may have been given the name Folly Mill because two previous buildings on this site had been washed away and a third

The Folly Mill ruin.

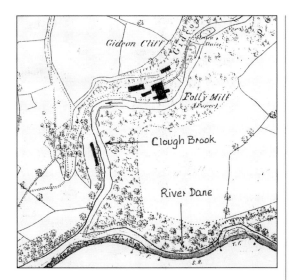

Ordnance Survey map 1876 showing the location of Folly Mill.

WINCLE (OR WHITELEE) MILL (SJ 957 642)

In the 15th century an agreement was obtained by the monks of Dieulacres Abbey, to have their 'watermill near Gighall' exempted from tithes. Gig Hall Farm is a property name on the Staffordshire side of the River Dane nearest to Whitelee on the Cheshire bank. Because a 'gig mill' was a machine used in the fulling process, this might suggest the monks from nearby Wincle Grange were mechanically fulling their woollen cloth at this site. Speculation about this site and its history is certainly plentiful.

A millwright and wheelwright named Abraham Bennett, who lived in Gurnet near Macclesfield in the early 18th century, was master to an apprentice, James Brindley jnr, who was to first make a name for himself designing and constructing water-powered factories (manufactories) in the area. This James Brindley was eventually to become one of the original driving forces in the construction of the British canal network.

During Brindley's apprenticeship (1733–40), Bennett was commissioned to build an 'engine paper mill on the River Dane' to a design probably based on a new device for pulping rags instead of the previously-used old technology of 'stamps' or hammers. The machine introduced into the industry around this time was the 'Hollander'. The story goes that Bennett was experiencing difficulties with the installation and young Brindley then travelled to Manchester to inspect a successful modern conversion before returning to inform Bennett where the problems lay. The Wincle Mill was being converted from a 'fulling' mill to a paper mill and it is now thought that Bennett and Brindley together completed the conversion to the proprietor's satisfaction. At the same time, Brindley was said to have made improvements to the paper press. He was recorded as being in his fourth year as an apprentice, which would make the date about 1737.

Wincle Mill continued as a paper-making mill throughout the 18th century, with various papermakers appearing in local parish registers – perhaps working at both the Wincle and Folly Mills. Wincle Mill certainly occupied the site when Yates drew his county map in 1775.

In 1824, after several failed attempts, the Trent and Mersey Canal Company completed a four-mile feeder from the Wincle Paper Mill's weir to their reservoir

attempt would be folly. The mill certainly appears to have been built around the end of the 18th century when paper-making was still a hand-made process with water power used to drive a 'hollander' to pulp the rags. By 1825 the mill may have passed to Thomas Hope, who also ran a paper mill at Whitelee (Wincle). The mill remained in fairly continuous use, the census returns of 1841 showing eight papermakers living in the area together with an excise officer living at the mill itself. In 1849, the mill was advertised under the name 'Folly Grove Mill'. In 1861, only four paper makers were shown in the census, but by this time, paper-making had become a fully mechanised industry and the Folly Mill was no longer competitive with mills using continuous process machinery. By 1868 the mill was listed as 'not in work' and in 1869 as 'unoccupied'. The mill may have been in use again in the 1920s to make coarse brown paper.

The three-storey, dressed-stone building has surviving wheelpit masonry suggesting the wheel to have been either overshot or pitchback with a diameter of about 16ft. Some of the walls still stand precariously but the floors have long gone. The weir, about 70m upstream and the headrace that enters the building through a low arch can still be found. Where the mill access road arrives at the valley bottom (subsequently washed away) are the thick, ruined drystone walls of a possible storage building connected with the mill. A detailed OS map of 1876 correctly shows both the location and the access road of this remote and barely accessible mill still intact at this time.

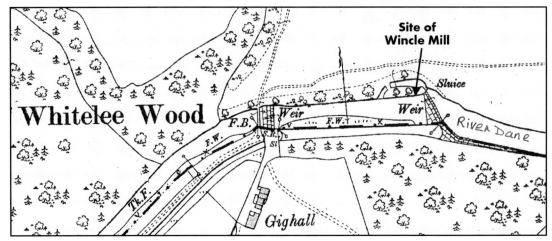

Ordnance Survey map 1910 showing the site of Wincle Mill.

known as Rudyard Lake. Rudyard fed the short Leek Canal, which in turn fed the Caldon Canal that empties into the summit level of the Trent and Mersey Canal at Hanley.

Any floodwater 6ins above the Wincle Paper Mill's normal weir height would flow into the Dane Feeder to help maintain the reservoir level at Rudyard. The original attempts to build a leat to the feeder were started from a newly constructed curved weir *downstream* of the mill. The flow of water was so poor that a further intake *above* the paper mill's weir was built, which not only preserved the mill's water supply but also vastly improved that to the feeder. By 1834, the machinery installed in the late 1730s by Bennett and Brindley had become obsolete due to the invention of continuous paper-making machines patented by the Fourdrinier Brothers. The mill was thus no longer competitive. At this time, the mill's water rights were transferred to the Trent and Mersey Canal Company but are now presumed to belong to British Waterways.

Although the mill ceased to operate after 1834, it was not demolished but allowed to fall down. The OS map of 1842 shows the site as 'old mill'. Apart from the recently repaired mill weir, the only evidence of Wincle Paper Mill today is a mound of grassed-over masonry almost isolated from the bank by the ruined tailrace and the similar channel where the headrace and wheelpit must have been. The Dane Feeder weir and the silted-up feeder itself running parallel with the river downstream of the mill and the extension leat running in the riverbed can both still be seen and followed on foot.

That the Wincle Paper Mill was associated with James Brindley jnr (1716–72) and Abraham Bennett was never questioned in reports and biographies of the 19th century – the mill fulfilling all the elements of the story. It was certainly recognised up until the early 20th century as the 'fulling mill that Brindley had converted'. However, later 20th-century writers have located the mill 'on the River Dane in Wildboarclough' or else at Folly Mill, which (again) is not on the River Dane. More recently, 'Brindley's paper mill' has been located by local tradition on the site of the later Crag Works on the Clough Brook – but the mill was clearly at Wincle.

DANEBRIDGE MILL (SJ 963 651)

In a deed dated 1652, Danebridge Mill is mentioned as a paper mill and a corn mill. In 1671, the paper mill at Danebridge is said to 'adjoin a corn mill and a fulling mill'. These mills (or a single mill building with water-powered machinery to make paper, mill corn and full cloth) may well have existed long before these dates and the location suggests possible ownership by the Dieulacres Abbey near Leek until the Dissolution in the 1530s. It was not uncommon for paper mills and corn or fulling mills to be built adjacent to each other or even under the same roof but using separate wheels.

The present mill site can be found on a semicircle of land created by river meanders, about 200m downstream of the Dane Bridge. By 1716, the site consisted of a dwelling, a corn mill, a paper mill and a fulling mill. Around 1740, the three concerns were split between two estates and in 1742, James

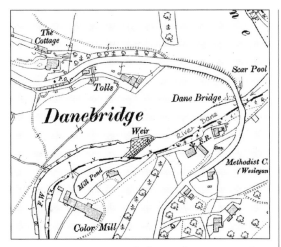

Ordnance Survey map 1897
showing location of Danebridge Mill.

Brindley, yeoman of Low, near Leek, leased the properties. This James Brindley was the father of the famous engineer and canal builder – also James Brindley – who early in his career was involved in converting Wincle Mill (see above). It is possible that Brindley, father and son, worked together at times in the Danebridge Mill and that James jnr instructed his father and his younger siblings in the skills of mill engineering. By 1754, the paper mill and fulling mill had been demolished and the remaining corn mill probably modified and improved by young Brindley's brother Henry, the new mill owner. The mill was leased to a cotton spinner in 1784 but by 1791 the mill was again advertised, this time in the *Manchester Mercury* as 'a cotton water mill newly erected and factories . . . four storeys in height, situate at Dane Bridge with Heaton . . . with two dwellings on two acres of land'. Given the size of the mill in the 1791 advertisement, it must surely have been rebuilt before this date.

The land tax records continue to show Brindley as owner of the mill until at least 1831. There was a succession of tenants, including James Simmister from 1809 to 1821, and John and James Berisford and Company from 1822 until at least 1831. Danebridge Mill continued as a cotton mill until 1851 and after a period of closure, as a waste silk spinning mill until 1860, from which time Bowden Bower Dakeyne was spinning silk here, as he was at Gradbach Mill. Presumably he ceased operations at Danebridge in 1868 when spinning at Gradbach was discontinued. The mill was only one and a half miles from the Congleton and Buxton turnpike – a significant transport route. By 1870, the mill was reopened by John Birch and by

1876 his son, John, was operating it as a 'color' mill where coal slack was ground to a fine powder and sold as 'dye' to the Leek silk makers. This powder was also used in the manufacture of shoe blacking, stove polish and for black lead pencils. The mill appears to continue as a 'paint manufacturer' until 1898 when it was sold and used as a smithy but eventually fell into disrepair. Gradual disintegration then occurred until the ruins were finally removed in 1976. The weir was dismantled to ease flooding and the mill pool is now dry and overgrown.

GOYT VALLEY

THE FERNILEE POWDER MILLS (SK 0130 7725)

Although there is evidence for blasting in Peak District mines and quarries as early as the 17th century, industrial production of gunpowder only spread to Derbyshire early in the 19th century with the establishment of water-driven powder mills at Fernilee. The mills were built in response to new markets provided by developing industries and an expanding network of roads and railways. These mills on the upper River Goyt were built on a small plateau of land leased from Francis Jodrell, at a safe but convenient distance from the nearest settlement of Fernilee. Coppices of alder, willow and alder buckthorn, planted around the mills to provide some screening and protection for the nearby farms, would also provide a renewable source of suitable wood for charcoal used in the manufacture of gunpowder and fuse powders. The tree species are still in evidence by Fernilee Reservoir today. All the bark was removed before kilning and the charcoal carefully examined to ensure that no grit, stone or metal particles that might cause a spark were introduced into the powder mills.

Thomas Williamson of Grappenhall, Cheshire, applied for a licence to produce gunpowder at Fernilee and this was granted in 1801. Part of Williamson's application suggested 'That the Manufacture of Gunpowder will be very useful and beneficial to the Neighbourhood on Account of the great Number of Coal and other Mines hereabouts, in the working whereof great Quantities of Gunpowder are used' etc., and to 'erect Gunpowder Mills with proper Offices to adjoin thereto upon the said Lands lying in Shalcross aforesaid, called by the several names of the "Geldee Warth", the "Mill Warth", and the "Warth

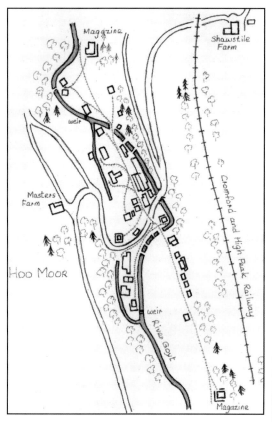

Fernilee Gunpowder Mills. Site map of the later phase showing tramways, canals etc.

were laid out to connect the different buildings, with the trams pulled by horses or pushed by workmen. Gunpowder was stored in magazines while awaiting dispatch.

Apart from charcoal, materials would have been brought in and the finished products taken out from the mills by road and later by rail. Carriage was at first by horse and wagon, using the old lane that connected the nearby farms on either side of the River Goyt to the Manchester to Buxton turnpike (1724) – the old lane meandering through the powder mills site (see map). Given the obvious dangers, public access to this lane would seem unlikely. The tramway linking the various site buildings extended to the Cromford and High Peak Railway, as this passed within 100m of the mills when it opened in 1831. This rail transport link would then have been eagerly adopted until the Shallcross Yard to Ladmanlow section was discontinued in 1892. Thereafter, the gunpowder was again taken by road to Whaley Bridge Station for onward dispatch.

In the 1851 census, ten Powder Mill employees are shown working at Fernilee. By 1861, the numbers had risen to fourteen. Their addresses show them to have been residents of Rainow, Taxal, Stockport, Chapel-en-le-Frith and Fernilee.

The Fernilee Mills acquired more modern machinery and expanded, taking on a much larger workforce when the company became a subsidiary of the Chilworth Gunpowder Company Ltd in 1888. A total of thirty employees are recorded. Three years later, many workers from far afield had moved to work at the mills. Men came from Surrey, Sussex, Cumberland and Westmorland.

EXPLOSIONS

Minor accidents were routine and most powder mills would experience a fatal explosion occasionally. The Fernilee Powder Mills were no exception when three workers were killed in an explosion in 1909. The plan of the Powder Mills, showing the widely spaced nature of the buildings layout, reflects the sequence of necessary stages of gunpowder production and the combustible nature of the processes.

Many Acts of Parliament dealing with public safety were passed to regulate the manufacturing practices. To bring about rigorous plant inspections, a licensing system evolved that required all accidents to be notified and investigated. The Parliamentary Acts also

on the other side of the Water'" ('warth' probably from 'wath' – a water meadow). Although no mention was made in the petition regarding military use, it is perhaps safe to assume that British infantry in the Napoleonic wars used Fernilee gunpowder. In 1848, the Post Office Directory states that 'There is a gunpowder mill in Fernilee near the C&HP Railway . . . '. White's Directory of 1857 lists Thomas Williamson (son of the founder) as one of the nine principal landholders in Fernilee. At this time the total workforce at the mills consisted of about a dozen workers.

PACKING AND TRANSPORT

Gunpowder was traditionally packed in oak barrels and kegs of various sizes, the 100lb (44kg) barrel being used as the standard unit of weight in marketing. The Fernilee Mills had its own cooperage that employed a large proportion of the overall workforce. For transport within the complex, punts were used on the millstreams wherever possible and tramways regulated the safe carriage of gunpowder and insisted that magazines for storage should be remote from the mills and shielded behind sturdy walls (see map).

Even after the slump in the industry following the armistice in 1918, 'Black powder', as it was called, was still in use for fuses and fireworks and for blasting in some quarries where it was favoured for its clean heaving action. However, gunpowder was already becoming obsolete for most purposes as a new high explosives industry, based on a more modern technology, made rapid progress. The Fernilee Mills, not wishing to embrace this new technology and redevelop the factory, closed for good in 1920. Immediately after closure, the entire complex was deliberately pulled down because it was believed that the impregnation of the building's fabric by gunpowder could constitute a permanent explosion hazard. However, six years later, the new Fernilee Village Hall opened, built with bricks salvaged from the gunpowder mills. This old industrial site now lies beneath the waters of Fernilee Reservoir and was the only example of a gunpowder mill in the Peak District.

GOYTSCLOUGH MILL (SK 011 733)

At the southern end of Goytsclough Quarry are the ephemeral remains of Goytsclough Mill and its small row of workers' cottages. The mill and cottages were already in ruins when they were finally dismantled during the 1930s, as that end of the quarry reopened briefly to provide additional dressed stone for Stockport Corporation to build a small covered reservoir behind the old millpond. The reservoir was constructed to ensure a head of water to supply properties in Higher Disley, the water being piped alongside the valley road down to the Fernilee Water Treatment Works and boosted from here to its customers. This reservoir, a millpond and the remains of leats from both Deep Clough and the River Goyt upstream, survive on the hillside, while a flume still carries the Deep Clough stream down to join the river below the road.

Goytsclough Mill was water-

powered, probably built in the late 18th or early 19th century. With the arrival of the turnpike road between Buxton and Macclesfield in 1759, and the Cromford and High Peak railway in the early 19th century, products from both quarry and mill could be transported by horse and cart and then by rail. The *Baines Directory of London Carriers* 1807 gives 'T and M Pickford and Co. – The London to Manchester Carrier'. This would be Thomas and Matthew Pickford, who had been loaned money by the Goytsclough Quarry owner, Joseph Marchington, to help them expand a transport venture. An 1831 Estate map shows 'polishing mill' but by 1842, the OS one-inch map shows it as a 'scouring mill'.

Perhaps we can safely assume the early phases of operation of the mill and adjacent quarry to have been a joint enterprise at that time when high-quality paving stones were being produced. At one stage there were proposals to construct a canal to serve the quarry, perhaps to boat the stone down to the railhead by Goytsbridge hamlet, and amazingly, a railway was proposed from near Leek (Harris), but neither materialised.

By 1860, *White's Cheshire Directory* suggests a change of product by listing 'Ellam and Jones, manufacturers of barytes, Goitsclough'. The local name for barytes was *caulk*. The 1861 census for Taxal lists the fourteen residents of the mill cottages called Slate

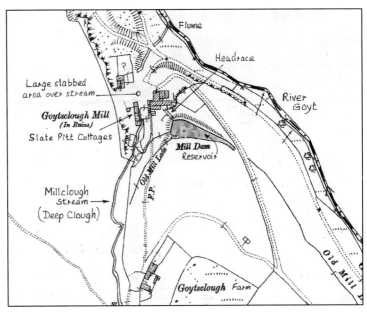

Ordnance Survey map 1925 showing Goytsclough Mill and Quarry.

Pitte Cottages. Five of the resident men listed were Barytes Mill labourers, a James Embery was the Barytes Mill Manager and a further man was a Barytes Mill carter. The remaining seven residents were wives, children and 'boarders'.

The mill is shown on the 1881 OS six-inch map as a 'paint mill', when its reputedly enormous overshot waterwheel was used to power grinding machinery to wash and crush the barytes (barium sulphate, $BaSO_4$), obtained from the Ladmanlow lead mines. This produced a source of pigment used in the manufacture of paint, glossy paper and as a dressing for calico. In the 1890s, barytes was still being processed here. Twice a day, some at least of the twenty-two workers must have walked considerable distances along the valley or over the moors – in darkness in winter – to and from the Goytsclough Mill. The 'paint mill' ceased production at the very end of the 19th century. There was also a 'paint mill' at Shallcross.

QUARNFORD

GRADBACH MILL (SJ 994 661)

Gradbach Mill, four miles from the source of the River Dane, lies on the river's south bank and was built on Harpur-Crewe land. To enable an efficient power system to be employed, a millpond was dug and a lengthy headrace excavated along the hillside to drive an overshot wheel. The wheelhouse was built below a bank on the southern gable-end furthest from the river, the wheelshaft position being situated at about ground level. A tailrace tunnel was driven under the mill frontage to an outfall downstream of the mill. A modern footbridge has replaced the old horse bridge over the river. This leads up a very steep packhorse track past a group of water troughs to what had been a smithy and the 'Eagle and Child' farm at Burntcliffe Top. The earliest lease to this farm was granted to Joseph Hatfield in 1737. The stone above the front door bears a motif taken from the Stanley crest and the initials of Hatfield and his wife. From here a substantial cart track runs past the abandoned shafts of Greenhills Colliery to the 1792 Congleton to Buxton turnpike at its nearest point. The building of the turnpike may have been the impetus for the construction of the mill, benefiting its fortunes considerably.

No evidence for a mill appears on Yates's 1775 map of Staffordshire, nor on his 1777 map of Cheshire, but on a 31-year lease dated 1792, three named partners, described as cotton manufacturers, built a mill 'for working and spinning cotton, wool or silk into twist or yarn and to make dams, weirs, cut sluices, floodgates and wheels to be driven by the River

Gradbach Mill.

The Eagle and Child.

102

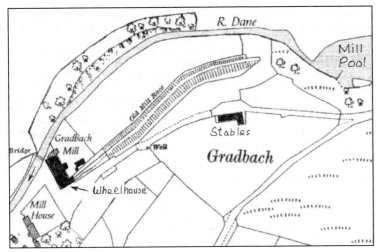

Ordnance Survey map 1925 showing Gradbach House and Mill.

into a sawmill for their estate. By the end of the 19th century, the mill was being used as a barn.

In the 1930s, a local farmer who grazed cattle on land surrounding the mill constructed watercress beds in the running water of the disused millpond. The beds provided five crops of watercress a year to be transported to Buxton and Macclesfield markets in a large box attached to the front of a pedal tricycle – each a distance of some ten miles.

In 1951 the Calke Abbey estate finally sold the property, which slowly decayed until 1978 when the mill buildings were purchased by the Youth Hostel Association, who undertook the necessary renovation of the mill's fabric and conversion of the interior into a hostel. Mill records from the early 1950s state that the waterwheel then in position was breastshot, being 38ft in diameter and having 96 buckets with a capacity of 35 gallons per bucket. The wheel was fed through a 5in diameter pipe from the leat that, although now dry, still exists and can be followed for 250m east of the mill to where the weir and pool were once situated. Although the mill was built by 1792, its large windows and cast-iron columns (now plastered) supporting the first floor are typically mid-19th century. So was the mill rebuilt sometime after the John Dekeyne and Co. bankruptcy and subsequent sale in 1837 – and if so, why and by whom? Despite the removal (sometime in the 1950s) of a smaller, narrow, two-storey extension with a chimney at the river end of the mill, there seems no evidence to support claims, however popular, that the mill was built in 1640, that Thomas Dekeyne came to the mill in 1780, or that the mill burnt down in 1785 and was then rebuilt. An increase in the waterwheel's diameter by 14ft and a change to a breastshot design sometime between the description in the 1837 sale notice and the 1950s records does point to a post-1837 rebuild. It may have been a simple improvement in technology during a change in the mill's usage when perhaps the wheelhouse was modified, although to change the wheel's diameter by this much would involve a major rebuild of the wheelhouse at least. The mill once employed a great many workers; some walked from Flash village while others were housed in Doublers Row

Dane'. They were to pay a rent of £20 p.a. Despite the bankruptcy of these partners only two years later, they took over the completed mill to try to recoup some of their outstanding debts.

By 1798, the Dakeyne family of Two Dales, Matlock, had acquired the remainder of the lease, built a warehouse and introduced the spinning of prepared flax and 'tow' using a new (patented by the Dakeynes) flax-spinning machine called the 'Equilinum'. From 1823 the business traded under the name of 'John Dakeyne and Co.', but by 1837, the company was declared bankrupt and the lease was again advertised for sale. The building was then described as 'being two storeys high comprising: mechanics shop, drying store, bleach house and yarn room, overshot waterwheel 24ft in diameter and 6ft wide with a 30ft fall, a two storey flax warehouse, a "heckling shop", 34 acres of meadow and pasture with barn, stables and cottages'. In 1838 the mill is described as 'working', employing 64 people and having seventeen years of unexpired lease. Whether a buyer was found is not known but the Dakeyne family remained at Gradbach and continued to work the mill.

Between 1850 and 1860 there was a boom in silk spinning, so the mill turned to both flax *and* silk spinning. By 1860, Bowden Bower Dakeyne had also leased the Danebridge Mill downstream, intending to spin silk there also, but the industry had declined by this date. The Dakeyne era ended in 1868, after which, in 1872, the mill was recorded as 'vacant'. In 1884, the mill was still 'not in use' and it reverted to the Harpur-Crewe family who converted the building cottages slightly upstream of the mill building where the footings still exist. At the top of the access road was accommodation for apprentices and stabling for horses. The buildings were removed in the 1990s although a water trough flanked by stone seats can be found at the roadside.

WILDBOARCLOUGH

CRAG WORKS (SJ 983 687)

Situated in a steep-sided valley at Crag, in Wildboarclough, Cheshire near to Macclesfield Forest, are the remains of a group of impressive dressed stone buildings representing all that survives of the former Crag Works started in the 1790s. The two main buildings were powered by twin waterwheels, side by side, driven from a millpond fed by the Clough Brook, a tributary of the River Dane. The buildings, known as Upper Mill and Lower Mill, were constructed as fireproof mills employing cast-iron pillars and beams and can be considered as two of the first iron-framed buildings in the world. The premises were on land owned by the Earl of Derby and were purpose-built for cotton spinning by the first leaseholders. The business, however, soon experienced financial problems.

It is often claimed that watermills had existed here from at least the middle of the 18th century but there seems no evidence for this. None are shown on Burdett's map of 1777. In 1799, a sale notice in the *Macclesfield Courier* by Francis Heywood and George Palfreyman, two of the three bankrupt leaseholders (the third was an eleven-year-old boy), describes the mill complex as: 'a very good new built dwelling house [Crag Hall, built by Palfreyman as his own residence, by 1803] . . . Also that large building lately used as a cotton mill and printing shop, 65yds long by 12yds wide, four storeys high with twin waterwheels . . . Also a dye house, an overlooker's house, twelve good cottages, an apprentice house, all of free stone erected within the last six years.' The building work must therefore have started in 1793 with confirmation of this appearing in the Wildboarclough Land Tax returns for that year, when the building and its purpose are first specified. Further confirmation is available from the Customs and Excise 'paper duty' records of the 18th century, that show entries for other mills in the area but nothing at Crag. The 1799 sale advertisement and a further one the following year were both unsuccessful but Palfreyman, one of the original builders, became bankrupt yet seems to have worked the mill until 1813 when it was again offered for sale. By this time the mill had acquired a bleaching house, three dye houses and a blacksmith's shop. From 1839, the works was heated by steam boilers with coal gas being manufactured and stored in a gasholder for use in lighting the works.

Palfreyman somehow became sole owner and operated the mill as a bleaching and calico-printing works with some success throughout the early 1830s. During this period, woven calico, a form of coarse cotton cloth, was obtained from manufacturers in Macclesfield to be printed in one or more colours with designs cut on blocks or rollers. However, by 1840, the mills were listed as 'not at work'. At this time, a colour mill operator, Joseph Burch of Froghall, North Staffordshire, bought the lease. Burch was a respected inventor and eventually patented an improved machine for printing pattern onto carpet.

Around 1848, Burch entered into a partnership with Bright and Co. of Rochdale, where plain carpets were made and then transported to Crag to be printed. The Crag machinery was now capable of printing six colours in one operation, while

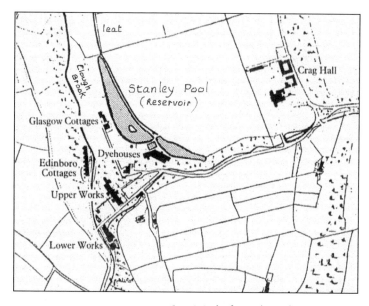

Crag Works from the Tithe Map, 1848.

a recorded influx of skilled workers into Wildboar-clough at this time suggests the business was becoming a great success. During the carpet boom years of the 1840s and 1850s, carpets made at Crag were in much demand, with the company even exhibiting (with small acclaim) at the Great Exhibition, London, in 1851. During this period, the works were employing hundreds of workers who came in from Macclesfield and neighbouring villages and farms – some wages helping to supplement income from small-holdings. Unfortunately this commercial success was comparatively short-lived. The 1861 census shows that skilled operators had now moved on and local people at the works were forced to revert to agricultural jobs or move away.

There are several reasons why this remarkable enterprise failed. The 1860 Free Trade Act caused many rifts in both political and commercial alliances. Both the deliberate denigration of the Crag product and a long patent court action by a pre-eminent rival stretched Burch's finances considerably and a subsequent total retreat to Rochdale by Bright and Co. to concentrate completely on woven carpets was to leave Burch completely out in the cold.

Crag Works never reopened for printed carpet manufacture or operated as a complete unit again. Towards the end of the 19th century, the leases of the now-closed works and of Crag Hall reverted to the Earl of Derby, who, in an attempt to revitalise the depressed local economy, made several important improvements to the village and the farms of the valley including the construction, using local labour, of a properly made road from the Crag Inn to Clough House. Various uses were made of some of the buildings. The Derby Estate used Lower Mill as an office and workshop; part of Upper Mill became a telegraph office and then a sub-post office. Village social activities were conducted in part of the mill, with other areas used variously for storage. During the Second World War, munitions stored at Crag were guarded by a detachment of Dutch soldiers based at Congleton. Consistent vandalism eventually made the buildings unsafe and in 1957 the local council demolished most of them.

The Upper Mill's water supply originated from a weir on the Clough Brook, over 1km north of the complex at the early 17th-century Clough House Farm. It can be followed along a contour above the brook as a covered leat through a field, then below a line of sycamore trees on the skyline to the reservoir known

Mill House, Crag.

as Stanley Pool just below Crag Hall. The pool supplied water to the dye house and powered the water-wheels of Upper Mill. Any overflow was directed into the little stream running down by the roadside to the Clough Brook where a storage pool powered Lower Mill's internal breastshot wheel.

The Upper Mill's dye house was demolished and replaced at the beginning of the 20th century by the little church of St Saviour.

Some idea of the size of the enterprise in its heyday can be gained from the remaining three-storey office building. A small two-storey block of Upper Mill remains, now converted into a dwelling called Mill House. The foundations and tailrace outlet of Lower Mill are still to be seen, while along the valley road beyond the bridge are some purpose-built workers' cottages known as Edinboro Row. A small school and a further terrace of workers' cottages were built below the Stanley Pool. They were known as Glasgow Cottages and later as Banking Edge. Pairs of all the surviving cottages have now been combined into single dwellings.

THE RAINOW MILLS

Straddling the Cheshire boundary of the Peak District National Park is the village of Rainow, where there were once extensive coal mines, quarries, an engineering works and more than a dozen factories and textile mills which grew to a peak during the

19th century – all concentrated around the village. Constructed of regular sandstone blocks with stone-flagged roofs, the mills at Bollington, Kettleshulme and Rainow would have been seen as a coherent architectural group.

As a general rule of mill construction, most multi-storey buildings were for spinning machines. Good lighting was absolutely essential for weaving, so that most weaving looms were installed either on the top floor of a spinning mill or in single-storey buildings with north-facing skylights.

Rainow's population grew significantly as opportunities for employment increased. The mills here were engaged in a changing variety of textile processing and manufacturing including cotton spinning, silk throwing and fustian cutting. A huge bleach works in Ingersley Vale stood close to the Rainow Mill – a silk-spinning factory completely destroyed by fire in 1908 (see also Chapter 5). There were silk mills at Kerridge End, Smithy Lane and Tower Hill. Some were relatively short-lived and many changed use over the years.

The local coal and textile industries of Rainow began to collapse, firstly with the opening of the Macclesfield Canal in 1831 and then with the arrival of the railway through Bollington – bypassing Rainow. The drift of capital and labour to Bollington and Macclesfield increased when larger cotton mills were built along the line of the new canal, which, together with the railway, were to provide cheaper and more convenient ways to bring in raw materials and distribute finished products. Only Gin Clough Mill still survives intact, but converted to other use. A number of the mill sites in, or near, Rainow village are described below.

GIN CLOUGH COTTON MILL (SK 9584 7644)

Originally 10 yds long by 8 yds wide, this tiny building still stands across the clough beyond Washpool Cottages. Built by John Lowe on the new turnpike road in 1794, it consisted of a cotton-spinning shed with cottage attached. It was powered by a 15ft diameter overshot waterwheel driven from a small pond, with water conveyed through an iron pipe from the Hayles Clough stream. The mill converted to silk throwing in 1824 and the building was extended by 1827. This extension was to leave the waterwheel at the centre of the building instead of at its original position at the northern end of the mill.

In the basement of the mill are the remains of the wheelpit that housed an overshot wooden wheel, the rim sections being held in place by wrought-iron straps.

In the 1850s or 1860s the mill converted to steam power when a boilerhouse and chimney (still intact) were added. The mill engine was provided with coal from mines at nearby Big Low, where old maps show other small mines and quarries in the vicinity of the mill.

Gin Clough, with its cottages, stables, public house and smithy (the building opposite the Highwayman pub) would have been a busy spot, positioned as it was on a turnpike road. Activity diminished here later in the century, Gin Clough Mill becoming a wheelwright's shop, a sawmill and finally a plumber's shop. It is now part of a private house.

COW LANE MILL (SJ 946 758)

This was just one of the nine water-powered cotton-spinning mills built on the River Dean and its tributaries between 1794 and 1806. The original 18ft diameter waterwheel was driven from a mill pool, which can be seen as a silted-up area containing trees on the

Gin Clough Mill.

far side of the ruins. In 1803 a second wheel, 25ft in diameter, was installed, fed by a hillside leat from a pool further upstream. Some heavy masonry, part of the three-storey ruins (probably the wheelhouse), can be found next to the track while a chimney on the site suggests a change to steam power some years later. By 1817 the mill had been converted to silk throwing but later that century became a bleachworks. By 1909 the site had been abandoned, the pools silted up and the buildings gradually fell to ruin. The chimney and the remaining mill walls were demolished and the stone removed in 1992.

MILLBROOK MILL (SJ 950 758)

Although the name 'Millbrook Mill' suggests an earlier mill, perhaps near the bridge over the nearby Mill Brook, John Gaskell built this mill in the late 18th century. It was quickly extended and in 1805 a second, supplementary mill pool was built upstream with a leat to power a 22ft wheel. The used water was then fed into the original pool behind the mill, this pool now feeding a 38ft wheel. At some later time, perhaps if water quantities continued to be critical, the twin-pool and twin-wheel arrangement was abandoned when the two pools were amalgamated into one raised pool. In 1806, Gaskell installed a steam engine 'for the purpose of working the machinery more effectually on these occasions'. One large pool still remains. The two mill pools must have been subsequently adjoined by raising the height of the original pool. The resultant large pool remains. Around 1868 part of the mill was destroyed by fire, after which the surviving portion of the mill was rebuilt and used for a time for fustian cutting. Bollington UDC demolished the mill in 1922 to make way for a borehole and pumping station. The filled-in windows of the ruined walls, now garden walls, can still be seen to the west of the pumping station.

LOWERHOUSE COTTON MILL (SJ 954 765)

This was a three-storey cotton mill in stone, built c.1792 but closed around 1825. Powered by the Hayles Clough stream, it was the first of Rainow's mills to close and stood directly below the dam. Bollington UDC demolished the ruins in 1899 and the mill pool was used to store water from nearby boreholes. Covered filtration beds were built on the area which had

been occupied by the mill building and only the old mill reservoir survives.

HOUGH HOLE MILL (SJ 947 764)

The mill was designed and built for cotton spinning in 1803 by James Mellor, farmer and builder. By 1806 the mill was leased to tenants but for part of the early 1800s at least, Mellor, assisted by his two sons James and William, worked it himself. William left to work elsewhere but returned to the mill in 1860 and with his four sons set up a successful engineering business. Messrs W Mellor and Co. of the 'White Shop' won a fine reputation for their precision lathes, steam hammers, drilling machines and, eventually, steam-powered road locomotives. James Mellor's other son, James, retired from business and devoted himself to religion, philosophy and garden design. The mill, which was used briefly in the 1920s and 1930s to produce 'tin foil', was demolished in the 1940s and nothing has been built on its site. A short terrace of cottages, the mill site and pool, the stone quarry, the remains of a coal mine, the mill road and stone-slabbed paths through the fields can all be considered as an interconnected historical site providing evidence of an early industrial enterprise.

In the secluded and wooded Brookhouse Clough, north of Bull Hill, there were two forges, two cotton-spinning mills (one c.1786–91 that became a dye works – SJ 947 751) and one in 1805 that was eventually used for hat making. Little remains of these mills and there is no public access to the sites. Not far away, late in the 19th century, a silk-throwing mill was built at this end of the village next to the Macclesfield turnpike. A house called 'Brooklands' now occupies the site.

RAINOW MILL (SJ 942 770)

Perhaps established in the 16th century, documents and a map of 1611 clearly show a manorial corn mill, 'Rainow Milne', tenanted by Rauf Thorley in Ingersley Clough on, or near the site later occupied by today's Waulkmill Farm. A 17th-century probate inventory lists goods in a later tenant or owner's 'dye-house and mill'. Research into the mid-18th-century phase of the mill indicates the erection of a 'bleaching works' at an extended 'fulling mill'. Burdett's 1777 Cheshire map shows 'Walk Mill' and a waterwheel symbol roughly near to the later Ingersley Vale Mill site. Between 1794 and 1796, the Rainow land tax returns describe Rainow Mill as being in the ownership and occupation of Joseph Wagstaff and later of Lawrence Plant Wagstaff and his partner William Watts. Part of an undated document in the Bollington Civic Society archive contains references to permission to dam the stream above Higher Mill 'near the said Joseph Wagstaff's *paper mill*'. This mill could be either Rainow Mill or a different mill on or near this site. It seems to have been converted by Wagstaff and Watts to cotton spinning around 1800 – a date stone on the weir, which reads '1801 LPW/WW', might support this assertion. These changes appear to coincide with Edward Collier, the new tenant of the Clough Mill (Ingersley Vale Cotton Mill) downstream, building a large reservoir above Rainow Mill. The two mills could now operate together. They are clearly shown as cotton mills on the 1871 OS six-inch map. A lease of 1822 refers to both a waterwheel and 'steam apparatus' at the mill. Although a tithe sale prospectus of 1844 listed 'Tenter Field' and 'Tenter Meadow' (implying open-air bleaching), by this date chemical bleaching would have been employed. Rainow Mill was rebuilt after burning down in 1856.

If the Waulkmill Farm site is the most likely location for Rainow Mill, the waterwheel arrangements would not have survived the construction of either the large reservoir above or the Clough Mill hillside leat in

c.1880. The mill burned down again in 1908 but this time was not rebuilt because the operators, Heathcote and Sons, had changed its use to silk spinning without informing the insurers, who refused to pay up. It may be that the farm has inherited the name of the old fulling mill.

KETTLESHULME

THE LUMBHOLE MILL (SJ 9882 8038)

At Kettleshulme, a two-storey mill called the Lumbhole Mill or the Candlewick Mill was probably designed and built for water-powered spinning. The mill is first mentioned in the land tax returns of 1798 when the owner, John Shird jnr, was apparently having difficulty finding tenants to use the mill for cotton spinning, as originally intended. Using an internal waterwheel, the mill was powered by a mill pool fed by underground pipes (not visible) from a reservoir upstream on the Todd Brook. When the mill was put up for sale in 1815, the advertiser suggested that it might 'at very moderate expense be converted into a corn mill'. It was bought by a George Brocklehurst of nearby Gap House and was extended from two to four storeys. It was then leased as a spinning mill, with a 10hp steam engine which 'may be useful when the

The Lumbhole Mill, Kettleshulme.

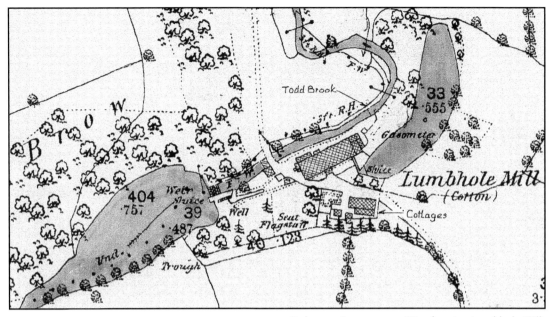

Ordnance Survey map 1880 showing Lumbhole Mill.

waterwheel is not in moving condition.' Subsequent leaseholders were Messrs Henshaws and 'Dean and Oldham', cotton spinners. In 1822 the mill burned down. John Sheldon bought the ruins one year later and in c.1830 the building was reconstructed in its present form as a three-storey mill. The rebuild is in local gritstone with a Kerridge stone-slate roof, stone ridge and two stone chimneys, both now reduced in height. Later, a one-bay, beam-engine house and lean-to boiler house containing a 'Cornish' boiler were added to the west end. The two bays added to the east end have a single-storey building at the front, which contained a hand-fired retort for making coal gas to light the mill. The south front has a projecting staircase tower under a gabled roof with loading bays. A steel launder carried water from the mill pool to the waterwheel at first-floor level. Housed at the east end is the 26ft diameter, all-iron overshot wheel which is twinned with a double-acting condensing beam engine by Sherratts of Salford added c.1840. Much of the gearing and drive is intact. There may have been an existing dual power system at the time of the 1822 fire. At some point in the 19th century the mill was making wicks for miners' safety lamps. The Grade II* Lumbhole Mill is considered to be the last example of a mill where water power and steam machinery were used together and survive intact.

THE UPPER HULME MILLS

By 1831 there was a four-storey silk mill with a house and four workers' cottages. By 1851 a mill here employed 18 workers. By 1860 this mill was used for spinning flax and for dyeing. From 1869, Leek based William Tatton used the works for dyeing silk and from 1924 for winding rayon filament yarn. From 1928 warping machines were introduced and operated until 1931, at which time a new factory was built to house all the machinery. The mill at (SK 012 600) survives but is now converted to other industrial uses. Tattons withdrew from the site in 1970.

POSTSCRIPT

Today, the upper reaches of the rivers and tributaries of the South-West Peak are characterised by pasture and isolated farms, revealing few signs of the historical importance of the exploitation of water power or of the early industrial mills and factories on the riverbanks. Although water power, which is usually associated with the major growth of industry, continued to play a vital role here throughout the 19th century, from as early as 1793 coal-fired Boulton and Watt-type steam engines were beginning to be installed at the mills in Rainow, Bollington and Macclesfield.

PART FIVE

THE EXTRACTIVE INDUSTRIES

Chapter 16. COAL, LIMESTONE AND GRITSTONE

COAL

THE GEOLOGY

On the western fringes of the Peak District, coal seams occur in the Namurian series of rocks formed from the vegetation of tropical forests that flourished over 300 million years ago during the appropriately named Carboniferous period.

One of the dominant geological structures of the South-West Peak is called the Goyt Syncline, one of a series of north–south aligned folds running northwards from Leek. It was recognised in the early 19th century by the surveyor, John Farey, as the 'Goyt Trough', where thick sandstones outcrop in craggy scarps that face outwards along both flanks of the syncline. Along with the associated sandstones, mudstones, shales and occasional thin beds of ironstone, the coal seams outcrop on opposite sides of the syncline. Coal formation, which seems to have taken place over a long period, appears as stratified deposits with many distinct seams showing throughout the rock sequence. The seams vary in thickness from a fraction of an inch to several feet, so that out of a total sequence of coal measures some hundreds of feet in depth, only a few tens of feet represent coal – and an even smaller proportion will be workable. Fireclay appears immediately below the coal, while a band of mudstone and blue shale in the roof of the coal is associated with the swamp where the forest grew. The coal measures occasionally contain 'ganister', a hard siliceous stone used for furnace linings. Although most workable coal seams in Britain range between two and six feet in thickness, some seams in the study area as narrow as one foot have been worked. The area under consideration forms the southern tip of the Cheshire coalfield.

LOCAL MINING HISTORY

During the Tudor period forests were cleared for agriculture; there was a large shipbuilding programme, an urgent need for housing and a new requirement for the commercial smelting of metals. Timber, still plentiful, was expensive and although the extraction of coal by digging or sinking shafts was difficult, it became a major and very necessary industry. Coal was to become the fuel of the Industrial Revolution.

As with many other extractive industries, coal mining has early origins. There is evidence of coal use in the Chesterton area of Staffordshire in Roman times but no similar evidence for actual mining, either there or in Derbyshire. Medieval and later mining would have selected that same outcropping coal and this has probably erased most, if not all opportunities to identify evidence for Roman exploitation. However, it is possible that coal from the study area may have been used for industrial purposes in the Roman settlement at Buxton. From the early post-medieval period onwards, it is likely that landowners would have exploited this coal for burning limestone both for lime mortar and for land improvement. Regular mining activity was to increase from about 1600 to the end of the 19th century. The most productive period, which was inextricably linked to the growth and decline of the local limeburning industry – particularly that at Grin – was from around 1780 to 1880. Compared with coal production at the major collieries of the adjacent lowlands, these mines west and south of Buxton were fairly modest enterprises. Even the larger mines here were completely overshadowed from the second half of the 19th century.

The earliest accounts of local mining are recorded in the 14th-century Macclesfield Forest, where at the halmote court it was possible to purchase the right to dig coal. In 1371 Nicholas Jolynet was fined for taking coal from the forest without licence. The account gives no location for this mining but there are early accounts of digging for coal both in the township of Pott Shrigley and north of Midgley in Quarnford. Digging for coal is recorded in 1401 near Goldsitch Moss, an area of Quarnford between The Roaches and Gib Tor. The Quarnford reference details a year's lease by Thomas Smythe, miner, of 'a vein of coal at Black Brook' (a tributary of the River Dane near Goldsitch Moss) and by Richard Strongarm, of 'two coal mines and a forge at Black Brook for 12d a year'.

The manorial lords were usually willing to allow their tenants to dig and raise coal for their own use and perhaps local sale without interference. This suggests that anyone who had common rights also had the right to dig coal. Some of these mines are associated with very small freeholds of land and although there are no known surviving accounts, those who worked the coal must have been prepared to invest money in the development of their mines. There seems no evidence until the peak of commercial coal exploitation (when the landowners saw profit in it) of any attempts to prevent customary access to this coal.

Rights of Turbary

Because of the sulphurous smell, the domestic use of coal in the early years of mining was limited to grand houses with chimneys. For the majority of people, it was far better to burn wood and turves that smell sweeter. The common 'Right of Turbary', granted by lords of the manor, allowed tenants to 'break the soil of the wastes' in order to cut peat for fuel, and turf and sods for a variety of purposes, including roofing and the repair of hedge banks. It was of particular importance to communities that relied on peat for fuel. Specific routes were sometimes designated down which individual tenants might bring their fuel. These 'turf gates', or 'peat gates', often doubled as 'drift ways' up which cattle were driven to the upland grazing. Small overgrown peat cuts identified in various parts of the South-West Peak illustrate that, for centuries, local farmers and cottagers had commonly used turves for fuel. On the Staffordshire moorlands there is good evidence that peat and turves continued to be dug and sold into the late 19th and in some cases 20th century. The gradual domestic rebuilding in stone, which took place over much of the region in the late-17th and 18th centuries, permitted the construction of chimneys in smaller houses where those who lived near to the coalfield or could afford its very high transport costs used coal. Coal was to become an acceptable fuel for domestic heating and cooking where wood, which became increasingly hard to obtain, and peat, that was plentiful, had previously been used. Much of the area's coal, however, was sulphurous and more suitable for industrial rather than domestic use.

INDUSTRIALISATION

It has been estimated that between 1451 and 1641, the price of firewood increased by a factor of eight where general prices increased by only a factor of three. Wood for charcoal (usually from coppicing) was a renewable resource used in the smelting and forging of metallic ores. However, from the early 18th century there came a change in technology when the metal producers gradually shifted to coke as the primary fuel.

The industrialisation of this part of the Peak District probably began with an increasing demand for its raw materials. This rapidly stimulated the extension of limestone quarrying and coal mining to fuel large-scale limeburning at such quarries. Also, as the textile industry itself developed, changing from water to steam power with the general adoption of the steam engine, a further requirement for coal was created. Pot manufacture and small-scale beer brewing were also to become dependent on coal or coke. For smiths' work, charcoal was used in forges but as wood became expensive and coppices depleted, a need was created for the better quality and less smoky coal often obtained at greater depths. By the 19th century, demands for coal were to come from the local limestone quarries to both fuel their limekilns and power their large steam drills, crushers and shovels. Ever-increasing industrial and domestic demand for local coal led to depletion of the shallower reserves and a tendency towards larger, deeper shafts and the driving of lengthy tunnels, some having their entrances close to the turnpike roads.

The Major Landowners

The major landowner, the Cavendish family (later, Dukes of Devonshire) purchased the manor of Hartington with the mineral rights in 1662 where in 1698, the Duke leased a mine (probably outcrops on Axe Edge) to the Brock family, together with the Grin limekilns which remained in their hands until 1789. The Stanley family (the earls of Derby) had leased land in Macclesfield Forest in 1684 and then acquired it following its subsequent discharge from rent. The

Harpur (later Harpur-Crewe) family acquired many of their north-east Staffordshire lands in c.1597 when Sir John Harpur purchased them from Sir John Savage of Clifton, near Crewe. These landowners were all keen to exploit the potential of their minerals, so that much of this activity was concentrated on these estates. With the arrival of the local turnpike road system, to avoid paying tolls to others they were anxious to lease the tollgates on the developing branch roads to and from their extraction sites. The majority of the coal output from these collieries was used in fuelling their limekilns.

THE LOCAL MINES

Coal was mined at Burbage, on Castids Common, in the upper Goyt Valley, on Axe Edge Moor, at Taxal, Shallcross and Fernilee, all around the upper River Dane at Knar, Holt, Orchard Common, Spar Bent, Dane Bower and Dane Thorn. It was mined in Blackclough, at Goldsitch Moss and Hazel Barrow, at Brink and in the Harrop Valley at Pott Shrigley (where coal served the local brick-making industry in the latter half of the 19th century). Mining also took place at Bakestonedale, both of coal and of the important siliceous fireclay deposits used by a brickworks that remained operative until the 1957. By 1808, the Bakestonedale Colliery was larger than any in the surrounding townships (except Worth and Poynton) and produced coal of a 'very superior quality'. There was also small-scale mining on the slopes of Big Low and extensive mining at Rainow, particularly on the east-facing slopes of Kerridge Hill. Coal was exploited on Sponds Hill above Kettleshulme (where fireclay was also dug from the Lower Measures), in Wildboarclough, Wincle, Birchen Booth (Diamond Hill and Robinsclough), Blue Hills, Green Hills, Whiteshaw, Lyme Park – in fact parts of the whole area are still pockmarked by shallow pits, capped-off shafts, sealed adits and debris from all this previous activity. Much of the coal was of poor quality and the mines were difficult to work, so that many were abandoned when faulting and/or flooding became a serious problem, or when rail transport eventually provided cheaper and better coal from further afield.

The early coal exploitation took place at, or close to, the surface but the seams often dipped quickly, becoming progressively deeper and requiring more sophisticated extraction and haulage techniques and the use of the real main drainage aid (from a very

early date) – the 'sough', or 'waterloose'. Soughs are drainage levels excavated up into the seams from nearby valleys.

The collieries on the gritstone moorland west of Buxton and the huge limestone hills to the east were less than two miles apart. This unique situation in the Peak District was to be one of the more significant factors in the development of the Derbyshire lime industry.

Much of the following text is based on the 1985 publication The Coal Mines of Buxton *by Alan Roberts and John Leach, and on more recent studies of the area's mines produced as papers for the Derbyshire Archaeological Journal by John Barnatt and John Leach, and in the newsletters of the Peak District Mines Historical Society by John Barnatt, Chris Heathcote and Phil Shaw (see Bibliography).*

THE MINING OPERATIONS

- Sinking shafts, cutting underground roadways or driving adits prior to coal extraction. This necessary but unproductive development could be very costly and was known as 'deadwork'.

- Mining of the coal itself by the methods described below and maintaining the workings both underground and on the surface to protect the capital outlay. This also provided a measure of safety for the miners.

- Once the coal from a particular colliery was worked-out, the miners would progressively retreat and in doing so they would rob the supporting pillars to gain more coal, thereby collapsing the exhausted workings. Adits would be blocked and old shafts backfilled.

'Pillar and Stall' working

Coal from underground was extracted by using the 'Pillar and Stall' method. This involved each hewer cutting his own small section of the coalface separate from his neighbour but leaving frequent pillars of coal to support the roof.

Groups of closely spaced shafts excavated down to the seam are all likely to be linked underground by pillar and stall working with short 'roadways' either following the seam or driven to where the seams were known to have existed. The reason the shafts are close together was one of practicality. Where the seam was close enough to the surface it would save on laborious underground haulage and would help ventilation. Shafts sunk specifically for ventilation do not occur until working from long adits, or tunnels, was adopted at a later date.

GETTING THE COAL

The two main coal seams, the 'Yard' and 'Ringin-glow' (geological names), whose depth varies due to their position in the syncline, were known locally as 'Goyt' and 'House'. The workings were either managed directly by the landowners, or leased to farmers or local lime and coal dealers on an annual or other fixed-term basis. The coal was obtained using the following working methods – not always in sequence or chronological order. This would depend on the size of the mine, the depth of the coal and the time involved in extracting it. Some of the later phases were not taken up at smaller mines, particularly as these might be quickly abandoned. Only at the larger mines are the phases chronological, although this might not be synchronous from mine to mine. Some of the earlier methods were to survive well into the 19th century:

Phase 1

By outcrop digging or 'trenching' where coal breaks the surface, sometimes following an inclined seam downwards. This early practice was eventually replaced by sinking small shafts down to the seam as surface exposures were worked out (see Phase 2).

Phase 2

Only where the seams were thick and of good quality was it economic to follow the coal to depth – and then only to the water table. Narrow vertical shafts were sunk, with the miners using ladders, or in some cases, either climbing bars of wood called 'stemples' set in the shaft at 2–3ft intervals or being lowered to the seam and wound to the surface using a wooden hand-windlass known locally as 'stowce' or 'stowes'. Broken coal in buckets or 'kibbles' was wound to the surface in this laborious manner. Unless the miners hit a fault, there would be no sudden flooding if the shafts were above the water table. Where coal seams dipped awkwardly below the water table, either such areas were abandoned or 'soughs' (mine drains) were driven up from valleys into the seam.

At this time, the most economical way of working

Shaft to deep mining, Burbage Moor.

the seam involved following the coal underground by progressively sinking new shafts. In this way, by keeping a number of shafts open at the same time, the new shaft(s) might be used for winding and others for maintaining through-draught. Underground transportation could therefore be reduced, and natural drainage improved, while haulage to the surface and ventilation were maintained close to the working area. A typical area of 'pillar and stall' working around the base of any shaft would perhaps be 50yds by 50yds – about 2,500sq yds.

Phase 3

Where 'stowes' became impractical for deeper Phase 2 type shafts sunk to below the water table, from the 18th century onwards, as with Phase 2 working, drainage soughs were driven up through adjoining hillsides and horse-engines employed for haulage.

The horse (or sometimes horses) was led around a 20–30ft-diameter gin circle by a boy to provide power for winding coal and men. A horse-engine or 'gin' consisted of a large wooden drum supported on a vertical spindle-like post resting in a metal bearing set in a flat stone on the ground. The horse, its harness attached to a rotating arm, circled the mechanism. Ropes or chains to a headgear with pulley over the shaft mouth were wound round the drum, thus bringing up the coal. As at Phase 2, the shafts would have timber props around the base and drystone 'ginging' at the mouth for stability. Again, as with Phase 2 working, these pits were closely spaced to overcome ventilation problems. Although this would vary from mine to mine, horse-gins were usually worth employing above a depth of about 50 feet, where the gin was

Above: Haulage level.

Left: Facimile Horse – engine, iron-ore mine.

used to speed production rather than out of practical necessity. At a depth of well over 100 feet, hand-windlasses became impracticable because of the weight of the rope. The use of horse-gins is known to have survived in this area well into the 19th century.

Phase 4

By 'drift mining' in narrow, sometimes self-supporting tunnels, or **levels**, driven into hillsides. Again, pillar and stall working with short roadways was used, either following the seam or driven to where the seams were known to have existed. The early drift mines, e.g. at Blackclough, Danethorn and Castedge, were often smaller, simpler versions of the larger ventures (see below) that were using long levels often to a considerable distance underground. In some cases the smaller drift mines were contemporary with and sometimes part of the deep-level mining. Absence of other coal-mining shafts across the immediate surrounding land indicates that when a particular level was active, the method of working from a number of interconnected shafts had been abandoned. At these situations, the colliery was ventilated from the level entrance and perhaps just an occasional discrete air-shaft sunk down to the level. Hillside mine entrances in the area were called 'day-eye' pits by the miners. At the end of a shift, they would be walking out towards a pinpoint of light – a 'day eye'.

THE GOYTS MOSS (BURBAGE COLLIERY/ CASTIDS COMMON) COLLIERY

The workings on Goyts Moss measured approximately 1km by 1.5km, and covered an extensive area of the basin near the head of the River Goyt centred on Derbyshire Bridge. Over 50 opencast pits at the edge of the basin were dug before the upper, or 'Yard' seam was exploited from underground by sinking closely spaced, interconnected shafts. Over 170 shafts of various ages, many with adjacent horse-gin mounds, have been identified. The depth of the seam varies due to its positions in the syncline. The shafts were progressively sunk and worked over a 120 to 150-year period – probably only one or two being dug per year, perhaps during the drier months because of the risk of collapse or flooding. The material removed from the shaft would have been in the ratio of about 5m of shales and mudstone to 1m of solid rock. The groups of shafts had one thing in common; they needed to be close together to overcome ventilation problems and to avoid the necessity to transport coal a long distance underground. The majority of the mines on Goyts Moss, Axe Edge and at nearby Black Clough on the River Dane were on land long owned by the Dukes of Devonshire and were for a time managed by the estate as one unit.

The 'Yard' coal cut here was generally sulphurous and of poor quality, 1 to 1.5m thick. At the heart of the colliery the seam is about 15 to 30m below the surface. Between here and the outcropping at its edge, because of rising ground, the seam is up to double this depth. In the later 19th century, remaining reserves were exploited via a long deep level driven from Burbage (see Coal Mining near Axe Edge below).

Shafts on Goyts Moss were probably first sunk in the late 17th or early 18th century, with coal being extracted by hand-winch. As shallow reserves became depleted by the 1770s and 1780s, deeper shafts were sunk and horse-powered winding engines (gins) were introduced.

Early transport to these pits was by packhorse. Transportation was radically improved with the building of the 1759 Macclesfield and Buxton turnpike, from which time production and therefore profits increased, with the coal now transported by horse and cart. In order to capture some of these profits, the very competitive Buxton and Leek Turnpike Trust was quick to build branch roads onto the colliery in the 1770s, parts of which can still be seen as hollow-ways and grassy tracks. The two turnpike trusts then competed to supply coal, principally to the Grin limeburners. Part of the colliery, including Moss House and adjacent land owned by the Dickensons, lords of the manor of Taxal, lay within Cheshire (the county boundary was moved up from the River Goyt to The Tors Ridge in 1936) and was at first worked as a separate enterprise known as the Castids Common Colliery. However, from 1780 it was all controlled by the Duke of Devonshire, the lord of the manor of Hartington, who owned the Derbyshire land and now purchased the lease of that in Cheshire from Messrs Dickinson for £2,300. From this date and until 1825, both areas supplied the Duke's limekilns at Grin Low.

Having leased out the 'Thatch Marsh and Goit [*sic*] Collieries', the Duke of Devonshire chose not to receive cash rents from his lessees; instead, he required payment in cartloads of lime to be spread on his tenanted limestone heathland and other poorer soils as a method of land improvement for growing hay, root crops and cereals – the improved yields thereby having a significant effect on the value of his land and creating an opportunity to raise rents at the next review.

Documentation from 1790 has shown that eight shafts were used at the colliery that year, with only two or three being worked at any one time. Twenty-three people were employed, about half of whom were working underground. Regardless whether above or below ground, the Duke's colliers worked twelve-hour shifts, six days a week. Unless the workings were flooded, these colliers were expected to both dig and transport coal even during the winter months. They were allowed one day off at Christmas!

A section of the western part of the Goyts Moss Colliery on Castids (Castedge) Common, within a small discrete area of walled fields, has a spread of old mining remains including shafts and interconnected old barrow-runs, cart tracks and old turnpike road branches. Designated as a Scheduled Monument (SAM), this can be found centred 200m southwest of Derbyshire Bridge at SK 014 717. Surface remains of this part of the colliery, which had been worked over several centuries, are considered to be representative of three phases of mining in the area. Mining probably began here in the 17th century. Most of the shafts are infilled or collapsed, some containing pools of water. The network of tracks running between the shafts, some of which have the remains of gin mounds, are connected to the two turnpike branches by causeways constructed from shaft spoil – a continuous, ongoing process.

Although coal was to become increasingly used for domestic use, the majority of the Goyts Moss output was used for limeburning at the nearby Grin Low kilns and by individual kilns across the region – Axe Edge probably providing the earliest coal for the Grin kilns. Closely spaced 18th- and early-19th-century shafts/upcast mounds can be seen today on the fields and moorland covering much of Goyts Moss and the adjacent Axe Edge Moor. Where horse-engines were used, they were often placed on the upslope side of the shaft on a flat-topped circular mound of spoil to increase clearance and help prevent surface water entering the shaft. As shafts fell out of use, most were blocked with timbers below the shaft top and then backfilled. These shafts are now collapsed and this, plus subsequent erosion in most cases, has left hollows 5 to 10m across which, if the shafts are sealed, now hold standing water. At any one time only a few shafts were in use.

Surface-working profits from this colliery peaked between 1790 and 1816 and by the mid-19th century all the coal close enough to the surface to be economically extracted by closely spaced shaft working had been removed. To the west and the south, two areas of reserves remained. Because this was mostly at greater depth, to extract the coal an existing deep level from Burbage needed to be extended (see Coal Mining near Axe Edge below).

From 1826, the colliery tenant was Thomas Boothman, a Manchester lime and coal dealer with other lime and coal interests at Whaley Bridge. Boothman and his son, John, worked the Duke's mines and Grin kilns until the younger Boothman retired in 1857. From 1859 the collieries at Goyts Moss and Axe Edge Moor were leased to the Buxton Lime Company, who invested money in the enterprises, revitalising the mines and also the kilns at Grin. These later colliery improvements were to include the sinking of new deep shafts. Some were airshafts; others were associated with steam engines on Burbage Moor, Axe Edge and at the top of Cisterns Clough (see below). The BLC also began to import Whaley Bridge coal along the Cromford & High Peak Railway to mix with the poorer-grade Goyts Moss/Axe Edge coal to fire the Grin kilns.

Associated with the Goyts Moss mines, a level, still recognisable as a drainage sough just above the flood-level of the River Goyt, was driven in 1750 to drain the Ravenslow Flat area. The gated sough tail, still issuing water, can be found 200m north of Derbyshire Bridge by the roadside.

Extract from Thos. Wyld's 'fortnightly reconing' for the Chatsworth Estate 12/3/1790

Thatch Marsh and Goite Colliery, showing range of tasks undertaken by mine workers

• **Buckett Engine**

Getting coal, banking coal, breaking coal, waiting over the men at night, filling and hooking of coals, repairing the 'Navvgation', boating coals, cleansing of lodge

and landing, ladeing water, repairing the boats at night, mending of roads.

• **The New Rise Pitt**

Sinking 20 yards, getting stone out of the pitt top, making three Flakes, geering the pitt, setting 15 pairs of timber.

• **Goit No 5 (shaft)**

Getting coals, raising shael.

• **Goit No 3**

Driving of endway 10 yards, getting coals.

• **Goit No 4**

Getting coals, sending shael, banking coal and driving the engine horse to Macclesfield to buy powder [gunpowder] for the works.

Wyld's accounts for 1790 also show that at this time there was considerable local demand for the coal, with a total yearly output figure of at least 14,000 tons produced by just five shafts. At this time, about 50 men and boys were working these Goyts Moss shafts but only 23 were employed on a permanent basis – about half of them underground.

COAL MINING NEAR AXE EDGE AND AT ORCHARD COMMON (SK 028 725 to SK 016 689)

These mines exploited the Ringinglow Seam. The outcrop runs southwards from north of the old Macclesfield to Buxton turnpike road between Burbage and Derbyshire Bridge (and beyond), to Orchard Common and Firestone Brook. There are a large number of features covering an extensive area. The seam outcrops on the moorland to the west of Burbage and then on Axe Edge Moor, Dane Head and Orchard Common, running in a north–south line. The earliest workings can be found near or at the outcrops. West of the area, the seam dips steeply and although soughs/levels were driven from the east, this coal became inaccessible because of its depth below the surface and water problems. The earliest mining documented is in the 16th/17th century and lower parts of the seam were variously worked into the 19th and early 20th centuries.

The dips in the seam restricted economic working to a relatively narrow band, 100 to 150m wide, over about a 4km length. Around 200 shafts/upcast mounds can be identified, together with numerous access causeways, earlier packhorse tracks, several horse-engine platforms, the sites of three 19th-century steam-engine houses, including that at the head of an inclined level into the workings, with a tramway running eastwards down Cisterns Clough.

A short distance westwards from the outcrop the shafts were deeper and some have access causeways. One shaft, which lies above the mid-18th-century upper level driven from Burbage, met the coal seam at depth and has a gin platform. There are three deep-shaft hillocks further west at SK 028 714. The most southerly, on a public path next to the road, was known in the late 18th century as the Bucket Engine (SK 029 714). What kind of engine was installed here is not known. Why there was a bucket engine is unclear as the two shafts here went down to the level/sough driven southwards to follow the seam started from Burbage in the mid-18th century. By the late 18th century, the 'engine' was apparently out of use and coal was certainly taken out down the level rather than up the shaft. This may have been the original intention, and perhaps the engine was associated with a change of level in the workings associated with an adjacent fault, some of which may have been below sough level and thus required pumping. At surface there are the ginged tops of two adjacent shafts in a hollow within a large flat-topped hillock.

Further north there are two shafts that are 19th-century in date, with a linking causeway from both ends. The northernmost lies above the lower level driven from Burbage in the 19th century at a position just east of the coal seam. It has a large gin platform. The other shaft, known at some time as Engine House Pit (SK 028 717), is probably of mid-19th-century date. Here there are slight footings of a steam winding-engine house and boiler house. These are sited close to the ginged top of an otherwise filled shaft.

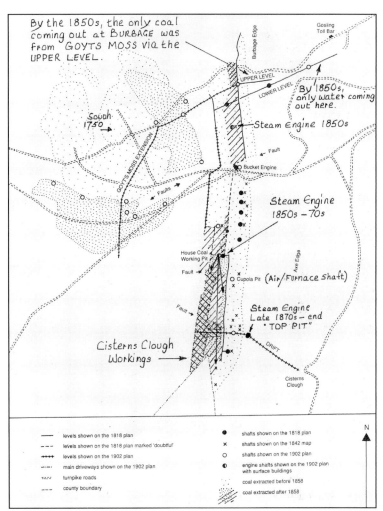

Above: Underground levels from Burbage to the Goyts Moss and Axe Edge Mines (after Barnatt and Leach 1997.)

Right: Layout at the entrance to the Goyt Colliery

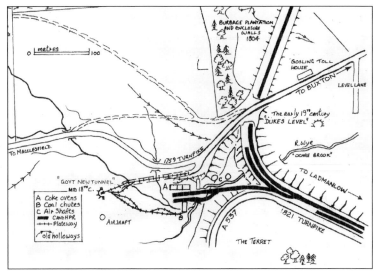

A coking oven, Goyt Colliery.

At Burbage, well to the east of the coal seam and on lower ground, are the entrances to the two major levels running deep under the moors. The upper Burbage level, in a small but deep valley, with its entrance (now collapsed) at SK 0370 7230, dates to the mid-18th century when it was driven to the Ringinglow Seam. From the point of intersection with the coal, these levels followed the seam north and south, acting as both haulage ways and soughs. The main level to the surface (and parts of the north/south levels?) may well have been converted to a short-lived underground canal later in the 18th century.

The passage was again remodelled in the mid-19th century when the main level was extended to the Goyts Moss Colliery well to the west of Axe Edge. From this date it became known as Goyt or New Tunnel. Running eastwards from the level mouth and near to a stream/leat, there is a badly eroded tramway bed of setts laid for the horses pulling tubs. The tramway led to a wide sidings platform close to the turnpike. Immediately downslope above the valley, there is a bank of three or four partially ruined 19th-century coking ovens. There is evidence nearby of a steep chute for coke/coal down to the well-preserved

C&HPR colliery siding, Burbage.

railway siding from the Cromford and High Peak Railway in the valley bottom. From a hillock near the level entrance there was a second narrow inclined tramway direct to the sidings. The lower part of the tramway bed is now masked by quarrying spoil but the upper part can be seen running diagonally down the steep slope. By the top are traces of a structure that may be the site of a small winding engine.

The entrance to the lower Burbage level, commonly referred to today as the Duke's Level, is now thought to have been started in the early 19th century and to have become largely disused in the second half of that century. The entrance lay well beyond the large C&HPR embankment on much lower ground to the east, south of Goslin Bar Farm, off Level Lane, quite near to the Wye but now obliterated by later development. Nearby, a large-diameter pipe in the riverbank issues water from the workings into the river, known locally as 'Ochre Brook'. On the moor between the upper level entrance and the coal outcrop there are two airshafts and associated hillocks. The smaller one lies over the upper level. The larger shaft, now capped with concrete, lies over the lower level.

Near to an intersection of public paths on Axe Edge Moor (SK 027 707) are two shafts associated with the 18th- and 19th-century Burbage levels at a point where, because of faulting, the earlier level turned briefly eastwards before running southwards back into the seam. In order to work the coal between these two levels, particularly from the fault southwards, a steam winding-engine was installed at the western shaft that had previously been used as a sough/ventilation shaft. Shown on the 1883 OS six-inch map as 'Thatch Marsh Colliery', it was known as the 'House Coal Working Pit'. Near to the shaft are two hillocks of spoil (one from its sinking, the other associated with drawing?). There are now few traces of the engine house and adjacent small buildings; they may have been demolished when the shaft(s) was backfilled. Close by are three deep shafts lying on the line of the mid-18th-century level. Two have gin circles, one was used later as an airshaft, while the third, named 'Cupola Pit' on a mine plan, was within a small building (only footings remain) with a walled-up 'flue' arch facing the shaft. This building is likely to have been a furnace house used to encourage updraft in the shaft.

Half a kilometre southeast of these workings, near to the seam outcrop, is the site of the 1-in-6 Burbage Colliery inclined drift (SK 027 706), known locally as 'Top Pit', driven by the Buxton Lime Firms Company from the top of Cisterns Clough in 1879. It was created to work the coal in an area below the mid-18th-century level/sough in the area up to the county boundary, beyond the point reached by the early-19th-century lower Burbage level. The workings were perhaps drained via this lower level. With the workable reserves depleted by 1917, the colliery closed in 1918. Existing blurred photographic evidence of the site shows a sturdy single-storey engine house and its large square chimney, a boiler house and a single-storey building with two chimney stacks indicating fireplaces within. A narrow-gauge inclined tramway, with a siding to one side, carried coal tubs down the clough to a loading yard and mine office/storage buildings by the Leek to Buxton road. Power for haulage was provided by a horizontal steam winding-engine. Between the buildings, a raised winding rope and an associated timber frame construction can be seen. The drift entrance has been backfilled and apart from the nearby large hillock of driving spoil and the footings of two buildings, there is little in the way of surface remains.

The extensive workings on Orchard Common appear to be mostly 19th-century in date. There are 25 to 27 shafts/upcast mounds and access causeways link most. The majority of the shafts (SK 023 694)

Broken engine bed, flue line and associated chimney, Dane Colliery.

lying to either side of the upper Firestone Brook were capped by the Coal Authority decades ago. The deep downstream part of Firestone Brook has further coal mining remains including shafts and the sites of a number of small drift entrances, several now only visible as slight hollows in the slopes just above the road.

At the bottom end of the valley, below Orchard Farm, are two ruined 'coes' and several documented drift mine entrances that have now disappeared. By the stream is the collapsed entrance to an earlier level, which issues water that contains ochre. This is known as 'Alum Spring' – possibly the main access level/sough for the documented 19th-century Penny-hole Mine.

THE DANE COLLIERY AND THE DANE THORN COLLIERY (SJ 999 699)

Whilst the workings at Blackclough, Goyts Moss and Axe Edge were all owned by the Dukes of Devonshire and either managed by the estate as one unit or leased to independent companies, the mines on the Cheshire side of the River Dane were mostly owned by Lord Derby and leased to independent (and often part-time) colliers.

The Dane (or Danebower) Colliery, the largest in the area of the upper Dane, worked the 'Ringinglow' coal of about two feet in thickness from 1746 (and possibly earlier), periodically until 1943. At this time, the colliery can be said to have provided the final major technical mining developments in the upper Dane Valley. The coal here was the deepest workable coal in the Dane area to be extracted. The workings appear to be very extensive and complex, and the chronologies are far from clear.

The surface remains of the mine can be located a mile upstream from Panniers Pool at SK 009 699. Some small ruined mine buildings, a shaft capped with concrete, a broken stone engine bed together with a long flue line and associated square chimney remain high on the Cheshire side of the valley. The 19th-century horizontal steam engine operated a haulage system via a surface channel to the now-capped (earlier?) shaft located on the same contour on the hillside approximately 30 yards away. The actual haulage, probably using a continuous rope, was in the level below, not in the shaft itself. Because the dip slope of the coal seam in this part of the colliery was too steep for either manual or horse haulage, the

tubs could be hooked onto the rope at the bottom of the slope and unhooked in a horizontal adit (see below) at its top. From here the full tubs would be pushed to the adit entrance. Downslope of the broken engine bed is a large grassed-over mound of cinders and clinker from the boiler furnace, the product of perhaps up to fifty years of mining. Separated from the capped shaft by a wall is a flat area suggestive of an earlier horse-gin circle. The footpath from the chimney joins the complex arrangement of grassed-over colliery tracks that zig-zag down from the turnpike above, to at least two lower adits, plus a further adit and stone-lined cutting just above the river's flood level. This was the lowest adit or 'tub track' into the mine, where coal was hauled to the entrance by horses and then weighed on the weighbridge before being loaded into carts. The use of horses in these small hillside adits or horizontal levels was very common where the steep valley sides made extraction of the deeper coal far easier than sinking vertical shafts on higher land.

Along the top of the slope and also along the shelf on the other side of the A54 are many shaft mounds associated with this colliery. There was apparently no firedamp in the mine and candles for illumination were usually fixed to the wall using imported clay. Removal of the coal pillars was a tempting, short-term profit measure but one which presented obvious dangers. When a colliery was abandoned the miners often retreated, either removing the pillars or reducing them to inverted pyramid shapes.

Markets for the Dane coal included domestic use, local limekilns and the mills at Gradbach and Wildboarclough, where, despite being powered by water, these mills had coal-fired steam boilers installed to heat the works. At the Crag Works, Wildboarclough, coal was also used to manufacture gas stored in a small gasholder and used for lighting the works.

Shown on some maps as Dane Bower Wharf (a term inherited from canal construction), this does not imply the use of underground boats to bring the coal to the mine entrance but only that coal could be loaded here onto wheeled transport. Boats were once used in the nearby Blackclough or 'Beat' mine over the hill on Devonshire land, boats being first mentioned in 1790 as adjoining the colliery at Orchard where the same Ringinglow coal seam was also mined. Farey, in 1811, tells us that this was worked by a 'Tunnell for Boats'. This was later confirmed in 1860 by Beresford, who says 'coals used to be boated out of this (Blackclough) pit into a canal'. The Dane colliery closed on 18 May 1925, as it was 'nearly exhausted and unprofitable'. It reopened twice, briefly, being abandoned in January 1928 and again in June 1943.

There is a firm possibility of an underground connection between the Dane Colliery and the Dane Thorn drift mine half a kilometre to the west. In fact, Dane Thorn (active in 1811, as Farey reports) may well never have been a separate colliery but only part of the 19th-century phase of Dane Colliery, working the same coal. There is no known documentation suggesting they were ever worked independently and it is quite possible that the colliery names were at one time interchangeable. The main entrance to Dane Thorn Colliery, on a shelf of land overlooking Cumberland Brook (SJ 9999 7000), has a prominent spoil heap to the west, two small, ruined drystone-wall sheds and a tramway bed leading into the level. This drift level and the complete absence of any nearby pre-19th-century coal-mining shafts, indicates that the colliery had gone over to long-adit working. It is likely that at least one or two of a group of earlier coal winding shafts down to the seam at roughly the halfway point between the Dane and Dane Thorn drift entrances may have provided some ventilation.

Underground evidence and recent studies of available documents suggests that the Dane Colliery had been active for over 200 years until final closure in 1943, during which time some of the Dane Thorn levels may have been kept open for ventilation.

The Dane/Blackclough Colliery Leat

Close to Dane Colliery on the eastern bank of the Dane, on Open Access land, is a very obvious excavated leat visible for about 200m, before flooding debris briefly obliterates it. At its upstream end (SK0095 6977), ochreous orange water weeps into the leat from a collapsed level or a sough. For the curious and determined – despite riverbed changes and landslips – the course of the leat may be followed intermittently for a mile southwards down the Dane towards the Backclough Colliery where presumably the water was put to good use. Following round the contours above the Fyrestone Brook the leat suddenly ends high above the stream opposite the small packhorse bridge at SK 0130 6876. Where sections are no longer visible across unstable ground or on steep profiles of the hillsides, wooden launders or troughs supported on posts may have carried the water.

There does seem to have been an underground connection between the Dane workings and the Blackclough mine, where colliers worked across seam faults. It is recorded that they used sometimes to meet and smoke their pipes together.

THE BLACKCLOUGH OR 'BEAT' MINE (SK 018 691)

The Ringinglow seam was mined from shafts here and then, for a period up to the 19th century, the coal was brought out by a canal tunnel. The exact location of the mine entrance(s) is uncertain but the fact that

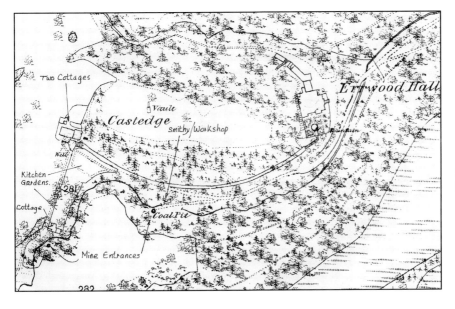

Castedge Colliery, Errwood Hall.

the Devonshire estate owned the colliery has ensured that a full run of accounts has survived – at least from 1790 until 1840, at which time all records cease. It is possible that to mine any reserves below the boat level and sough, considerable new pumping or drainage investment would have been required and, being part of a wider complex of mines on Axe Edge and Goyts Moss, it was perhaps abandoned in favour of the new Thatch Marsh Colliery then operating on nearby Axe Edge.

THE CASTEDGE MINE

Below Errwood Hall burial ground in the upper Goyt Valley, the Shooters Clough stream has carved deeply into the sandstones and soft shales leaving steep-sided banks of ferns, coarse grasses, nettles and rampant rhododendron. During the summer months all this vegetation hides a terraced track sloping down to a level platform and a ruined circular stone building on the north bank above the stream. The building was used as a colliery smithy, a store for a small amount of timber and as a shelter. Although there are surviving shaft mounds further up the valley, the terracing, ruin and the run-in entrances to two or three access tunnels across the stream (hidden by vegetation) are all that remain here of the former Castedge Mine, driven to exploit the Simmondley coal seam of 15 to 24 inches that also outcrops in Shooters Clough. This seam occurs slightly above the Ringinglow horizon and was not mined elsewhere in the study area to any great extent.

The overgrown and collapsed entrance to the main access tunnel can be found close to the small round building above stream level at SK 0064 7464. This mine was already open when John Farey published his list of mines in 1811 – well before the Grimshaw family bought the estate with all the mineral rights around 1835. While the mine only ever employed a small number of men, a large area of coal was extracted over many years.

Personal communications with men who had worked the mine and a BBC interview with Joe Hewitt, who had mined coal here in the 1920s, give us some idea of the mining techniques, conditions underground and the lives of the families who had worked and lived in this location in the early decades of the 20th century. Mr Jack Swindells, a tenant of the Errwood Estate living in the Goytsclough Cottages, worked the mine for the Grimshawes until his retirement in 1911, from which time he moved up the valley to live at Moss House Farm above Derbyshire Bridge, still an Estate tenant.

Peter Lomas then worked the mine until 1917. During this period, government legislation of 1915 had stipulated that all private mines should have a second entrance as an escape route and to provide improved air circulation. Upstream of the mine entrance, a second tunnel was excavated to connect with the main roadway and, fortunately, the miners broke through into an old sough or worked-out haulage level and probably repaired it – saving many weeks of toil. The short tramway bed and shale heap from this second entrance is still visible across the stream from the Shooters Clough Cottage ruin at SK 0050 7456.

Towards the end of Peter Lomas's employment, coal from the mine was sold at 4/6d per ton, while coal from the surrounding district was fetching 7/6d per ton. When Peter Lomas enquired of the Errwood Estate manager if he could increase his charge to Estate tenants, his request was turned down. This refusal resulted in the Lomas family leaving their home at Goytsclough Cottages to become tenants of the Duke of Devonshire at Goyts Moss Farm on the Chatsworth Estate. From this time, coal for the hall was transported from Whaley Bridge. This resulted in the Grimshawes persuading Jack Hewitt (a trained mining engineer) and his family to rent the vacant Shooters Clough Cottage and reopen the mine. Together with a Mr Massey, Jack Hewitt spent eight weeks completing necessary repairs and supporting the sagging roof with pit props. A prominent mines inspector and lead mining Barmaster, John Mort of Manchester, then inspected the mine and it was reopened. From about 1920, Castedge Mine was worked by Jack Hewitt and his son Joe, a boy of around 12 or 13 years of age.

The Hewitts, who would often start work around 10am, occasionally assisted by casual workers, would cut between four and six tubs of coal per day in the winter months both to supply the hall (for which they usually received a jug of beer) and to be sold at 12/6d per ton to the Estate farms and cottages and to the Gunpowder Mills down the valley. Castedge coal was also available to farms outside the valley, for example in Wildboarclough – usually in exchange for milk, butter, eggs or cheese. Summertime working, when less coal was required for domestic use, was a more leisurely affair. Days were often spent outside the mine doing necessary maintenance, cutting pit props, sawing boards for tub repairs on a circular-saw bench and sharpening tools. Faces would be blackened to convince the owners of continued industry!

The narrow coal seam, of 14 to 18ins thickness, sloped with the south bank of Shooters Clough stream but at a more acute angle. The main tunnel or roadway, which soon turned sharp left to follow the seam, had tramway rails to carry flanged-wheeled wooden tubs, each with a coal capacity of around 5cwt (275kg). At the working face, a groove was cut under the bottom of the coal and thin wedges driven in at the seam top a little at a time so that the face dropped in over a manageable length. The face, accessed through 'gates', or subsidiary tunnels, often extended 20 to 30 yards back from the roadway, widening out from about 8ft to 20ft. Sometimes, as a further safety measure, spaces were backfilled with packs of fallen stone from the tunnel headings. The roof would then gently settle over a period of time on the unmined coal pillars and on this packing.

The miner, lying on his side, placed the cut coal into a shallow wooden sledge fastened to his waist with a leather belt and chain. Dragging his full sledge, he would crawl back to the roadway and transfer the coal into a tub – two sledge-loads filling the tub. Lunch, consisting of a bottle of cold tea and some cheese sandwiches, was eaten underground. When coal was cut from the far end of the workings it would take 45 minutes to push the full tub to the mine entrance, the miner leaning over the tub and walking on the rails to help him maintain balance. Because the roadway was cut with a slight rise, any water present in the mine would drain down to the Shooters Clough stream. Tubs from the mine were pushed out of the entrance and tipped onto the level flagged area to enable the coal to be more easily loaded into horse carts, or onto a lorry. The stream was directed into a culvert under the edge of this flagged area.

The main roadway into the mine, in its last phases of use as described above, has a run-in adit approach of drystone walling hidden by bushes and was something like a mile long, the coal being extracted updip to the west. Further upstream, south of Castedge, there is the site of an earlier adit, later used as a return airway. A third possible level east of the main level may have been a sough. While the main roadway adit may also have acted as a sough when it was first driven, after the postulated lower sough was driven, it may have been used just for haulage and access.

Castedge coal was known to be good 'cakeing' or 'crozzling' coal, i.e. it caked on the fire into a flattish compact mass and could be eased and broken with an iron poker. It was eagerly sought by blacksmiths throughout the area for forge work, where the 'cake' would be subjected to regular watering and blowing.

There are groups of closely spaced collapsed shafts, including a track to a run-in early adit (centred at SK 003 742), to be found along the rising east bank of Shooters Clough, indicating an early-18th-century phase of mining activity before the two or three long levels from the streamside were driven.

Around 1918/19, a Model 'T' Ford motor vehicle replaced the horse and cart normally used to take coal to the hall, but it proved frail and unreliable. This vehicle, or a later Ford lorry, was washed away by floods following a huge cloudburst in 1930 when the Shooters Clough stream burst its banks.

Despite further problems with the mine entrance roof and the Hewitt family moving for a while to Furness Vale, the Castedge mine seems to have been worked fairly continuously until 1933. A survey plan commissioned by Stockport Corporation (the new landowners) showed it to have been last worked at this date.

GOLDSITCH MOSS COLLIERY

This colliery is at the southern end of the Goyt Syncline and is centred at SK 010 652. It is the location of the earliest known mining in the district and lies centrally between Gib Tor and The Roaches in Quarnford CP. Coal was worked here from the beginning of the 15th century to well into the 19th century.

The surface remains consist of numerous closely spaced shafts and upcast mounds on saturated pasture and heather moorland. Most of the coal was obtained by employing Phase 2 and Phase 3 working from sometimes very closely spaced shafts of varying depth. The colliery, which covers less than 2sq km of valley bottom, sloping gently westwards towards the Black Brook, was abruptly curtailed by faulting to the north. Deeply cut tributary streams, braided packhorse tracks, various branch turnpike access roads and old causewayed cart tracks, some with gateposts, bisect the colliery. There is no surviving surface evidence of horse-gins ever being employed at this colliery and little in the way of documentary evidence to give an accurate history of this long-worked former mining area.

The geology of gritstone and shales contains the

Yard, Simmondley, Ringinglow, White Ash, Red Ash and the Big Smut coal seams. The most extensively mined seam here was the Yard, reaching a thickness of 4 ft. Mining in this particular location is first recorded in the Alstonefield Manor Court Rolls in 1401 where it is stated: 'Thomas Smith takes from the lords a certain vein of coal at Blakbrok for one year beginning last Michaelmas for his own use paying 12 pence p/a to be paid by Richard Strongarme for two coalmines.' By 1564, Goldsitch Moss mining is recorded in chancery proceedings by Sir John Savage (see Chapter 1).

Coal was probably extracted here firstly by digging into outcrops. Subsequent phases appear to have all used regularly spaced shafts for haulage. The remarkable closeness of some shafts suggests at least two and probably more phases of working – firstly, early shallow shafts and, later, others to the deeper seams.

In order to exploit deeper coal at the northern extremity of the colliery, it became necessary to drive a major level to drain the workings. This sough, 4ft high and 3ft wide, was driven towards the colliery from the tail (SK 0036 6637), just above a side stream that joins the Flash Brook above Manor Farm. The collapsed tail is still obvious and can be found 100m up this stream from the confluence. Four or more air-shaft hillocks enable the course of the sough to be traced where the tops of two shafts can still be seen as large grassed-over mounds in rough pasture (SK 002 660) west of Bradley Howel. The initial 50m from the sough outfall was driven alongside the stream before turning uphill towards the colliery. A shaft mound and a small ruined building with a fireplace are still evident at this point. Due to a build-up of ochre, the sough now spews upwards from a hole before falling into the tributary stream and bringing with it an accumulation of thick, bright orange ochre (a mineral of clay and ferric oxide) that was collected at one time in the three large well-preserved, interconnected stone settling tanks by the Flash Brook confluence below. From here it was dried and sold, perhaps for use as a dyeing agent.

A braided packhorse route, with several clearly defined hollow-ways, runs from Goldsitch House and crosses the Black Brook before climbing to Lower Roach End to cut straight across the enclosures here, indicating that it certainly predates them. It forms a cross-country route of some importance and may have medieval origins and/or has been used for transporting coal from the Goldsitch Moss mines. It may be the well-documented 'coal road' from Goldsitch

Moss to Leek, shown on a Leek Enclosures map joining the old pre-turnpike road through Meerbrook to Dieulacres Abbey.

A lease from the Harpur Estate was drawn up in 1765 that covered both the Goldsitch and the Knotbury mines. The lessees were James Slack, George Goodwin and John Wheeldon. The 21-year lease included a forge at Quarnford (Gradbach?) worked by Slack (see Chapter 14, Iron Production). The Devonshire archive for 1782 reveals that these three men were paying £10-15s per annum for the Harpur lease and were delivering coal to the Ecton copper mine at 15 shillings per ton.

KERRIDGE HILL, RAINOW (centred SJ 943 762)

On the east side of the 2km-long ridge of Kerridge Hill, west of Rainow, there are extensive coal-mining remains where coal had been removed, probably from at least the late 17th century until the 19th century. The remains consist of opencast workings, at least forty shafts, drainage soughs and run-in adits. The colliery at North End is shown on Burdett's map of 1777. Documentation has been found that shows these workings as being active later in the 18th century and that in 1808 new owners started to drive a sough here. Mining at this location had ceased by the mid-19th century and no mining is shown anywhere at Kerridge on the first-edition OS map of 1842. However, the mines at East Side continued to be worked, perhaps intermittently, until the 1920s. At the start of the 19th century the mines here would have had a ready market in the textile mills at Rainow, Bollington and Macclesfield where, from 1793 onwards, Boulton and Watt-type steam engines had started to be installed. After the arrival of the canal to Bollington in 1831 and the construction of larger mills, the Kerridge mines would not have been able to satisfy the demand for coal in either quality nor quantity.

THE BAKESTONEDALE AND SPONDS MOOR COLLIERIES, POTT SHRIGLEY (centred SK 959 799)

Several coal seams were worked here, two of which are underlain by thick, high-quality fireclay, or ganister. Farey in 1811 refers to 'Spons Moor' colliery, producing both coal and 'crowstone' (ganister) and the Bakestonedale colliery, producing both coal and

Bakestonedale Colliery, shaft with ginged top.

WORKING CONDITIONS

Throughout all these mines, work was often interrupted by very wet underground conditions with the workings and shafts sometimes flooded. Before the arrival of efficient steam-engine pumping, soughs were driven into the workings from nearby valleys and excessive ground water was removed with rag-pumps or bucket chains wound by a hand-windlass worked by a number of men in succession. With the later shafts, even horse-gins hauling barrels of water could sometimes prove inadequate. Sufficient ventilation of the workings was also a problem and relied on various methods to divert the prevailing wind down the shafts. Convection currents could be created by using a furnace at the shaft top or by placing a brazier in one of the shafts.

Mining the deeper and extensive workings not only increased ventilation problems but increased the possibility of explosions due to the build-up of gases, although there are surprisingly few records of explosive or suffocating gases in these mines. The miners called the gas hazard 'damp'. The two main types of gas released as mining proceeded were 'choke damp', which snuffed out the candles by which the miner lit his work and then suffocated the miner unless he reached fresh air quickly, and the highly inflammable 'fire damp' or 'marsh gas' (methane). The remedy for 'damps' was a current of fresh air, which sometimes involved the sinking of an exclusive airshaft down to the workings.

Throughout their history these mines relied mainly on manpower, the miners daily facing the possibility of shaft or tunnel collapse, potential problems with gas, and flooding. Dragging their 'corves' (crude wooden box sledges) of coal from the face, either bent double or on hands and knees on the wet clay floor, they worked long hours with picks and shovels by the light of oil lamps or, in the later period, using tallow candles fixed to their 'Bradder' hats (thick felt hats – manufactured in Bradwell by William Walker & Son), packing any waste rock behind them and leaving pillars of coal to support the roof. The candles, usually bought in bulk by the mine owners, were sold to the miners at cost. Mine owners or leaseholders often employed women and children in their pits

'brasses' (iron pyrites). In addition to the coal, ganister and pyrites, a vast amount of shale was also excavated.

An 1881 OS map of the area shows limekilns, several brick-kilns, coal shafts and a smithy, all close to a 'Brick Works' (SJ 952 797) and situated in a wooded area alongside the narrow Bakestonedale valley road. A tramway (now masked by quarry spoil) is shown leading downslope to the brickworks from a shaft above, marked 'coal pit'. Bricks were eventually made exclusively by the large brickworks until the mid-20th century, during which time the colliery would have been mining both coal and fireclay. Beneath the brickworks were two water-balance winding engines.

The majority of the surface remains are found in a broad band between what is now called the 'Old Brickworks', running for about 1.5km north-east to the deer wall at the south end of Lyme Park. Features include possible opencast workings, capped or backfilled shafts to different depths, grassed-over spoil heaps and raised access causeways to the central track. Some of the shafts have gin circles and one reveals sandstone ginging at the shaft top. One of the gin circles retains its central bearing block complete with iron bearing. The site of an adit by the stream does not appear on maps until the mid-20th century – the entrance is now visible only as a hollow on the steep streamside slope. A detailed survey of these two collieries is nearing completion and is likely to be published as articles in the Peak District Mines Historical Society Journal.

until the *Mines and Collieries Act* of 1842 prohibited the work of women and girls and of boys under 10 years old.

Coal mining can be a very hazardous occupation. Typically, during the early years of the 19th century a number of people lost their lives in the local pits:

Aug. 1824. Abraham Brown – 'died by accident in coal work', aged 29 years.

Mar. 1825. Lucy Beiston – 'killed in the Penny Hole coalpit', aged 16 years.

Dec. 1834. Abraham Sigley of Newstone – 'suffocated in a coal mine', aged 13 years.

Oct. 1835. William Pickford of Leek Frith – 'killed at Goldsitch Coal Works', aged 37.

Sept. 1835. James Hudson of Back o'th Dane – 'crushed to death at work', aged 59.

GENERAL CONCLUSIONS

Due to the thinness of the seams and the 'pillar and stall' extraction techniques employed in the South-West Peak mines, there are none of the large tips associated with mining elsewhere, making it difficult to appreciate the scale of all this activity. The commonest surviving evidence is that of the shafts and surrounding upcast mounds, some with associated raised gin circles and causeways in groups in the fields and on the open moor. There were fewer adits and soughs and little now survives at their entrances. By the second half of the 19th century the canals and railways had arrived, bringing superior coal from further afield. With much of the local coal worked out, massive new investment would have been required for further drainage of the later deep-level workings, for example at Axe Edge, so decisions were made to close most of the mines. By the early years of the 20th century, all the area's mines had ceased production. Although these coal mines had no national significance, locally they were undoubtedly one of the two main industrial pursuits in a predominantly agricultural area. For hundreds of years mineshafts were sunk and adits driven to work the coal underneath. Although mining has finished, an unknown number of shafts remain whose location has been long forgotten except by a few industrial historians, archaeologists and local people. Thus, whilst enjoying your leisure in this area, at all times BE CAREFUL. Mining evidence in the neighbouring lowlands at the heart of this coalfield further south and west has usually been

The Great Stone.

126

swept away by later development and the remains described above are thus some of the most important survivals in the region.

Local pedestrian paths from this area to the collieries and quarries can be found passing the Great Stone (SK 0260 6895) on Drystone Edge and the ancient landmark of Fivestones. From here, miners' paths are found leading to 'Thatch Marsh', 'Top Pit' and the small Dane Head quarry before crossing towards the Congleton turnpike and the 1759 Macclesfield turnpike above Burbage. The causewayed coal road across Orchard Common below Fivestones is almost obliterated by marshy ground, haphazard 18th- and 19th century coal-mining activity and perhaps unsuccessful turnpike branch construction. A whole network of fractured causeways and faint tracks, some underlain with thick gritstone paving slabs, certainly indicates a variety of industrial activity here in the past. Some are abandoned or now improved as public bridleways or footpaths, including those more recently concerned with moorland management for commercial gun sport. For both men and women living and working around these high moors, unless there was access to a cart, getting to work and returning home would mean a long walk. This could be particularly onerous in winter or during prolonged periods of wet weather, when presumably they worked in wet clothes for hours on end.

Intimately connected with this network is the narrow tarmacked trans-moorland road connecting the Leek and the Congleton to Buxton roads north of Cheeks Hill. Its original purpose and whether or not it was turnpiked is open to question; it appears to have evolved rather than been built to a plan but its general direction suggests an early route to the Goyts Moss and Axe Edge Collieries. It has become a modern short-cut, avoiding the necessity of travelling to Ladmanlow to change roads.

LIMESTONE AND LIMEBURNING

GEOLOGY AND USAGE

Limestone is the oldest exposed rock in the Peak District and was formed over 300 million years ago when this part of Britain lay beneath an ancient sea. The limestone around Buxton and at Dove Holes, being deposited in clearer waters, is particularly pure in this respect. Although difficult to shape and therefore not ideal, limestone is a good building stone, wearing better than sandstones that can absorb water and lead to damp problems. As bedrock its structure is susceptible to slightly acid rainwater and as this water percolates downwards through vertical joints and bedding planes, so hairline cracks tend to gradually widen over time to create an intricate network of underground passages, potholes and cave systems such as Poole's Cavern at Buxton. Sometimes the limestones contain corals and form poorly bedded reef limestones that are harder and more resilient to erosion. Good examples of this are the pointed hills above the River Dove near the village of Hollinsclough.

Besides its value as a solid building material, limestone could be calcined (roasted) in kilns. This involved the liberation of carbon dioxide and the formation of 'quicklime', a caustic, alkaline substance. 'Slaked lime' is 'quicklime' in chemical combination with water. Both forms of lime were to have a wide variety of uses such as in traditional mortar, as a fertiliser and in the chemical industry.

From prehistory, limestone has been used by people in the construction of barrows, stone circles and enclosures and from the first millennium AD onwards, as the building material for forts, castles, dwellings, church building, barns and bridges, etc. Limestone is still occasionally employed for building, usually at the insistence of the planners. It is used for walling, as railway ballast and as aggregate in concrete, while its crushable strength has made it of huge importance as road metal, currently transported far afield.

History

The earliest archaeological evidence for limeburning in Britain is found in the Roman period, where extensive use of mortar and cement is apparent in surviving structures from the time. A Roman bath made from solid limestone and cemented with strong water-resistant cement was discovered during excavations for The Crescent, Buxton. The Romans had also developed an excellent form of concrete, which sometimes survives.

There are Saxon church-building references to lime and mortar. In a 12th-century document, a statement that 'the church of York had been whitewashed with lime in AD 690' also indicates that limeburning was practised.

Huge amounts of mortar were used in the medieval period for castles, abbeys and churches. Lime was often made in pits or earth clamps, which, together with early stone-built kilns are specifically mentioned in medieval MSS and confirmed by excavation. By the 16th century large quantities of mortar were made at the building sites of the great royal palaces and for the gradual replacement of timber halls (and eventually numbers of humbler dwellings) with stone buildings. By the 19th century, in places like the Peak District, this replacement was universal. Rural limeburning became more common as private farmers became interested in methods of improving yields. With the increasing enclosures of the commons between the 17th and early 19th centuries, huge amounts of lime were applied as a fertiliser on agricultural land, especially towards the end of this period.

The kilns came in a variety of types and sizes. An **intermittent** kiln was loaded, fired, cooled and emptied, then reloaded for the next firing. A **continuous running**, or **draw kiln**, usually with a stone-built interior, was kept burning and further supplies of limestone and coal could be fed in as the quicklime is drawn off. To make this possible, these kilns had to be taller.

The process of lime production by farmers appears in *The Boke of Surveyinge and Improvements*, written in 1523 by Anthony Fitzherbert, a relative of the lord of the manor of Tissington, Derbyshire. This outstanding agricultural writer stated that '. . . another manner of mending of arable land is to make it, marl it, lime it and dung it'. Fitzherbert describes the process and how nearly every farm on the limestone plateau was equipped with one or more limekilns. There appears to have existed a common right for people to 'get limestone and make lime for their own use' within the local manors. Usually the work of firing and feeding the kilns alternated with other farm jobs and was done in the less busy times of the year. Over a long period, lime mixed with horsehair and clay or dung had produced 'daub' for buildings employing 'wattle and daub' structures.

Lime was used in large quantities to defoliate coarse vegetation, especially when land had just been taken in from common and in smaller quantities to counter the natural acidity of the local soils and improve the grazing capacity of pasture. This application of lime was necessary both on the gritstone and the limestone areas, the latter usually having acid soils despite the alkaline bedrock. Lime will also break down heavy clay soils, making them more porous and better draining.

LOCAL FIELD KILNS

Solitary field kilns seem to have been associated exclusively with individual farms and were built by individual farmers for their own use. Although few of these kilns (common enough on the limestone plateau) were ever built on the gritstone of the South-West Peak, there are individual kiln sites, for example at Edge Top west of Hollinsclough village, at Manor Farm, Quarnford (SK 0037 6634) and a fine example in the upper Goyt Valley (see below) which all attest to the economy of carrying limestone onto gritstone land to be burned with local coal. References in Wildboarclough to 'new limed ground' in 1628 and 'new limed piece' in 1721 confirm its early use and may suggest a nearby field kiln or the purchase of ready-burned lime from Grin.

From the 16th century and perhaps earlier, lime from small groups of 'sale' kilns (see below) was sold to builders for use in mortar and plaster, as a wash to waterproof walls and lighten interiors and for lime-water taken as a medicine. It was sold to tanners and candlemakers and to smelters of metals for use as a flux in the removal of impurities. It was used in the glass industry, as bleach for paper and in soap production or sold to local farmers and those in other districts who had no local limestone from which to make their own lime. Building in stone became common in the Peak District from the 17th century. From the 18th century onwards, lime was used for industrial purposes such as bleaching and a variety of chemical processes.

THE GOYTS LANE FIELD KILN (SK 0162 7475)

A small, intermittent limekiln above the Wildmoorstone Brook in the upper Goyt Valley would have burned limestone brought down Goyts Lane from the Buxton/Burbage area – the nearest source of limestone – while coal to fire the kiln probably came from nearby shafts that exploited the 23-inch Ringinglow seam a short distance up Wildmoorstone Clough.

This rare example of a field kiln on a gritstone area of the Peak District is built into a bank below Goyts Lane and is drystone-wall-retained to a thickness of 8ft, standing almost to its original height (see photo and drawing). In the centre of the wall is a bottle-shaped stoke-hole with a passage leading to the internal base of the kiln, where a simple wooden frame

The Goyts Lane field kiln.

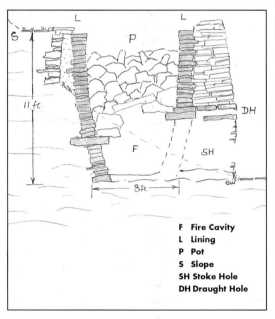

F   Fire Cavity
L   Lining
P   Pot
S   Slope
SH Stoke Hole
DH Draught Hole

The Goyts Lane agricultural field kiln, Goyt Valley.

may have supported the initial load of coal and limestone, forming a dome over the fire cavity. A fire was lit and modest heat maintained initially to dry and set the charge, then fierce heat was generated until calcining was complete. Directly above the stoke-hole is a small draught-hole 'stepped' internally from the stoke-hole by large flat stones. The kiln would

have been loaded from the top via the short terraced approach track from the lane above but may have been emptied from the track below the kiln, where, after a lengthy cooling period, the ashes and burned limestone would have been raked out. Long-handled tools were used for raking and clearing – perhaps into a shallow pit by the stoke-hole. These field kilns have no waste heaps because normal agricultural practice was to spread both the lime and ashes onto the fields. It was only the commercial kilns that separated out a purer product.

The process of calcining often took from 36 to 48 hours and completion was indicated by a clear red fire at the kiln top. The cooling-down period seems to have taken another 48 hours – the complete operation taking some five days. No weather protection near the kiln is apparent, although a simple shelter may have been erected. To reduce the draught during calcining, the stoke-hole would have been partially blocked with earth and stone. The lime from this kiln was presumably used in the valley below in the fields around Goytsbridge hamlet. The burned product was 'quick' or 'lump lime' and resembled the unburned material in size and shape – but with reduced weight. It was common practice for farmers to take 'lump lime' straight from the kiln to the fields. This had its dangers, since the heat generated if it started to slake could set fire to packhorse panniers or the wooden cart or sledge – yet they would risk carrying it long distances. Furthermore, this 'lump lime' was chemically caustic and would burn the handler's skin. The burned product, which contained a useful percentage of potash, would be dispersed in small heaps over a field, often covered with earth and left to slake, in due course falling to a powder that could be ploughed in. Mixing the slaked lime with riddled ashes and limestone dust was used to make excellent mortar.

The Goyts Lane kiln would probably have been built and used by one enterprising, improving tenant. It might have been built at the instigation of the Chatsworth Estate but this seems unlikely as they may well have promoted or allowed the use of lime from their kilns at Grin. The pot of the kiln has been filled in, a common practice at abandoned kiln sites. Of the few surviving kilns with a stone outer face still intact today, most are no older than the late 18th century.

Much of the following text is based on studies of the quarries and limeburning at both Grin Low and Peak Forest, produced as papers for the Derbyshire

Archaeological Journal by John Barnatt, Anthony Dickson and John Leach (see Bibliography).

INTERMITTENT 'SALE KILNS'

These were often circular, earthen and of the so-called 'pudding pie' type used intermittently for single firings. Farey, writing in 1813, referred to them as 'sale kilns' (as distinct from private farm kilns), where lime was burned, sieved and then sold as either quicklime or slaked lime. These kilns are usually quite small and may have waste heaps downslope of the draw-hole. Their remains are often found in groups at the edges of shallow quarries. Such sale kilns are found in quite specific places in the Peak District from the 17th century onwards – at Buxton, Peak Forest and Cauldon Low. They were built, fired and then allowed to cool when the lime was dug out on the downslope side. A well-built stone-lined kiln could be used several times before needing a rebuild.

COMMERCIAL LIME PRODUCTION

Fully commercialised production of lime was to become very different both in scale and character, when a whole series of markets for this lime was created. From the late 18th century, banks of kilns were built at limestone quarries and beside the new turnpike roads, tramways and canals, as the expansion of the transport infrastructure allowed the raw materials for lime production to be economically carried long distances from their sources. Some canals were even cut specifically for this lime trade. Rather than use their own field kilns, local farmers were now buying lime from these complexes – or else taking away (at a reduced price) the large waste-heaps of ash that still contained a useful percentage of lime and potash.

Replacing the 'traditional' intermittent sale kilns came the **continuous running** sale kilns, with pots lined with hard stone or firebrick and capable of continuous firing over many years. The conical or egg-shaped pot was loaded with alternate layers of limestone and coal in the ratio of three, four, or five parts of limestone to one of coal. Movable iron bars at the base of the pot provided support for the charge and could be adjusted for drawing off the lime. After initial lighting the fire spread progressively through the kiln, which would be loaded gradually as the fire spread. As the 'quicklime' was drawn off, fresh layers of coal and stone were loaded into the top. These kilns were generally built against hillsides or banks,

giving easy access to the charging level at the top. Because a purer product was required (as with the earlier 'sale' kilns), waste heaps were often present at these kiln complexes. Lime could be spoiled by wet weather, so it is assumed that some protection for the burned product was provided at the kilns. Perhaps crude wooden temporary shelters were erected?

GRIN LOW, A LIMESTONE HILL

HISTORY

Derbyshire's embryonic industrial limeburning centres grew up around Buxton in the 17th century, with small groups of kilns at Dove Holes, Grin Low, Thirkelow Frith and Peak Forest, the last comparable in both size and output to Grin by the 18th century. At these locations are the remains of intermittent 'pie' kilns set in circular earthen mounds, often close together, each with its own small limestone quarry normally upslope of the kiln, and occasional small heaps of ash, slag and part-burned coal on the downslope side. In contrast, later kiln mounds and waste heaps are usually large and often linked to turnpike roads by carefully built access tracks.

Limekilns cover much of the northern and eastern aspect of Grin hill, centred at SK 045 725, where, with mid-19th-century outliers on adjacent Stanley Moor, they represent all that has survived subsequent quarrying. Because of its proximity to a coal source and a developing communication network, this hill on the south-west edge of Buxton soon became one of the main focal points for the Derbyshire lime industry. By 1704, Grin lime was being carried into Cheshire and by 1734 into Lancashire. Coal from the nearby Goyts Moss and Axe Edge mines, although of poor calorific value, was used to fire the kilns and was initially brought in by packhorses.

The name Grin is derived from Grene or Green Hill, formerly located in Hartington Parish. Together with Stanley Moor it comprised part of the ancient Hartington Common, lying on limestone. The earliest reference to limeburning here occurs in a 17th-century manorial dispute over rights and royalties to 'dig coal and get stone and burn and get lime to sell . . . near a place called Buxton within the manor of Hartington'. In 1662, the third Duke of Devonshire purchased the manor for £20,000, where, six years later, a rental table reveals that tenants had 'several Lime Kilns on the Commons and Wastes there, with

Grin Low limekiln with wheel-barrow run.

Liberty to make other kilns and get stone and burn and make lime to sell'. The table gives details for coal-mines and limekilns and mentions Thatch Marsh and the location of the kilns including Grin Hill and part of adjoining Stanley Moor. Correspondence from a Buxton visitor in 1704 reveals that 'the hill called Buxton-Grene is covered with Lime Kilns' and relates how distant parts of Cheshire had become a market for the lime. This reinforces the likelihood that Grin was producing lime for agricultural *and* commercial use in the late 17th century, underlining its early importance as a limeburning centre.

The partly wooded gradients of today's Poole's Cavern woodland are still covered with the remains of 17th- to mid-19th-century kilns and their spoil heaps. The surveyor, John Farey, confirms early-19th-century kilns, while mid-19th-century dating is confirmed by detail on the 1840 one-inch OS map. No history of the area around the upper Goyt Valley and Axe Edge can be complete without some understanding of the importance of the limeburning industry on the hill of Grin Low, where the remains of at least 120 survivors of a possible 200 of these 'sale' kilns can still be found.

The Brock and Dickenson Families

A Hartington Parish Rental for 1698 gives details of rents for mines at Thatch Marsh and for kilns tenanted by the Brock family. The actual location of the kilns is not given but part of 'the common' centred on Axe Edge and Grin is quoted – a likely further indicator to the importance of Grin at this time. For almost all of the 18th century, the Brocks leased kilns on Grin Low, but they were not the only family burning lime here for retail. In 1738, John Dickenson, Lord of the Manor of Taxal (and Manchester merchant) purchased a small freehold at Grin and erected kilns in competition with the Duke's tenant (the Brocks) to burn lime with coal from his (Dickenson's) mines on Castids Common, west of Derbyshire Bridge. The Brocks, believing they had sole right to retail lime from Grin, were outraged and the series of disputes over custom and usage etc. went on for over 20 years.

A valuation completed in 1766 reveals that Brock's main income was from his coal mines while his eight kilns, served by five men each, were sublet for seven months of the year (presumably the drier months). By employing an agent to look after the limeworks, Brock was able to personally seek outlets for his lime. Further evidence to support this valuation came from a House of Commons committee enquiry regarding the proposed *Macclesfield Canal Bill, 1766*, when Brock's eight kilns, together with Dickenson's four, plus four kilns at Peak Forest were shown to be producing nearly 11,500 tons of lime annually. This huge amount of trade was a major factor in the promotion of, and investment in, the turnpike roads across the area.

Traffic in this lime trade was dispersed throughout Cheshire, Lancashire and Staffordshire – Derbyshire's agricultural requirements on the limestone plateau of the Peak at least were largely met through output from the many local field kilns – except for those farms close to Grin. The retirement of the Brocks in 1789 from both coal mining and limeburning after nearly a century as tenants on the Duke's hill happened at a high point in activity at Grin. The Dickenson involvement with these industries came to an end in 1793 when the family died out.

DEVONSHIRE MANAGEMENT

Following the retirement of the Brocks, the Devonshire Estate directly operated the local coal mines and limekilns, from which time greater historical accuracy becomes available through detailed Estate accounts for both industries. Thomas Wild managed the Duke's collieries from 1790–2. George Dickens

managed them thereafter for a long period. The Estate also owned the large limeburning complex at Peak Forest, but abandoned both these and the Grin kilns in the early 19th century.

In 1805 (the most profitable year for the Duke), there were five kilns in operation on Grin. These kilns had distinctive names: 'Old Spy', 'New Spy', 'Boson Hole', 'Cotton Shop' and 'Red Bull'. They were sublet to teams of independent limeburners who produced 8,000 tons of lime that year for the Duke's development of the Buxton Spa and for sale in Cheshire, Staffordshire and a small amount in Derbyshire.

When the Hartington Enclosure Award was executed in 1807, the fifth Duke received 267 acres that included Grin Hill. These enclosures coincided with the continuing development of Buxton as an inland Spa and in the following two decades, there was widespread tree planting on Grin, Corbar and at Burbage by the sixth Duke to landscape the ugly ash tips from the sensitive gaze of the spa patrons.

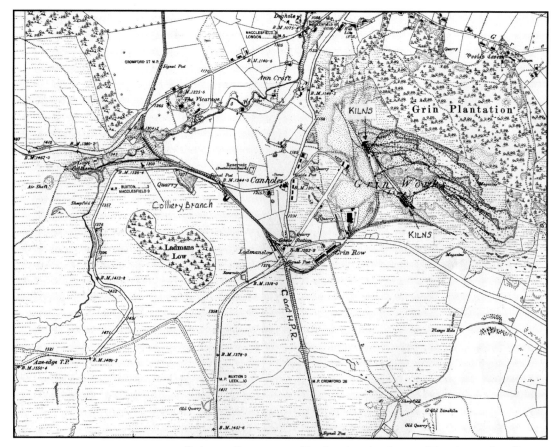

Ordnance Survey map 1883 showing the Goyt and Thatch Marsh Collieries, the Grin Limeworks and the rail and Tramway network.

Perhaps a more significant effect of this tree planting was that lime production now transferred to the west and south sides of the hill – the shallow quarry on the north side was in any case worked out.

The success of the expanding lime trade along the Peak Forest Canal and the withdrawal from direct management of the Grin kilns by the Devonshire estate in 1817 added further to a gradual decline in profits at Grin. Here we find a reduction in the number of working kilns and a proportional decline in the toll receipts from the Buxton toll bars that controlled the turnpike access to and from Grin, namely Green Lane, Grin End and Ladmanlow.

In 1826, the Devonshire mines were leased to Thomas Boothman of Manchester. The following year, Boothman leased the Grin kilns and for the next thirty years worked both concerns with his son, John. By 1823 the route of the Buxton to Macclesfield turnpike had been improved and in 1831 the northern section of the Cromford and High Peak Railway opened, providing quicker and cheaper transport. By 1857 the C&HPR was carrying superior coal from Whaley Bridge directly to Grin, where it was mixed with local coal to fire the kilns – but despite these improvements, lime prodution was relatively low.

In sharp contrast to this situation at Grin, large masonry kilns were being erected in the quarry at nearby Harpur Hill. More importantly, between 1799 and 1840 had come the development of large, deep quarries in Dove Holes Dale and banks of large masonry kilns built on, or alongside, the Peak Forest Tramway at Dove Holes and Small Dale. This, together with a further developed roads network and the opening in 1863 of the Stockport, Disley and Whaley Bridge Railway (see below) to give access to Buxton from the north, was to eclipse much of the early pre-eminence of Grin. From this time, the turnpikes were increasingly bypassed as carriers of lime, gradually reverting to local and agricultural needs.

In the 1830s, a stone-built viewing tower was constructed upon the Bronze Age burial mound on the summit of Grin Low. The barrow centre was excavated in the late 19th century. The present tower is a replacement, built in 1896 by a local man, Solomon Mycock – hence its name, 'Solomon's Temple' – and was last restored in 1987. Popular with tourists and a focal point for those who climb the wooded slopes, Grin Low Tower continues to attract visitors.

In 1852, the Duke of Devonshire commissioned a Mr Stephen Eddy to report on the state of his mines and limeworks. Eddy's report concluded that the Duke's tenant Boothman, who was also operating extensive limeworks at Bugsworth using Dove Holes stone, was selling lime from there as a superior product, 'Buxton Lime', and at a high price. Boothman was in fact merely holding possession of the Duke's Axe Edge mines to prevent other parties from working both the coal and the Grin kilns.

Large collapsed limekiln near Grin Low Tower (Solomon's Temple.)

THE BUXTON LIME COMPANY

In 1855 the Buxton Lime Co. (BL Co.) was formed and operated both the Grin and the recently opened Harpur Hill works. It was a separate but parallel company to the Cromford and High Peak Railway with offices, a warehouse and stables at the Whaley Bridge trans-shipment complex. In 1857, a direct C&HPR rail branch was made into Grin from Ladmanlow – the BL Co. having purchased some small C&HPR wagons and 1600 yards of rail, together with the redundant Bunsal Incline 'middle engine' (for £25) for use by the Grin works to power a lime-crushing machine. A connection sponsored by the C&HPR into the main rail network (the new Stockport, Disley and Whaley Bridge Railway) was then made at Whaley Bridge.

Most of the limestone excavation at Grin was now taking place on the south side of the hill within the extensive deep quarry that had developed. Large, continuously-running vertical masonry kilns were in use by 1858 and thus the character of the extraction changed radically.

In 1859 the BL Co. acquired the lease to the Goyts Moss and Axe Edge Collieries. By 1861, the BL Co. held capital of £25,000 and was providing employment for a large workforce at its quarries, mines and at the Whaley trans-shipment wharf. Its chief markets for lime were still the rapidly expanding Liverpool and Manchester industrial regions, but when the Midland Railway reached Buxton in the 1860s, this was to provide the company with opportunities to exploit new markets further afield.

By 1866 the company had increased the number of kilns to a maximum of eleven. By 1880, these eleven kilns appear on the first 25-inch OS map as a bank of four, a bank of six plus one individual kiln – all positioned directly by the branch railway track. These masonry kilns were about 45ft in height, open at the top, lined with gritstone and could be operated night and day for periods of many years. Because of exposure to cold and rain, the kiln tops frequently needed repair, but the 20th-century addition of large steel 'cans' largely removed this problem. Coal and crushed limestone in tramway wagons was hoisted to the kiln tops and fed in by chutes. Each kiln was capable of producing about 12 tons of lime per day. With the maximum of eleven kilns in operation, the total daily output of the limeworks would be around 130 tons of lime.

By the early 1890s, with recession affecting both agriculture and industry, associations were formed to provide mutual protection from hard times. Thirteen separate local lime companies, including the Grin and Harpur Hill limeworks, amalgamated to form the 'Buxton Lime Firms Company' (BLF Co.). By 1905, only 'chemical lime' was produced at Grin and supplied to a large alkali works at Northwich in Cheshire. This works was later to be taken over by ICI.

TRANSPORT

Until the mid-18th century, lime, limestone and coal would have been carried in the panniers of packhorses along traditional tracks, but with the emergence of the turnpike road system, these (and other commodities) were increasingly transported to customers by horse and cart. The 1724 Act of Parliament for the creation of the Buxton to Manchester turnpike had not stipulated collection of tolls on the carriage of either agricultural lime or coal but tolls were levied on the Buxton to Macclesfield (1759) and the Buxton to Leek (1765) turnpikes on which agricultural lime and coal were the principal commodities.

Because of improvements in production methods, a more efficient turnpike road system and therefore a better distribution of lime, it is generally considered that the larger kilns at the top of the hill on the east side of Grin were built in response to this increased demand. With a much-improved transport system in place by the late 18th century, Grin lime output expanded and was able to better serve the burgeoning industries of Manchester and Liverpool. By this time, canals had become established as mass carriers of bulk materials and a branch of the Peak Forest Canal from Bugsworth (now Buxworth) to Whaley Bridge opened in c.1796 connecting with a tramway from the Dove Holes limestone quarries. Large-scale limeburning became concentrated alongside these transport links using coal from the Whaley Bridge collieries. From here on the Manchester lime trade in particular made a gradual transfer to the Dove Holes Dale quarries and the Dove Holes Dale, Marple and Bugsworth kilns, resulting in a gradual reduction in the requirement from Grin.

Of enormous significance to the long history of limeburning at Grin had been the opening of the Cromford and High Peak Railway in 1831, giving the kilns access to the Whaley Bridge collieries and the Peak Forest Canal, with direct access by 1857 to coal from the nearby Goyt Colliery at Ladmanlow via a private branch line.

THE GRIN RAIL BRANCH

To increase efficiency and output, estimates and plans had been drawn up in 1830 for 'a branch railway into the Grin limeworks from the wharf at Ladmanlow' (SK 041 708). This was not built until 1857, when the BL Co. extended their private branch line from Grin to the Goyt Colliery level entrance below Ladmanlow. Despite this advancement, with coal and lime now directly transported on the new rail link, output at Grin remained disappointing.

The initial curve of the branch where it left the main line can still be found barely 100m south of the level-crossing keeper's house at Ladmanlow on the Leek to Buxton road. The shallow cutting of the curve soon fades behind the gardens of the nearby Grin Row cottages, beyond which the rails crossed the Grin Low Road towards the bank of large kilns at SK 044 722. The branch had sidings and shunting lengths at the kilns and at the company's workshops (SK 043 719). At these locations, both track and kilns were lost during the 1979–80 demolition and land-scaping (see below).

In the surviving trackbed of the branch, just beyond its junction, can be found a few of the typical single-hole gritstone blocks used to secure the L&NWR–type 15ft wrought–iron rails. These had been employed as replacements for the Butterley Co.'s rudimentary 4ft cast-iron 'fishbellied' rails, which on sharp curves of other sections of the railway had proved too brittle to support the speed and weight of the early locomotive steam engines. However, photographs taken about 1950, when the Clay Cross Co. were still operating the branch, show modern long steel rails and wooden transverse sleepers. Before the branch closed in the early 1950s, twelve miles of internal railtrack and tramways were serving the large Grin works.

A Parliament Act of 1892 had allowed the L&NWR to open a new Buxton–Hurdlow–Harpur Hill section and dispense with the (old C&HPR) line north of Ladmanlow (see below). The Ladmanlow 'halt', sidings and coal yard closed in 1954 and the level crossing was removed in 1958 together with the nearby wrought-iron skew bridge that had carried the rails across the A54 towards the colliery branch and the main line northwards through the Burbage tunnel.

AN OUTLINE OF THE LATER LIMEWORKS

After 1866, although no further kilns were built at Grin, limeburning continued in the existing kilns. The internal tramway section, still visible around the south end of the quarry was built for tipping after 1880 but abandoned before 1921. By Stables Lane were the stables and workshops for the new quarry complex, while alongside the Ladmanlow branch line were the wagon repair shops.

After 1880, the BL Co. was using coal from the deep mining of the Axe Edge Collieries and from Whaley Bridge (until 1892) to burn in their improved banks of kilns. In the quarry, men were employed in the several processes of drilling, stone breaking, wagon loading and tipping the beds of soil and clay that separate the beds of limestone. At this time, drilling holes for blasting with the Fernilee Mill's gunpowder was still done manually, using short steel jumpers and hammers.

Motive Power

Horses provided much of the motive power in the BLF Co. limeworks. How many there had been before the introduction of steam power for haulage is not known but in 1906 there were still twelve horses employed. The ages of the horses is recorded. Two (still working) had reached the ripe old ages of nineteen and twenty-two years respectively – a remarkable testament to the treatment and management of these hard-working animals.

It is not known exactly when steam locomotives were introduced at Grin but by 1887 the C&HPR had been absorbed by the London and North Western Railway. In 1892 the amalgamated BLF Co. paid £20 for a 'Loco shed' and £100 for laying rails – perhaps to extend the internal tramway.

By 1907 the horses had been either sold or transferred to other quarries and a 12hp stationary Robey engine was installed. It would haul 200 wagons of stone up the internal tramway from the quarry to the kilns and move 60 wagons of soil and clay to the tips daily. Altogether there were four boilers at Grin: the stationary Robey, a locomotive, and boilers at the crusher and in the wagon shops. In 1919 the BLF Co. purchased a 'Grin Loco' for £2,300.

THE WORKFORCE

By the latter half of the 19th century, although some agricultural workers still worked half-time in the quarries, an independent and quite large labour force was required. Despite the dust and explosions (blasting was frequent and minor accidents very common) there were seldom periods of high unemployment in spite of any fluctuations in trade. Large numbers of men traditionally walked great distances to work in the two quarries at Grin and Harpur Hill and the company's books for 1861 show a total workforce (including the Whaley Bridge Basin staff) of 290. Census returns from the nearby village of Burbage for the same year record only eleven lime-trade operatives. However, by 1880 most of the passengers on the C&HPR were BL Co. employees on their way to and from work at the Harpur Hill and Grin limeworks – perhaps men living anywhere south of Ladmanlow who were within walking distance of a C&HPR 'halt'. Photographs of the quarry workforce taken in the latter years of the 19th century reveal that a considerable number of the workers were children of school age, possibly employed on a half-time basis. We do know that the work was back-breaking, tedious, exposed to the elements and dangerous, with a regular flow of accident reports appearing in the local press.

MINERAL EXTRACTION

Small-scale extraction of lead and its associated gangue minerals including barytes (caulk), was also carried out on Stanley Moor, Grin Hill and at the margins of the gritstone on Axe Edge. Workings on lead veins were described in use in the period 1835–41 on Grin Common and the lower slopes of Ladmanlow. There are also references to lead mines at Grin End, Solomon's Temple and an area adjoining the Ladmanlow toll bar.

THE 'ASH HOUSES'

Covering parts of the slopes of Grin Hill and at other limeburning locations were 'rooms' hollowed out of old lime-ash tips that had formed hardened crusts through slaking. Many were used as tool stores and shelters related to quarrying and limeburning. Some of these 'ash houses', sometimes 'ess-houses' in local dialect, became an unusual form of habitation for the limeburners and their families, some having two or three small rooms lighted by a round hole pierced through the hard crust of the roof. They had doors and some had windows. It is thought that in the 18th century, up to 200 people lived on Grin Hill. They were an obvious curiosity to visitors to the area but by the mid-19th century, perhaps because of Victorian taste and upper class sensibilities, wherever possible occupants were rehoused. Evidence of these dwellings can still be found in Grin Plantation along with their garden walls and gooseberry and blackcurrant bushes.

GRIN IN DECLINE

The abandonment of the old C&HPR north of Ladmanlow in 1892 had cut off the direct supply of the better quality Whaley Bridge coal to the Grin kilns. In the final years of the 19th century, the BLF Co.'s own colliery at Burbage was deep-mining the last viable coal reserves under Axe Edge. With the 'Top Pit' (Cisterns Clough) coal reserves depleted by 1917, lime production at Grin eventually collapsed. 'Final' production figures occur in 1920 and again show the limeworks in terminal decline. In 1922, the last year of the lease for the BLF Co., there was no production at Grin at all.

THE FINAL DECADES –
A BRIEF RESURGENCE

When the BLF Co. abandoned Grin in 1922, the lease was taken in 1923 by the Clay Cross Co., who were operating limestone quarries at Ambergate and Ashover. This company purchased the obsolete plant and somehow worked the kilns again fairly successfully despite awkward blackout restrictions throughout the Second World War until 1952, when once again all quarrying and limeburning at the limeworks ceased. Much of the obsolete plant including the Grin rail branch (then LMS) was dismantled and the internal tramway transferred to Hindlow Quarry.

A huge white hill of lime-ash waste now dominated the south-western end of Grin Low but it would be another thirty years before this mound, considered an eyesore, was levelled and landscaped. This was of course the industrial archaeology of the future and in time might have been seen as a landmark of great interest.

With the nationalisation of the coal industry and a government policy to increase production, Grin Quarry was used briefly in the early 1950s to stockpile coal. Then, for over a decade it lay idle until a spurt in the major road and motorway-building programme of the time saw it re-opened by a new Buxton Lime Co. as a roadstone quarry. Despite subsequent acquisition by other quarry companies including, finally, the Tarmac Group, the huge output of quarried stone was still generating thousands of tonnes of waste soil, stone and clay, thin beds of which are interspersed between the five exposed beds of limestone. This waste increasingly complicated extraction and increased road transportation. Following local pressure, Grin Quarry closed for good in January 1972. Large, long-standing limestone quarries have since been developed around Buxton and in the Hope valley, around Matlock, Wirksworth and west of Ashbourne.

By 1970, the woods on the north side of the Grin hill had become Buxton Country Park, focused upon Poole's Cavern. In 1979–80 the site of the plant, within the main quarry and the tips of waste both on the western side and southern aspect of the hill, over which today's modern access road runs, were planted with trees as part of a reclamation scheme and landscaped by Derbyshire County Council at a cost of £700,000 – at the expense of the ratepayers, not Tarmac, the final lessee. In so doing, the council regrettably destroyed much of archaeological interest, including the banks of large masonry running-kilns built in the mid-19th century. The quarry floor has been transformed into a large caravan site and car park conveniently hidden by the quarry edges.

Postscript

In the past, a fine lime powder could only be obtained by burning limestone (or chalk) in kilns. Today, limestone is ground to a powder at an economic cost and, even allowing for transport and handling, is available at an acceptable price to agriculture and horticulture. There are still extensive applications for lime in the chemical industry, in water purification and in effluent treatment.

GRITSTONE AND LOCAL QUARRY PRODUCTS

It would be difficult to imagine anything more harmonious with a south Pennine landscape than a remote farm or tiny hamlet roofed and walled in local gritstone. This fissile sandstone from the Millstone Grit Series of the region best displays the 'spirit of place'. It is strong and will carry weight and resist the effects of atmospheric erosion. The use of gritstone for making quern stones (stones for the hand-grinding of cereals) is known from prehistory. This vital task was undertaken in later centuries by the use of wind-driven or, more usually, water-driven pairs of large circular stones fashioned locally from suitable beds of gritstone. On the eastern edges of the Peak District, an industry developed where particularly suitable beds of millstone grit were once fashioned into such millstones and grindstones.

LOCAL QUARRYING

Although occasionally used to drop a particular section of quarry face, explosives (usually gunpowder) were generally considered too wasteful of valuable stone, so blocks were broken from the parent rock by the careful insertion of wedges. The quarries provided employment for many workers but conditions were very hard. The quarrymen and masons worked outdoors on exposed hillsides with little shelter for much of the year, working long shifts with hammers, chisels and saws, cutting and shaping the stone in open dressing-sheds and moving enormous amounts of waste. They were commonly paid only for usable stone quarried and dressed – not for breakage. Accidents caused by falling rock, by machinery, and eye injuries obtained whilst dressing stone, were common. There was also the long-term danger of silicosis from inhaling stone dust. Coroners' reports in local newspapers regularly listed this as a contributory factor in the early deaths of many ex-quarrymen.

The age of most gritstone quarries is often difficult to ascertain and they leave few clues as to the time of their abandonment. Although it is largely uncertain how blocks of stone and slates were transported from the large older quarries we can assume that they were taken down inclines on a variety of sledges and/or carried in robust animal-drawn wagons to the nearest road.

With the industrialisation of the region came new commercial ventures requiring huge amounts of stone for building factories, mills, new homes and for road and railway construction. The making of the reservoirs and the construction of dams in the 20th century were to draw further on the reserves of the old quarries. From this period, photographs reveal the use of engine-powered inclined planes and steam locomotive haulage on temporary networks of narrow gauge railtrack.

Grey Slates for roofing, produced from bedded gritstone of varying thickness, were cut at Flash, Goytsclough, Macclesfield Common, Pott Shrigley (Bakestonedale), Wincle, Reeve Edge, Danebower, Blackclough and at Rainow (Kerridge), from where, in 1416–17, nineteen carts transported 2,000 'sclatestones' to Kinderton, near Middlewich (Cheshire). The slates cost 6s 2d per thousand and an additional shilling was charged for their carriage. A few years later the churchwardens of Mobberley (Cheshire) paid 5 shillings for 1,000 'sclatestones' to reroof their church.

Freestone, which can be worked in any direction, was used for quoins, gateposts, lintels, sills and flags and as a material both locally and in the growing manufacturing areas beyond the region for kerbstones and setts for paving streets. The railway companies were to take huge amounts of stone for bridges, viaducts, station buildings and platforms. Freestone of good quality was quarried at Danebridge, Disley (Jackson's Edge), Forest Chapel (Stoneyway Gate), Macclesfield Common, Pott Shrigley (The Nab) and at Kerridge where the Bollington flank of the hill has been completely devastated by quarrying. Improved transport links were to prolong the working life of many quarries.

Bakestones. In the days before mass production and long-distance transportation of food, the South-West Peak shared with the rest of upland Britain a climate that imposed on its inhabitants a dependence upon oat and (to a lesser extent barley) bread in place of the wheaten bread of lowland areas. In Derbyshire and in North Staffordshire in particular, the staple bread took the form of soft circular oatcakes of varying thickness and diameter. These could be baked and eaten daily or baked in batches to keep for up to a week in a wooden chest called an 'ark'. A number of shale beds in the area were particularly well known for producing smooth bakestones that could be polished into a cooking surface. Farey describes in 1811 how 'Bakestones are made from a particular kind of dark-grey shale in long flakes which are so soft they can be easily shaved by a drawing-knife to the proper shape. These are dried to anneal them. Often 15in to 16in diameter, they are sold to the cottagers for a shilling for baking their Oat Cakes upon'. Farey also describes such a use of 'fine-grained

stones from Bakestonedale that are either thin and round for the cottage trivet or large and square for setting on the top of a stove'.

These bakestones or 'backstones' were either permanent features built into a farmhouse kitchen alongside the washing furnace or were placed on griddles hung from a pot-hook or stood on a trivet over an open fire. Bakestones could also be made from iron or fired clay.

Domestic oatcake-making is now the exception rather than the rule; most oatcakes eaten in Staffordshire, Derbyshire and nearby Cheshire are commercially produced.

Pavers. Quarries producing paving stone could be found at Goytsclough, Reeve Edge, Danebower, Macclesfield Common and Rainow (Kerridge), where in 1811, pavers 1.5in to 2.0in thick were sold at '16 pence per yard super'. The steep diagonal tracks still to be seen crossing the hillside of Kerridge suggest the use of sleds for moving the stone.

Cisterns or troughs, for milk, ale, pigswill, for salting and for edge-running grindstones, were cut from very fine freestone found at a number of quarries including that at Corbar, Buxton. In the upper Goyt Valley alone, there are over twenty-five sizeable gritstone quarries, the larger ones producing stone for local road, railway and reservoir building. A quarry, 300m north-west of the triangulation pillar on Burbage Edge, provided stone for lining and facing the nearby 500m-long tunnel constructed in the 1820s by the Cromford and High Peak Railway. The line of a tramway from the quarry to both tunnel entrances is still identifiable.

GOYTSCLOUGH QUARRY (SK 012 733)

Goytsclough Quarry is a large gritstone quarry cut into the hillside above the upper River Goyt. The work faces of the quarry show the useless, friable overburden, the thinner strata that might have been used for roofing slates or flagstones and the massive blocks of freestone. Below the dressing floor and road, large amounts of this waste freestone now litter the steep valley side.

The quarry certainly seems to have produced pavers cut from suitable beds of freestone. This is confirmed in 1811 by Farey after visiting the quarry. Also evident are elongated shotholes in the quarry face showing radial cracks. These provide evidence of blasting with powder to drop large sections of the face. At the time of Farey's visit, a Joseph Marchington was working the quarry. Production here ceased entirely early in the 20th century, with the ledges of the quarry face now colonised by heather and other wild plants.

Whilst the traditional accounts of the quarry being worked by a variety of people called Pickford from the 17th century onwards (see Chapter 19) cannot be entirely disproved, the earlier, northern end of the quarry probably began in the later 18th or early 19th century. Its finished products would have been transported out of the valley by wagon using the turnpike roads, or moved on the C&HPR from the Bunsal 'halt'. By 1880, the six-inch OS map depicts the quarry site as 'Paint Mill' (see also Chapter 15, Directory of Mills).

REEVE EDGE SLATE QUARRY (SK 012 698)

A map of 1599 (PRO London, ref. MPC 274 (1)), illustrating lands in dispute between John Claye and William Gilbert, was produced at the time to support a claimant's right to 'a p'cell [parcel] of Wharnford pasture wch Hartington mene make clayme unto'. The River Dane is shown as the boundary between Macclesfield Forest in Cheshire and the Quarnford area of Staffordshire. Immediately south of 'the hed of the Ryver of dane where 3 shires meete', a simple ridge with scattered stones is depicted as 'Ryve edge whear sclates are gotten'. This is surely the now-abandoned Reeve Edge Quarry on land owned by the Devonshire

estate, and suggests that stone for roofing had been taken from here for hundreds of years. The first actual reference to a 'quarry' at Reeve Edge appears in the 1740s, where the first Quarry Master (lessee) was a William Brown who worked the quarry between 1742 and 1744. In the quarry accounts for 1746 he was referred to as 'being broke and run away' – he owed two years' rent!

Judging from its layout, this quarry has the appearance of one worked to remove one or two particular groups of thin beds, the huge overburden of freestone being discarded and left in mounds in the excavated areas, or used during a later period of quarrying to construct waste-tipping causeways. The waste freestone blocks, together with paver and slate production waste, tower over the ruined mining office and dressing-sheds, litter the slopes down to the infant Dane or have been built into long, finger-like causeways stretching out over the valley. Level grassed-over tramway beds run along their tops, while in between the 'fingers', re-vegetation is occurring. In places, faint remnants of constructed tracks of cart-width can be seen disappearing under the waste of later periods, again suggesting that this quarry has a long history.

Distinct beds of the hard but strongly laminate gritstone known as Rough Rock were split evenly to form good roofing slates known locally as 'grey slates'. Parts of the site contain recognisable open-fronted dressing sheds. There are small ruined buildings of drys-

Reeve Edge Quarry, Upper Dane.

Ruined circular building, Danebower Quarry.

tone construction, some with their north-facing sides curved to deflect the harsh winter winds. At a focal point of quarry tracks and facing the A54 is the ruin of a larger building of both mortared and drystone construction, perhaps the quarry office. There are unstable piles of stone – so visitors to the site should exercise caution. The quarry seems to have only had cart access to the Leek to Buxton turnpike (now the A53) north of Flash via the level terraced cart track above Blackclough and the narrow road through Readyleech Green (see also Chapter 18, The Later Turnpikes).

DANE BOWER SLATE QUARRY (SK 013 700)

Immediately across the river from Reeve Edge, the abandoned Dane Bower Quarry can also be visited from public paths. Here, as at nearby Reeve Edge, extraction has taken place in several phases with adjacent areas covered with the overburden of subsequent excavations and dressing waste. Huge amounts have also been tipped into the valley restricting the

infant Dane, or have been built into causeways supporting barrow-runs. The amount of waste provides evidence of considerable production in the past. A small, ruined circular building, probably of 19th-century date, at the eastern edge of the quarry, might have been the powder-house. Such stone-built magazines were designed with stout walls supporting a flimsy wooden roof that would disintegrate easily, dispersing the blast upwards in the event of an accidental gunpowder explosion. This particular example, however, is of insubstantial unmortared construction, thereby throwing doubt on the powder-house theory.

At most of these quarries, the output of quality stone reached a peak at the end of the 19th century, after which decline became rapid in the face of the development of mechanical brick and tile making. A few quarries, including the one north of Bakestonedale at Moorside, continued to produce cut stone for local building and repair well into the 20th century, but with the exception of those on the western flank of the Saddle of Kerridge, Rainow, most in the study area have closed because of cheaper 20th century materials.

PART SIX

COMMUNICATIONS FROM THE 18TH CENTURY ONWARDS

Chapter 17. ENCLOSURE

PEAK DISTRICT ENCLOSURES AND RESTRICTIONS

Between the 17th and the early 19th centuries the Peak District became an increasingly changed landscape dominated by drystone walls, largely a product of land enclosures. The earlier enclosures brought about by private improvement schemes had taken place either by agreement on individual farms, or were imposed by large estates. This trend amongst landowners to extensively enclose common land (not all settled areas were subjected to this) and what remained of the medieval-type **open fields** led to the disenfranchisement of some of the poorer people of the region. Over time, where change was resisted or allocations could not be agreed, villagers went to Parliament for an Act to appoint commissioners. These commissioners made Awards, allocating blocks of land to people with local rights. This improved the fortunes of many farmers and landowners by allowing them to increase agricultural efficiency. But poorer people, now unable to make a living in the countryside, were often left in real hardship and were forced to move to industrial areas.

In the twenty years from 1760 to 1780, over a thousand Enclosures Acts were passed. A successful Enclosures Act did not require local unanimity but it did require enough money to pay lawyers' and surveyors' fees and for walls etc., cart roads and drainage after the bill had been passed. This was largely a formality since the Enclosure Commissioners appointed to survey the land invariably favoured the parties wishing to enclose and, by doing so, heightened suspicion by the dispossessed of both the law itself and the JP's who administered it.

LOCAL ENCLOSURE

In 1760 in the central part of the South-West Peak for example, 12 acres of land were enclosed on Axe Edge and 29 acres at Turn Edge. At Goldsitch, some 127 acres were enclosed. Most of this 'privatised' land was to remain either as rough grazing, or become grouse-shooting moorland. By 1801, the passage of the General Enclosures Act ensured that enclosure procedures became simplified and that by the middle of the 19th century, the whole of agricultural England was converted to enclosed farms. The Parliamentary Enclosure Award for the large parish of Hartington was implemented in 1807 using plans dated 1804.

A three-volume work from the early 19th century, entitled *A General View of the Agriculture and Minerals of Derbyshire*, sponsored by the Board of Agriculture and written by the Mineral Surveyor, John Farey, is quite revealing. He writes, 'In the course of my Survey, I heard none of those complaints so industriously sought, of injury done to the poor by Inclosures, that have rarely any foundation in justice or reason. Phantoms . . . have possessed some men's imaginations to an extent which makes them overlook . . . the essential points of justice, and the principle, which is the very foundation of society, the inviolable right of property. There cannot remain a doubt but Inclosures have been and continue to be highly beneficial, in *every point of view.*'

During this later period of enclosure, when villagers might be awarded blocks of land away from the village, new farmsteads were built amongst the newly created fields. However, those whose holdings were so small that access to common land was of vital importance to them often had no capital to construct buildings, drains and barns. The squatters subsisting on these commons undoubtedly suffered the most; they had no legal rights and were often evicted without ceremony. For a time, the process of enclosure itself provided them with work, but it then left many of them as paupers. Although the local communities would have at the very least experienced some severance of their sense of territory, Farey appears to have seen enclosure purely in terms of the process of agricultural improvement. He may have felt the commissioners had done their best in difficult circumstances to maintain an even-handed approach.

ENCLOSURE WALLS

This 'privatisation' of the land and the building of defining walls and roads would change the Peak District landscape forever. It was the golden age of the professional waller, sometimes local and sometimes nomadic. They worked to surveyors' specifications and built many miles of walls across former commons and wastes in some of the most remote regions of the Peak District. The walls are built in local stone

and are a useful guide to the underlying geology. The vast majority of agricultural walls standing today originated before the middle of the 19th century. They sometimes remain untouched and are now dilapidated in remoter areas but elsewhere, piecemeal repair and renovation has taken place. These straight 'enclosures' walls can be seen on maps of the South-West Peak in stark contrast to the more organic curving shapes of the smaller fields around the older farmsteads in the valleys, where the art of making walls had commonly been practised for centuries.

The modern perception of field walls is often that they impose a 'natural' pattern and give a sense of scale to an otherwise nondescript view without detracting from the beauty of the landscape. Imagine the Peak District without its walls. However, the reality is that many of the larger enclosures from common imposed a new rigid scheme of straight walls onto the landscape so that in certain situations beyond the improved farmland, landowners have been able to develop vast tracts of moorland for grouse shooting. It also defined the route of the roads in the area,

Blackclough Farm, Axe Edge. The boundary wall marks an enclosure out of the common existing in 1614 and owned by the Duke of Devonshire. CLM Porter photo.

Chapter 18. A NEW ROADS NETWORK

INTRODUCTION

Even allowing for some exaggeration, the published accounts of 17th- and 18th-century travellers making horseback journeys through the Peak District reveal difficulties and mortal dangers unimagined by modern walkers and motorists.

The journalist and political satirist, Daniel Defoe, wrote that the Peak was 'inhospitable, a houling wilderness and the most desolate, wild and abandoned country in all England'. On the other hand, he admired the markets, the ale and the mining folk.

In the final decade of the 17th century, the woman traveller, Celia Fiennes, begins with a general comment that 'all Derbyshire is but a world of peaked hills'. She describes her journey on horseback from Haddon Hall to Buxton. 'Its very difficult to find the Wayes here for you see only tops of hills and so many roads by reason of ye best wayes up and down, that its impossible for Coach or Waggon to pass some of them, and you scarce see a tree and No hedges all over ye Country, only dry stone walls that inclose ground no other ffence. Buxton we saw 2 or 3 tymes and then Lost ye sight of it as often, and at last did not See it till just you came upon it – that 9 mile we were above 6 hours going it.'

The region was of course thinly settled, where the few roads would be rutted from the passage of robust wagons pulled by heavy horses or oxen. For the horseback rider unfamiliar with high moorland and the severity of winter weather it could be foolhardy to travel without the services of a guide. Burial registers in local churches reveal instances of people lost and 'perished' or 'starved to death' in the severe cold and terrible storms on the high moors. Even groups of people travelling together for security might meet their death whilst travelling even comparatively short distances in winter.

Nevertheless, many journeys were made by local people with purchases to make and produce to sell in market towns. Friends and relatives would be visited and despite the poor conditions of the highways such routes were undoubtedly well used. Many tracts of wild and inhospitable land had became criss-crossed by the routes of salters, 'badgers', tinkers and general carriers who cannot have felt the same dread experienced by strangers. They took their goods to towns, markets and ports, returning with a variety of back-carriage across the stark but sometimes familiar moors, often in unpredictable weather, until the arrival of the turnpikes slowly put their packhorses out of business.

TURNPIKE TRUSTS

It had become evident that a comprehensive network of adequately maintained all-weather roads, capable of carrying wheeled vehicles, was an urgent necessity to transport raw materials and finished products, including heavy goods to extended markets – and at lower costs. It was also needed to transport goods and services for the growing workforce of the industrial towns. In this region, as in many others throughout Britain during the 18th and early 19th centuries, an important transport revolution took place through the creation of Turnpike Trusts. Established by Acts of Parliament, these Trusts were empowered to charge tolls in accordance with stipulated rates on specified lengths of the King's highway and to borrow money for the maintenance and improvement of the roads in their charge. Existing roads were to be improved or new ones constructed and managed to standards laid down in private bills presented to Parliament. Listed trustees would be appointed to control the finances and set out the traffic tolls. The construction of this network with its associated industries was to create increasing demands for manpower and make sizeable contributions to local economies.

These business trusts, which developed rapidly from the mid-18th century, were supposed to be independent. They were comprised of eminent local residents who had a strong self-interest in road improvements, paid for, for the first time, by the road users. The trustees, inefficient, amateurish and often corrupt, were granted their powers usually for a 21-year period, by the end of which it was intended that tollgates be removed and travel would become free again. Bitter experience was to show that road maintenance could be as expensive as the initial improvements so that tolls came to be levied indefinitely.

The trusts were given, typically, authority to widen any existing roads to a maximum of 15 yards, to obtain road materials from the waste or common land of the parishes through which the road passed, to make drains, bridges and paved paths, to remove rubbish and to set up turnpikes or gates where tolls would be taken. There was little co-operation between neighbouring trusts and, at first, the short-term 'improvements' to existing roads proved little better than the parochial maintenance they replaced.

Many of these earlier turnpikes were merely narrow, upgraded horse or cart routes, followed slavishly irrespective of the terrain. Even on those roads supposedly improved by the turnpike trusts, conditions could still be poor, hindering trade and industry and inhibiting commercial development. A few improved roads, some with increased width, were built with drainage ditches and ran on causeways across boggy ground, although not surprisingly, when camber angles were sometimes constructed too steeply, forcing vehicles down the centre of the roads, conditions further deteriorated and traffic chaos increased. Drainage was a continual problem for the pioneers. Angled ridges of setts were used to divert the water on hilly sections where ditches and culverts were rare. Raised footways ('ploddings') impeded wheeled traffic and so did 'scotching stones', used by carters to wedge their wagon wheels on hills but then casually discarded. The introduction of improved horse-drawn coaches, however, soon convinced both the travelling public and merchants that more carefully planned and constructed roads were an urgent necessity. Later Acts of Parliament were passed where the instructions were 'to amend the dangerous, narrow and at times impassable roads'. To widen the roads, many turnpikes had any constricting hedges grubbed out. The roads were then walled or fenced to prevent illicit traffic entering or leaving them between tollgates.

This chapter describes important local routes and route changes that were dictated by the evolution of road transport, the levying of tolls and competition from neighbouring Trusts. These new roads, together with the canals beyond the region that were built to serve the transport needs of the 18th century, would eventually be eclipsed by the emergence of an even more spectacular transport system: the railways.

In the Peak District as a whole, a few sections of old traditional roads, roughly maintained during the Stuart period, were improved and turnpiked under Parliamentary Acts during the first half of the 18th century, the earliest being the Chesterfield to Bakewell road in 1739 and part of the Derby to Manchester road ('The Street') from 1724 (see Chapter 3, Roman Roads).

The term **turnpike** is derived from the toll bar (the bars placed across the road at the toll house or gate) in a shape resembling a pike – an infantry weapon with a long wooden shaft and a pointed iron or steel head. Samuel Johnson's English Dictionary of 1755 gives the meaning of turnpike as: 'A cross of two bars armed with spikes at the end and turning on a pin, fixed to hinder horses from entering.' The number of toll bars or gates was usually specified within a particular Act.

Although much Statute labour for road maintenance continued throughout the turnpike period, a proportion of toll income was also set aside for this purpose, reflecting the amount of traffic and the degree of local support for the particular section. In the latter half of the 18th century, general Turnpike Acts permitted those liable for Statute labour on the roads to pay money in lieu.

THE LOCAL TURNPIKE ROAD BUILDERS

Local surveyors appointed by the parishes were responsible for the early turnpike roads. They were hampered by lack of precedents, limited skill and small budgets. Traditional attitudes of the packhorse fraternity were brought to the problem and the difficulties of steep gradients were ignored in order to save money and time. These pioneer road builders evolved their own techniques that were, unfortunately, often a process of trial and error, for wrecked wagons and dead animals soon became commonplace.

Making lasting improvements to old routes and building durable new roads was at first largely experimental, but by the early 19th century, as turnpike trusts acquired wealth or perhaps amalgamated with others, some were able to abandon the 'hit and miss' methods of road construction and raise funds to appoint competent civil engineers. Two famous road-builders, John Metcalf and John Macadam, were responsible for many roads in the Peak District, particularly those around Macclesfield and Buxton.

John Metcalf of Knaresborough (1717–1810) was blinded by smallpox as a child and not until he was 47 years old, with several career changes behind him, did he experiment with the early turnpike road-building techniques. He became the most prolific road-builder of the 18th century and, despite his disability, developed legendary road-building skills. His most famous technique was to use a specially adapted 'viameter' for measuring distances, which he was able to 'read' by touch. He was one of the first road-builders to recognise the need for solid foundations and good drainage. On a road through a marshy region or across wet moorland he constructed his roads by 'floating' them on a raft of heather, gorse or wood with stone above and a topping of gravel cambered to carry off surface water into the ditches dug alongside. 'Blind Jack' retired from road-making aged 72 to return to Yorkshire, where he died at Spofforth aged 93.

John Loudon Macadam (1756-1836), who had some training as an engineer, was a road-builder of the later turnpike period and his contribution to the techniques of road-making and repair came during the second decade of the 19th century. Macadam dispensed with the solid foundations employed by John Metcalf and the famous Thomas Telford and instead realised that, given a firm and dry base for a road, all that was necessary was to provide a good surface that would be impervious to weather. If the subsoil could be kept dry it would support any normal road traffic. He considered, therefore, that drainage was vitally important and was particularly concerned with keeping gradients as gentle as possible. Because his construction methods were cheaper, he became very popular with the Turnpike Trusts – his roads being called 'Macadamised'. 'Macadamising', incidentally, did not involve the use of tar but employed graded stones with the smaller ones at the top, laid dry and hammered down to form a watertight mass to be consolidated by horses' hooves and the metal rims of wheels. Such a surface is called the 'road metal' or 'metalling' – not an ideal term. The improving roads network was to make the pack train redundant, as wheeled transport for longer journeys now became a viable alternative.

Macadamised roads were eventually replaced over time by mechanically rolling-in the roadstone with a coal tar binding and dressing the surface with sand – hence the name 'Tarmacadam'. 'Tarmac' was first used in English towns in the 1830s. Its general use in the countryside was to come much later, after the introduction of the motor car.

In the study area, and particularly on Axe Edge Moor, there was progressive and aggressive disruption of the regular horse routes used by the carriers when the road builders cut straight across them. Prior to the turnpike era, a regular packhorse trade to traditional markets had developed around these moors, with eastbound packhorse trains taking coal from the Goyt, Axe Edge and Dane Collieries to the Grin Low limekiln, and westbound trains taking lime to Macclesfield, Congleton, Knutsford and beyond. By the values of their day, road tolls could be very high. For example, in 1830, a cart drawn by one horse would have to pay fivepence or sixpence. As this roughly equalled one quarter of a miner's pay for a day, regular use of the turnpike roads might be considered as the preserve of the commercial user and the wealthy traveller. To evade the toll keepers, the packmen would occasionally pull down sections of wall or fencing between tollgates and take the packhorse trains on mixed routes to their destinations.

Nine distinct major stages in the development of the study area's communication system occurred, all of which can be identified from the maps:

1. Improvements to 'The Street' between Buxton and Manchester, Act of 1724.

2. Construction of a new route between Macclesfield and Buxton, Act of 1758.

3. Construction of a new route between Leek and Buxton, Act of 1765.

4. Improvements to a route between Macclesfield and Whaley Bridge, Act of 1770.

5. Construction of a new route between Ladmanlow and Brierlow, Act of 1773.

6. Construction of the Ladmanlow to Goyts Moss Colliery branch of the Leek and Buxton Turnpike c.1773.

7. The extension of a route from Congleton to Buxton, Act of 1789.

8. Construction of the 'New Cut' on the Terret, c.1790.

9. Re-routing an earlier turnpike between Macclesfield and Buxton, Act of 1821.

To these must be added the provision of numerous branch turnpikes to the moorland quarries, collieries and limekiln complexes and, by 1831, the completion of the Cromford and High Peak Railway. This railway, connecting two of the region's canals, was to have sidings to local quarries and coal mines.

The complexity of the road junctions, tollgates and successive developments and disputes, particularly those created by the Macclesfield and Buxton and the Leek and Buxton Turnpike Trusts over the years at Burbage and Ladmanlow – the focal points for much of the coal and lime traffic – are not described here in great detail. These constant changes were, however, considerable and frustrating, especially to the carriers.

THE MANCHESTER AND BUXTON TURNPIKE, 1724–1873 ('THE STREET')

THE PRE-TURNPIKE ROUTE

At the turn of the 18th century, the fractured remains of a Roman highway known as 'The Street' (see Chapter 3) was still one of the few routes of any significance through the relatively underdeveloped Peak District, where it formed part of a much longer route from London to Carlisle. Over the hundred and fifty or so years of route changes and improvements undertaken by various turnpike trusts on this major highway, only those in the vicinity of the study area are dealt with here.

In 1704 William Nicholson, the Bishop of Carlisle, had found the old highway 'mountainous and rough'. Although the route, narrow and sometimes impassable in winter, had endured centuries of neglect, parts of it appear to have remained in use right up to the turnpike era. It is shown on an Estate map of the small settlement of Buxton of 1631, a regional map of 1640, on John Ogilby's strip-maps published in 1675 and on Overton's Derbyshire map dated 1712, where it appears as one of only five highways shown as 'the Post roads and cross roads'. This and later 18th-century maps lay out the ground for the statute mile and are a useful introduction to the nature of travel at that time.

Ogilby's maps were the first collection of road maps of the kingdom and show seventy-five principal highways in simplified strip form accompanied by notes for the traveller. On the strip depicting the Derby to Manchester highway via Brassington and Buxton (on the line of the Roman road), a side road south of Buxton (at Brierlow Bar) is labelled 'to ye Cole Pits'. The map also shows the old highway crossing the River Goyt on a stone bridge before heading through Whaley Bridge, where it veered to the west over Longside above Disley and continued via 'Hesselgrove', through 'Stockport alias Stopford', past 'Ancots Hall' into Manchester.

Between Buxton and a crossroads at Shallcross Hall the map depicts two prominent rocks east of the old highway. These are the prominent gritstone outcrops at SK 043 745 and the Hanging Rock SK 027 767, both positions roughly corresponding to the still-visible remains of Ogilby's pre-turnpike route and the mileages shown on his map. North-west of the White Hall Centre the hollow-ways of this old braided route can be seen in steep, rough grass either side of improved pasture east of Hanging Rock at the southern end of the flattened Wainstones ridge.

Climbing out of Ogilby's route towards 'a rock' (see above.)

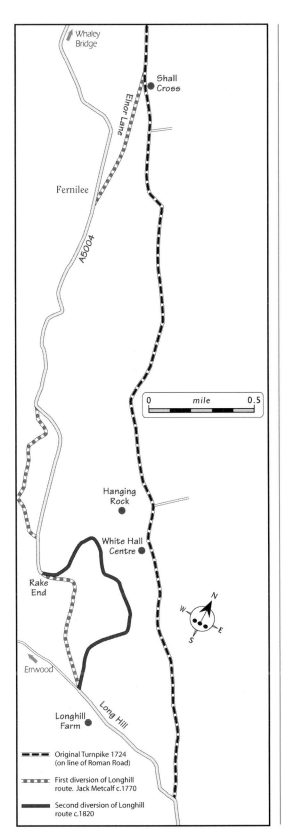

Whaley
Bridge

Shall
Cross

Elnor Lane

Fernilee

A5004

0   mile   0.5

Hanging
Rock

White Hall
Centre

Rake
End

N
W   E
S

Errwood

Long Hill

Longhill
Farm

—■—■— Original Turnpike 1724
(on line of Roman Road)

—✳—✳— First diversion of Longhill
route. Jack Metcalf c.1770

▬▬▬ Second diversion of Longhill
route c.1820

Map: Part of the Buxton and
Manchester Turnpike 1724 – c.1820.

THE TURNPIKE

On the current White Peak OS map the minor road leaving the A5004 above Cold Springs Farm (SK 044 744) for Shallcross village (SK 016 798) is shown as 'Roman Road' at its southern end and 'Old Road' 3km further north. This narrow road represents part of the resurfacing and improvements carried out from May 1725 as a rationalisation of the old traditional rutted highway through the deep and heavy soils between Buxton and Manchester. It was an extension of the Manchester and Stockport turnpike to the top of Sherbrook Hill, Buxton, and was in fact the first turnpiked road in Derbyshire. Between Round the Bend (SK 0358 7594) and Wythen Lache (SK 0270 7767) it follows a parish boundary for 3km, beyond which it forms a boundary to Long Edge Plantation before descending gradually to Elnor Lane, Shallcross. The cutting, forced through the natural ridge barrier at Wainstones, is part of the original turnpike, not the much earlier traditional highway. A turnpike branch between Whaley Bridge and Chapel-en-le-Frith over Eccles Pike was also constructed within the terms of the 1724 Act, to replace an established packhorse route.

By 1730, powers were sought to widen and improve this road north of Buxton because, by then, Statute work had proved insufficient to cope with the damage done by increasing numbers of wheeled vehicles – something the road planners had not anticipated. For the sparsely populated parishes of this area, few

Hollow-ways, top of Goyts Lane.

Long Hill, The Metcalf diversion (foreground) with the 2nd in the background.

of which actually lie on the road, these improvements to such an important through route often proved particularly irritating and time-consuming, any necessary work performed being slipshod and superficial. In 1749 a link was made from Hurdlow (SK 12 66) to Sherbrook Hill, Buxton (see above), thus completing the main through-route from Derby to Manchester.

In accordance with a Renewal Act of 1764, tolls were increased sharply to allow the turnpike trustees to keep up with interest payments and increase their borrowing capacity. Sometime between 1767 and 1776, the original version of the turnpike was rerouted north of Buxton for some 5km between Cold Springs Farm and Fernilee and became the first version of the so-called 'Long Hill' road (now the A5004), the contractor for this work being John Metcalf. This diversion began at the sharply defined set of hollow-ways (SK 0310 7520) representing the medieval route across the upper Goyt Valley. From this position at the top of Goyts Lane, the Metcalf diversion veers northwards from the hollow-ways down a steep descent and ascent to Rake End. Although offering few problems to packhorses or light wheeled traffic, it was to prove a serious obstacle to a heavily laden coach or wagon on an average gradient as steep as 1 in 6.

An article on 'Roads and Travelling' in the *Buxton Advertiser* in 1937 quotes a lady travelling from Northampton in 1776 who had found the road from Derby to Buxton via Ashbourne 'excellent without rut or stones . . . used a drag'd wheel down hills' – and from a later report, 'indirect evidence of the Manchester to Buxton road in May 1817, is that Absolam Watkin was able to read on the four-hour journey'.

Buxton became confirmed as the natural focus of the western part of the South-West Peak, replacing the village of Longnor, which was already on the Newcastle-under-Lyme to Hassop turnpike via Leek. Buxton was to become a prospering new resort and market town with a growing lime and limestone industry.

The former Fernilee toll house.

A further diversion, involving a 2km loop north of Longhill Farm, was constructed sometime around 1820. This eased the average gradient of Metcalf's earlier diversion to about 1 in 44. This second diversion appears on a plan for the Cromford and High Peak Railway dated 1824. Because Metcalf's diversion is not shown, this may indicate that it was already out of use. A sandstone milestone with a curved top survives at the roadside in long grass just south of the modern viewpoint and lay-by (part of the second diversion) at SK 0194 7715. The only known tollgate on this road that falls within the study area was set up in 1823 at Fernilee and remained in use until 1872. An earlier tollgate authorised in 1793 was probably set up at Brierlow Bar, but was called Buxton Bar.

In 1821 there was a new Act specifically mentioning the Hurdlow House (Bull i'th Thorn Inn). This Act, perhaps for the first time, excluded innkeepers from being trustees or toll collectors. Clause 99 of the Act mentions what the trustees thought were road nuisances that could be abated by fines, e.g. 'for damaging or defacing guide posts or milestones, breaking or turning out the lamps at the toll houses, driving except on the left and causing horses carrying milk pans or panniers drawing abreast of similarly laden horses'.

Despite traffic increases as a result of road improvements, particularly in Stockport, the resultant increases in tolls again proved insufficient to keep up with the interest payments and in 1828 the Turnpike Trust experienced severe financial difficulties. Notwithstanding the aggravation of railway competition and a period of financial stringency, by 1872 the Trust had commendably paid off its debts. Its responsibilities for maintenance and road improvements were then taken over by local government.

Although there had been two diversions north of Buxton, some of the earlier road sections are still in use as minor roads. A narrow Metcalf section from Fernilee off the existing A5004 that joins the 1724 road by the Shall Cross and descends into Whaley Bridge, for example, is now called Elnor Lane. Other short, grassy, abandoned sections still survive above the Fernilee Reservoir and below the modern road as part of the footpaths network of the area.

Centuries after the Roman departure, 'The Street' from Derby to Manchester is still used by several parishes as a boundary along which some elements of the Roman road remain incorporated into the modern roads network.

THE MACCLESFIELD AND WHALEY BRIDGE TURNPIKE, 1770–1820

Macclesfield had flourished as a trading centre for the produce from arable lowlands to the west and the pastoral uplands to the east. Until the building of the modern road system, the town was on the principal highways between Leek, Derby and The Midlands to the south, and Stockport and Manchester to the north. This route to the north had been used for many hundreds of years, its importance probably increasing with the development of Macclesfield in the Anglo-Saxon period. Many traders will have passed this way, including the salters' packhorse trains from Cheshire, some turning east in Rainow through Saltersford, others continuing via Salter's Green to Kettleshulme and through Whaley Bridge to Salter's Knowl at Chapel-en-le-Frith. At SK 973 793, Sester Bridge carries this old route round a hairpin bend over the Gnathole Brook. The bridge was 'Chester Breads' in 1611, from *bred*, meaning 'a plank or board' – i.e. a plank-bridge on the route westwards via Macclesfield, Middlewich, Kelsall and Tarvin, to Chester.

By the late 1760s, Macclesfield was an expanding and industrial market town with good turnpike road connections including that to the port of Liverpool via Knutsford and Warrington. Jobs were plentiful and an improved road to Whaley Bridge and the market town of Chapel-en le-Frith would link up to canals and roads from other prosperous and developing northern industrial towns. The old route was turnpiked by an Act of Parliament in 1770 but not entirely completed until 1779. Cutting across the north-west corner of the South-West Peak this road served as an artery for the Macclesfield area's finished textiles, stone, lime, bricks, coal and, quite importantly, the raw materials and finished products of the Macclesfield Copper Company (see below). This road was, like the Buxton and Manchester 1724 turnpike, distinctive in the sense of being built along the line of an already well-documented and ancient route. The distances to Chapel-en-le-Frith, Sheffield and Chesterfield are shown on the complete set of refurbished milestones. Either constructed, or just surveyed, by John Metcalf, this road originally ran via Rainow, Four Lane Ends, between Further Harrop Farm and Harrop House Farm, up to Charles Head, down into the Gnathole Brook Valley and over the Reed Bridge (SJ

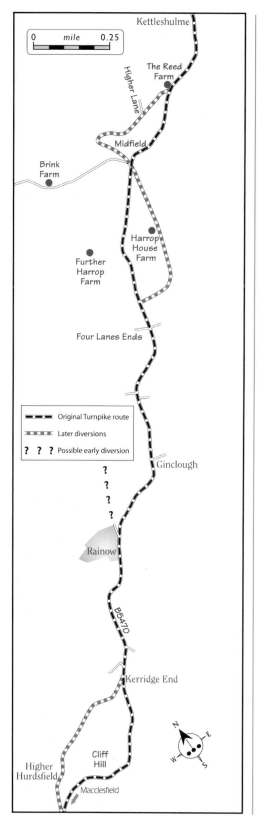

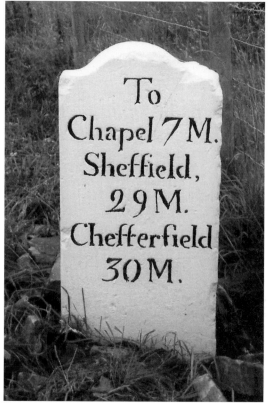

18th century milestone near 'The Highwayman'.

9820 7930) into Kettleshulme. From here the turn-pike continued through Taxal to Randle Carr Lane Head above Whaley Bridge, where the authority of the Trust ended.

The original turnpike had steep stretches that in places were rerouted, as for example north of Rainow between the Highwayman Inn and Charles Head where the older version (now a track) drops down into the Harrop Valley and climbs out again. Both routes are shown on Burdett's Cheshire map, published in 1777 but probably surveyed earlier. The diversion is perhaps Metcalf's work.

Through Rainow itself, the turnpike seems to have followed the line of the old route except for a pos-sible diversion passing to the east of the Rainow Institute which may never have gone further than Rainowlow. A further change was made in Higher Hurdsfield, with the original road bending east along Cliff Lane and skirting Cliff Hill to follow Calrowfold

Map: Part of the Macclesfield and Whaley Bridge Turnpike, 1770.

Lane to Kerridge End. Despite being widened more than once, the bridge across the Mill Brook in Rainow village still retains an 18th-century construction style. A cottage, No.1, Hawkins Lane, opposite the Rising Sun Inn, was an early tollhouse with a chain or bar across the road. The auction of tolls for 1790 lists the Hawkins Lane chain, together with bars at Hurdsfield and at Gap House, Kettleshulme. The Rainow chain and bar are again mentioned in 1820, by which time the Kettleshulme bar had apparently been replaced.

Between the bottom of Bull Hill Lane and the north end of Rainow village, this road, now the B5470, forms part of the south-western boundary of the Peak District National Park. The stretch through the village of Rainow goes under the various names of Hawkins Lane, then Tower Hill, then Pedley Hill.

THE MACCLESFIELD COPPER COMPANY

By 1696, a brickworks had been established on Macclesfield's common land. In 1758, land was again appropriated, this time by Charles Roe on the edge of the common near the boundary with Sutton, for the foundation of a smelting works. This suggests a further invasion of common pasture for industry. There was coal on the common and the possibility of getting copper supplies from Alderley Edge, but neither source proved to be sufficient and both materials were soon brought in from further afield such as the Duke of Devonshire's Ecton Copper mine. There was a large windmill to grind ore and abundant water, but by the mid-1760s, supplies of coal from the common were dwindling. As this became exhausted, coal was obtained from near Poynton – a distance of seven miles. Other copper works were established by Roe at Havannah, near Congleton, at Bosley and at Liverpool. Following the failure of the Alderley Edge ore supplies, copper ore was obtained from Coniston in the Lake District, from the Duke of Devonshire's Ecton Hill mine (pre1760) and from Parys Mountain, Anglesey. As well as smelting and working copper, Roe's company

manufactured brass – an alloy of copper and zinc. Zinc was obtained by smelting calamine ore, which came from Mold in Flintshire and from Oswestry. At this time the advantages of a canal that would have altered, perhaps improved, the industrial development of Macclesfield, were denied by the intervention of the Duke of Bridgewater. Roe's Macclesfield copper works, which then covered an area of 12 acres, closed in 1801, but the ore-grinding windmill was converted to corn milling and was 'in full work' by 1806.

As previously suggested, Macclesfield quickly became a town that was well served by the early turnpike road system. By 1759 there was a turnpike road to Buxton. In addition to the Macclesfield and Whaley Bridge turnpike described above; the Stockport–Macclesfield–Leek road to the south and London was turnpiked in 1762, while to the west, the Macclesfield–Knutsford road to Chester was turnpiked in 1769. In 1796, the road to Congleton was turnpiked. Communications were further enhanced in 1831 with the completion of the long-awaited Macclesfield Canal, which connected with the Peak Forest Canal at Marple and with the Trent and Mersey Canal at Talke in Staffordshire.

LINKS FROM BOLLINGTON

From the position once occupied by the Orme Smithy (SJ 945 780), an old metalled roadway leads eastwards across pasture and through woodland up the Harrop

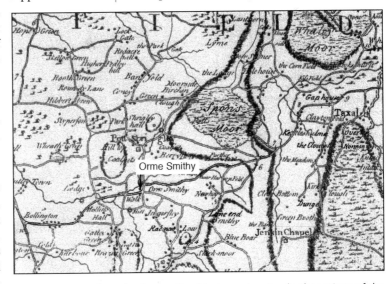

Part of Burdett's 1777 Cheshire map showing both versions of the Macclesfield and Whaley Bridge turnpike and the old road from Bollington to Kettleshulme via Orm Smithy.

Valley, before turning north over the Black Brook in front of Further Harrop Farm. Clearly shown on Burdett's Cheshire map, the old road sections, sometimes part of, sometimes adjacent to other ancient trackways, are now choked with vegetation or in places flooded where overflowing streams reveal the stoned foundations. Climbing up to Charles Head, it crosses the Macclesfield turnpike before plunging down past Slaters (once Salters) Green Farm to the Reed Bridge and north-east to Kettleshulme. These old roads from Macclesfield and Bollington, which served the quarries and coal mines in the Harrop Valley, formed a link between the Derby to Manchester (via Buxton) and the Macclesfield to Sheffield and Chesterfield ancient roads that were eventually improved and turnpiked. Much of the old Higher Lane link to Disley, with its severe gradients, can still be used today as an effective Whaley Bridge bypass. A route from Sowcar (SJ 943 778) that climbs to Brink Farm (SJ 967 793) has become the modern Gritstone Trail and turns north to pass the Bow Stones.

AXE EDGE MOOR AND ITS EARLY TURNPIKES

Some of the following text is based on the comprehensive 1992 publication Turnpike Roads Around Buxton by Alan Roberts (see Bibliography).

The interaction of the Macclesfield, Leek and Congleton to Buxton turnpikes makes it necessary to consider them together – firstly up to the year 1780.

THE MACCLESFIELD AND BUXTON TURNPIKE, 1758–1830

Prior to the construction of the turnpikes, the treacherous high moorland of Axe Edge and Goyts Moss had acted as a barrier to a direct route for wheeled vehicles between the two towns of Buxton and Macclesfield. From Macclesfield, an older horse route can be found shadowing the line of this old turnpike here and there, but only as far as Stake Clough northwest of the Cat and Fiddle Inn (see Chapter 8, Between Macclesfield and Buxton)._Known locally as the 'Buxton [or Macclesfield] Old Road', this turnpike road, authorised by an Act of Parliament in 1758,

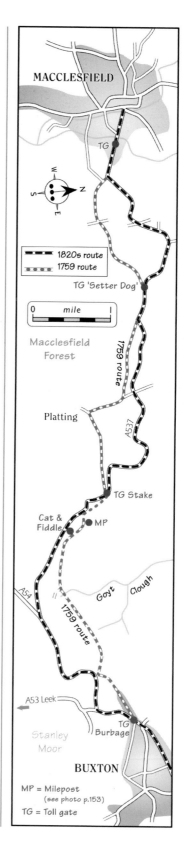

Map: Macclesfield to Buxton Turnpike of 1759 and 1821.

was completed by 1759. In places an entirely new cut was made. From Stake Clough to Buxton the final 5km of road was laid down in peat with double ditches and culverts across the easier gradients of Goyts Moss. From here it climbed the ridge before descending to Burbage and Buxton.

This early turnpike was the best road between Cheshire, the East Midlands and (briefly) London. However, its pre-eminence in this respect was diminished after four years when the gentler overall gradient of an old road from Macclesfield through Bosley to Leek was turnpiked. Now replaced as a main road, the 1759 route still exists as a rough road between Burbage and Derbyshire Bridge, from where it climbs as a tarmac road to join the A537 south of the Cat and Fiddle Inn. A diverted section can be seen as a broad stripe of altered vegetation behind the position now occupied by the inn (which had not then been built). A further abandoned section, part of a public

The Macclesfield / Buxton 'old road' west of the 'Cat and Fiddle'.

footpath, is picked up north-west of the inn, where its original width of 30ft and metalled surface still exists to provide a good example of what an early turnpike looked like. There is a contemporary milestone here (Macclesfield 6, London 164). The old road then dips left past the Peak View Tea Rooms to cross the A537 and descend steeply downhill, cutting through the earlier traditional route towards the Stanley Arms pub. From here it climbs north-west to Walker Barn and then west over Macclesfield Common to Macclesfield. When this road was disturnpiked in 1824 and its surface maintenance withdrawn, it acquired the name 'Stoneyway Gate', a name given to many redundant sections of 18th- or 19th-century turnpikes. Between Macclesfield and Derbyshire Bridge, this old turnpike was eventually tarmacked and is still in use today, linking here and there with the A537 but providing a quieter alternative.

In a sheltered dip where the 1759 road follows the infant River Goyt, five buildings were erected by the roadside in the late 18th or early 19th century. They were demolished in the 1930s when Fernilee reservoir was

built. The easternmost building was Goyts Moss Farm, the site now occupied by the Peak District National Park Ranger building (SK 013 716). To the west of this and having, like the others, surviving footings, was a large L-shaped building (a barn?); next came Moss Hall, then Moss House and furthest west Marchington Farm, once possibly the Coach and Horses Inn, with the extensive fields behind presumably walled-out after the shafts at the Castids Common part of the Goyts Moss Colliery had been abandoned. None of these buildings appears to have been for direct use by the colliery. Moss House is shown on Burdett's County map of 1767 – the only building shown – and Moss Hall and Goyts Moss Farm are shown for the first time on an early-19th-century colliery plan. All the buildings appear on the detailed Taxal Tithe map of 1845. The sites can be recognised by surviving stone footings, some with small stands of trees.

A similar milestone to the existing one on 'Stoneyway' is shown on 19th-century maps as being adjacent to the Marchington Farm ruin at SK 0127 7147. The distance is exact but where is the stone? The building of this turnpike made it possible to replace packhorses with carts and encouraged the sinking of deeper shafts with horse-gins to wind up the coal. This road was not completely walled-out until sometime after the 1804 enclosures.

The locations of three local tollgates for the 1759 road are known. They were at (1) Walker Barn (1823–33) by the roads junction; (2) Stoneyway (1759–1833), 1km west of the Cat and Fiddle; and (3) at Gosling (1759–1824), very close to the C&HPR access bridge where the building still exists as Goslin Bar Farm, Burbage.

THE MIDDLE HILLS AND HASSOP TURNPIKE, 1765–79

Today's motorist, passing the Winking Man pub on the A53 from Leek to Buxton, could be forgiven for assuming that the winding moorland road forking east to Longnor at Middle Hills had always been a minor route avoiding the head waters of the River Churnet. The first kilometre however was an entirely new cut over difficult ground to Ridge Head (SK 038 644) where it would pick up the line of a traditional route from Longnor via Merril Grove Farm, Morridge Top and Flash Bottom to Macclesfield (see also Chapt. 8, The Greenway Cross). In 1765 a turnpike road was authorised by Parliamentary Act to repair and widen this traditional route to Longnor and extend it through Crowdecote, Monyash and Ashford to Hassop where it would join an existing turnpike between Chesterfield and Peak Forest. Bridges were built over the stream at Hardings Booth and the River Manifold at Longnor, the Crowdecote bridge on the Dove was moved upstream and the Ashford bridge repaired. Branches were to be set up to Burslem and to the Uttoxeter turnpike at Sheldon. The 25ft wide roads were to be made at £160 per mile by Henry Watts. These roads would generate profits by helping to distribute products west into Cheshire and north-west to Stockport and Manchester. Some of the capital for this venture was put up by Josiah Wedgwood (1730–95), whose designs were to give pottery manufacture a new impetus. In addition to the usual provision of Acts for turnpikes, the trustees were given power 'to make walls or fences by the sides of the roads'. This clause was to have repercussions later on.

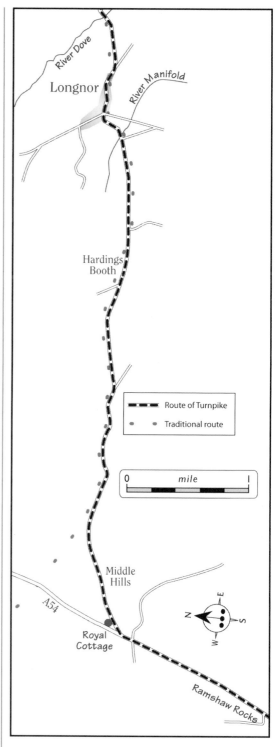

Map: Part of the Newcastle-under-Lyme and Hassop Turnpike, 1765.

New roads were therefore urgently required that would:

a) Take wheeled vehicles to carry foodstuffs for the workforce,

b) Connect with existing turnpikes and cut transport costs,

c) Give better access to sources of raw materials: **lead** could be obtained from around Monyash and Ashford, **chert** from Bakewell and Longstone Edge near Hassop (an important ingredient in pottery production), **lime** was available from the Buxton kilns and **coal** from the Axe Edge and Goldsitch Moss pits.

To the south-west of Leek, the six towns that became known as The Potteries were already the centres of pottery production for England with growing populations. Industrial potteries were making hygienic earthenware dishes and cups available to all social classes, underpinning the sanitary revolution of the 19th century which depended upon mass-produced drainage pipes, sinks, basins, chamber pots and WC bowls. In addition to capital investment and a labour force with some expertise, the large-scale production of pottery depended upon the transport of raw materials such as clay, flint, lead, coal and chert and markets for competitively priced finished goods. Although James Brindley's Trent and Mersey (Grand Trunk) canal, the first totally artificial waterway of the industrial age, was under construction to provide a much-needed trade route, it was not completed until 1777.

Near to its junction with the A53, the Longnor road verge is flanked by a number of stone pillars. They still indicate the width and general direction of the road, coming into their own under snowy conditions. The road was finally opened in November 1779. Thus there was a gap of some 14 years between the authorisation of the route and its completion – by which time it was facing competition from the recently opened Trent and Mersey Canal.

When the Trust was set up, Leek was developing as a textile town and agricultural centre. To its north there was only the traditional horse route from Abbey Green to Meerbrook, through the Windygates gap between The Roaches and Hen Cloud to Goldsitch and then north to Flash. Beyond the Flash area, the

Part of Bowen's 1749 map of Staffordshire showing the pre-turnpike route between Leek and Buxton.

Buxton traditional route over the county boundary is evident from the deep hollow-ways through Gamballs Green, Brand Side and Countess Cliff. This important old highway is shown on Emanuel Bowen's 1749 Staffordshire map (reissued successively at various dates up to 1800) and in editions of *The Large English Atlas* by Bowen and Kitchin. The Act of 1765 therefore included authorisation to construct a completely new 'turnpike branch from Middlehills [a name for the area east of Royal Cottage] to join the Macclesfield turnpike at Buxton' (see below).

THE LEEK AND BUXTON TURNPIKE, 1765–1875

At the time of the Turnpike Act, perhaps because Buxton had yet to be fully developed, this road (now the A53) was to be the least significant. With the rapid establishment of a comprehensive roads network at the burgeoning spa town of Buxton and the development of the Grin limeworks and nearby coalfield, it was to become the more important road. The Leek to Longnor section of the Hassop turnpike eventually

The Cisterns Clough embankment.

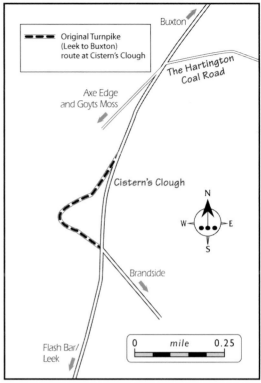

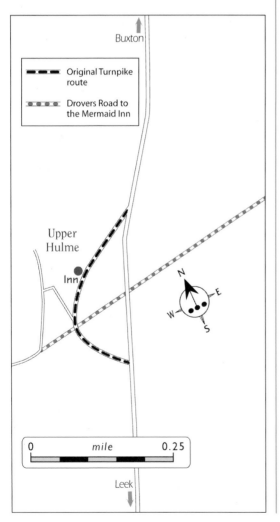

Map above: Road improvements at Cisterns Clough.

Map left: Road improvements at Upper Hulme.

became relegated to become today's minor moorland road, still flanked in places by the hollow-ways of old traditional routes.

Coming north from Royal Cottage, the Leek and Buxton turnpike passed along a broad ridge between Middlehills and Flash beyond which, at Cisterns Clough, it crossed the line of an established east–west route recorded c.1600 as a 'road to the cole pitts'. What would at this time have been a deeply hollowed road, climbing from Dove Head to the Cisterns Clough loop (SK 034 698), is now a banked causeway rising evenly to join the straightened and elevated A53.

The A53 follows the turnpike (except for minor road straightening at Solomon's Hollow, Upper Hulme and Cisterns Clough) as far as Flash Bar, where on his 1767 map Peter Burdett shows the road going straight on downhill past Gamballs Green and Dove Head before ascending to Cisterns Clough, which it would have crossed with a bridge or short embankment before

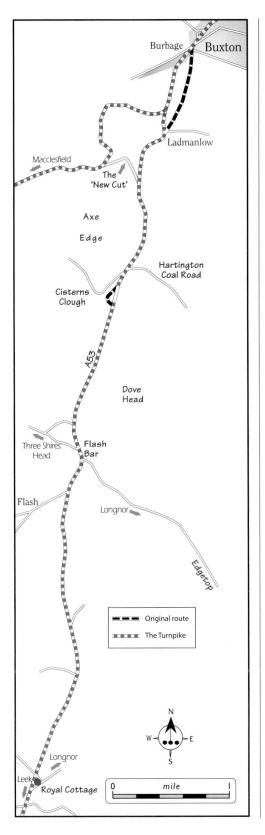

Map: The Leek and Buxton
Turnpike, 1765-1875.

continuing to the Ladmanlow tollgate. This particular section, based on pre-existing packhorse ways, may have been used to avoid enclosed land north of Flash Bar, but with only two years between the passing of the Leek Turnpike Act and the publication of Burdett's map, it is almost certain that road construction had not yet progressed to this location. In 1771 a toll-house and gate called Flash Bar were built north-east of Flash at the junction of the turnpike with the aptly named Edgetop road to Longnor (SK 032 679). The final stage was not reached until March 1772 when it was ordered that 'the junction of the turnpike branch with the Macclesfield road be brought forward on a lane known as Green Lane to form the Macclesfield road at Buxton'. Orders were also followed for the Grin tollgate to be built. It seems likely therefore that total completion of this turnpike could not have occurred until at least 1773.

The coal-mining areas lay to the west of this road while the limestone area was to the east. The original 1765 Act had contained a clause permitting the trustees to fence the road to prevent toll evasion 'near Buxton'. By fencing the road entirely between its London Road, Buxton termination and Flash Bar, the turnpike trustees blocked the access from all existing west–east tracks between the mines and kilns, thus funnelling all this traffic onto their strategically positioned Green Lane, Grin End and Ladmanlow tollgates at Buxton. This interpretation of the clause was to give the Trust a quite legal but unfair opportunity to coerce additional lucrative traffic.

The series of disputes over many years between the local turnpike trusts were nearly all to do with access to the Grin kilns. These were exemplified by proposals and counter-proposals for new and advantageous Acts of Parliament for provision of additional tollgates and turnpike branches to the coal extraction sites. To compound the problems, petitions to Parliament were also made by numerous residents of Hartington parish and collectively by several townships east of Buxton for these Acts to contain access provision beneficial to themselves. Although some petitions were refused, many were accepted and road sections diverted. Clauses to existing Acts were sometimes obtained whereby certain toll-free passage was allowed when only a certain length of a competitor's road was travelled (see below).

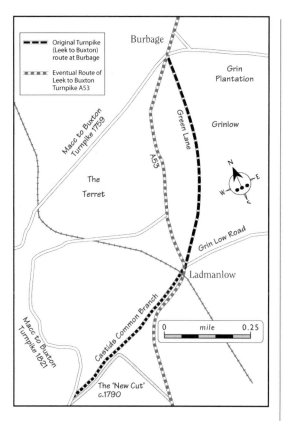

Map: Turnpike rationalisation at Burbage.

LEEK AND BUXTON TURNPIKE BRANCHES

In 1773, five new branch turnpikes, some with their own tollgates and one with a short spur, were authorised for the Turnpike Trust by a Parliamentary Act – but only four were constructed:

(1) Surviving today as an obvious grassy cut terrace on the southern slopes of The Terret, from the Ladmanlow tollhouse, a branch was built to the Castids Common area of the Goyts Moss Colliery. It turned through the gap between Axe Edge and the Terret, descending towards the Macclesfield to Buxton turnpike at the River Goyt (SK 0153 7145) by Moss Hall. From this date, the two turnpike trusts competed for trade. To bring coal from this part of the colliery to the branch, it was necessary to negotiate the very steep north bank of the infant River Goyt. To overcome the difficulty, in March 1778 a short extension spur was created from Moss Hall, crossing the River Goyt

at SK 0158 7150 and rising up to the coalfield. The gently rising curve of the spur, abandoned by 1842, can still be seen just left of the mature trees. A ruined bridge abutment can be found in the riverbank below. A further spur from this branch to access the Ravenslow coal pits, again cutting straight across the existing Macclesfield turnpike east of the Derbyshire Bridge area at SK 0200 7165, was included in the Act. Its aggressive route was hotly disputed although its actual completion date is uncertain. It can still be identified for part of its length, as a very boggy public footpath.

(2) A branch onto the Goldsitch Moss colliery was provided for in the Act. It was an extension of a proposed branch to 'Gibtor', and joined the main turnpike immediately south of Ramshaw Rocks where 'Rocks Bar' cottage now stands (SK 0189 6194).

(3) Seventeenth-century maps of Buxton reveal an old route shown as the 'cole road' running from Ladmanlow to join the important Derby to Manchester ancient road at Brieryfoot (Brierlow Bar). This minor road, which appears as 'lime road' on later maps, still exists as Burlow Road and Grinlow Road. Although it had to cross a very steep dry dale east of Harpur Hill, it was improved and turnpiked within the 1773 Act because of upheld parish objections to the proposed route of the main Leek Turnpike via Green Lane and Cote Heath to connect with the above main road – which by then was the main turnpike to Ashbourne. The Ladmanlow tollgate controlled both roads.

(4) The final branch to be built begins at the Middlehills to Hassop turnpike near to its junction with the Leek and Buxton turnpike at Royal Cottage, but cutting back westwards across it. This was to create the roads triangle immediately north of the Winking Man pub to facilitate traffic movements in all directions. The branch continued westwards across Goldsitch Moss and down to bridge the Flash Brook (at SK 0045 6640) above Manor Farm, Quarnford. A tollgate was ordered at Gib Tor in 1775 but in 1825 this was moved to the Hazelbarrow road junction, at which time a gate at Goldsitch Moss was removed.

Other changes included the authorisation of a small tollbooth (recently restored) at John Bradley's house (Bradley Howell) at SK 0060 6585. In 1842, this was replaced by the Flash Brook tollhouse and gate at the road junction 400m further north.

At the request of the Macclesfield and Buxton Turnpike Trustees, a provisional clause was inserted into the 1773 Act which granted toll-free passage between the Macclesfield road and the Thatch Marsh, Goyt and Ravenslow coal pits 'for horses or carts carrying coal, and from the Macclesfield road at Grin End to the Grin kilns for horses or carts carrying lime, provided they did not travel for more than four hundred yards on the Leek and Buxton Turnpike or one of its branches'.

The 1773 Act also incorporated a branch from Flash Bar via Knotbury and Oxensitch, to the Blackclough coal pits, which followed exactly a route shown on the Ogilby Map of 1675, although it was never turnpiked or had tollgates. By 1829, a tollgate and house

had been ordered for this road, to be let with the Flash tollgate, but again, their position or existence is yet to be established. Today, this tarmac road below Orchard Farm is just an access road that runs close to, and parallel with, the Black Brook. This flows south through Orchard common to join the Fyrestone Brook from Cheeks Hill, entering the River Dane below at Panniers Pool. How long the stream has been called Firestone Brook, indicating the known presence of coal, is not known. It certainly appears as such on an undated map, probably from the late 16th or early 17th century, with the position of the 'cole pitte' shown on either bank of the stream.

In 1777 a further branch to the Knotbury mines was constructed. Its route is not recorded. An additional branch was proposed from 'Axedge to Hirkillow Frith and the High Edge limekilns'. Although an east–west 'coal road' immediately north of Cisterns Clough, flanked by many old hollow-ways and remains of limekilns, exists, there are no records of tollgates or

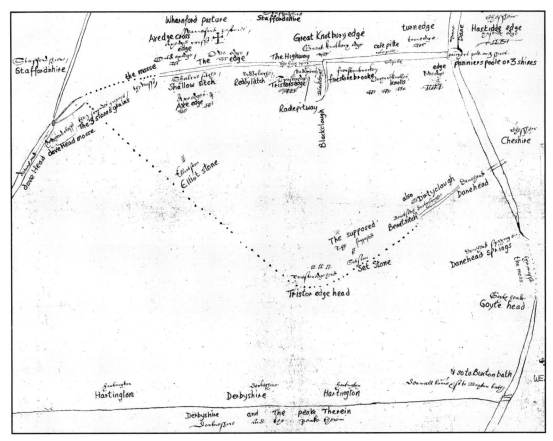

Undated map, possibly late 16th century or early 17th century affirming coal mining near Panniers Pool, Quarnford.

payments. This suggests it may never have been turnpiked.

The disputes between the Turnpike Trusts continued, with proposals for additional branches to be blocked, walls erected, tolls raised to unreasonable levels and compromises sometimes effected. From about 1780 an adequate settlement seems to have been reached, bringing a relative peace, at least to the Axe Edge and Thatch Marsh area.

In 1792, a branch was proposed from 'Nithing End near Buxton to Grin End'. This proposed branch would have linked the Grin kilns to the 1724 Manchester and Buxton turnpike by an existing route shown on the 1776 Fernilee and Fairfield Enclosures map as 'Fairfield Lane – to the lime kilns'. The proposed branch follows part of what is now Gadley Lane and although it would have provided a much shorter alternative to the existing turnpikes through the town, it was not included in the 1793 Renewal Act. It seems possible, however, that the Leek and Buxton Turnpike Trust may have upgraded the lower part of Gadley Lane, as the present stretch between the golf course and the Wye has been substantially improved at some time with a wide stoned surface and a retaining wall on the downslope side. However, the upper section below its junction with the A5004 at Nithen End (SK 048 739) is steep and narrow and would have been unsuitable for horses and carts.

LATER TURNPIKES AND BRANCHES FROM 1780

FURTHER LEEK AND BUXTON TURNPIKE BRANCHES

In January 1783, the trustees successfully applied to Parliament for a further five new turnpike branches including one 'from Flash toll bar and Axe Edge to Sonxedge [Oxensitch?] and from there to the Knotbury and Blackclough Coal Pits – and the road branching out of the said road between Middlehills and Hassop Farm from Isaac Billing's house to Goldsitch'. This was the road past Gib Tor (where the tollgate was positioned in 1775) across Goldsitch Moss and down to the Flash Brook near Manor Farm. This tollgate was shifted to Hazelbarrow in 1825. New gates

had been created at (1) the Knotbury turn-off in 1773, at (2) Saltwell (1815–29) and at (3) Oxensitch (1829–?). There was obviously complex retail coal traffic in this area well into the 19th century and it is still crisscrossed by a network of narrow public roads today.

The Leek and Buxton turnpike branches were never walled out but had freestanding gateposts at the entrances to their colliery causeways. Three sets still survive on the bleak moorland branches leading to the Ravens Low and Goyts Moss mines.

At a trustees meeting in 1792, proposals were received for a turnpike branch at Middlehills to connect to the Blue Hills, Milward, Hazelbarrow, Blackclough and Goldsitch coal pits. With the exception of Blackclough, all these pits are in the area between Ramshaw Rocks and Goldsitch Moss. In the event, only one short branch (authorised by an Act of 1793) was constructed from the Blue Hills area to connect with the earlier 1773 branch to Manor Farm.

In 1813. and again in 1818, an extension was planned from the existing branch to Blackclough to connect with the Dane Colliery and the Danebower tollgate on the Buxton and Congleton turnpike. This was to cross two county boundaries on land in two different ownerships. A viable route would have already existed to the Reeve Edge Quarry from Blackclough. However, to reach the Congleton turnpike, a mere 350m away, a bridge over the upper Dane and access to the nearby Danebower Quarry track would have enabled the Reeve Edge Quarry's products to more easily reach additional markets in Cheshire. The exact route of the proposed 1813 extension is shown on a map but, despite the likely benefits for the pits and quarries and increases in royalties for the two landowners, no such undertakings are apparent and the branch extension never materialised.

'THE NEW CUT' c.1790

In a suspiciously charitable move, the Leek and Buxton Turnpike Trustees decided to offer reduced tolls for coal and lime traffic travelling between the Thatch Marsh termination of the Congleton turnpike and the Grin Low kilns. This would be made possible by constructing an alternative route across the Terret to ease the gradient to/from Ladmanlow. Completed around 1790 (at the time of the completion of the Congleton and Buxton turnpike), this 'new cut' turned onto their Buxton turnpike where a chain was erected (1791–1814) to prevent toll evasion by traffic escaping southwards, perhaps with coal for the High Edge kilns? The 'new cut', which remained in use for many years as a road and still exists as a track, is shown on the 1804 Hartington Enclosure Award maps.

Railway competition, bringing high-quality coal from Whaley Bridge and beyond for both domestic use and the Grin kilns, gradually reduced coal traffic on the Leek and Buxton Turnpike branches to Goyts Moss, Thatch Marsh, Orchard Common and Knotbury. In 1852, a Renewal Act reduced the responsibilities of the Trust to caring for the main turnpike only, leaving the maintenance of all the branch roads dependent upon the unreliability of statute labour. The long and detailed series of records for the Leek to Buxton Turnpike reveal a huge complexity of toll changes and tollgate names and locations due to its fortunes being most strongly linked to the state of the local mineral extraction industries and the aggressive and convoluted policies of its Trust. Known tollgates at the Buxton end of this road around Grin Quarry and the Terret, where many road diversions have taken place, include Ladmanlow, Green Lane, Grin End and Park Chain.

THE CONGLETON AND BUXTON TURNPIKE, 1789–1882

In 1789 a turnpike extension across the moors from Bosley crossroads via Cleulow Cross to Thatchmarsh Bottom was authorised by Parliament, giving the town of Congleton access to the mineral resources of the South-West Peak. It was described in the Act as 'from Smithy Green [Bosley crossroads] to Tinkers Pit Gutter, which divides the Counties of Chester and Derby, and from thence to join a branch from the Leek Turnpike Road at a place called Thatchmarsh Bottom to open a Communication with certain Lime Kilns in the said Parish of Hartington; which would be a great benefit to the several Owners of Lands and Grounds through which such road is proposed to be made'. This was to be an entirely new road extension, built to increase the flow of lime, coal and stone from Derbyshire to south-east Cheshire, stimulate the paper, textiles and mineral industries of the upper Dane and improve communications to Congleton where a variety of industries – also relying on the water power provided by the Dane – were rapidly developing.

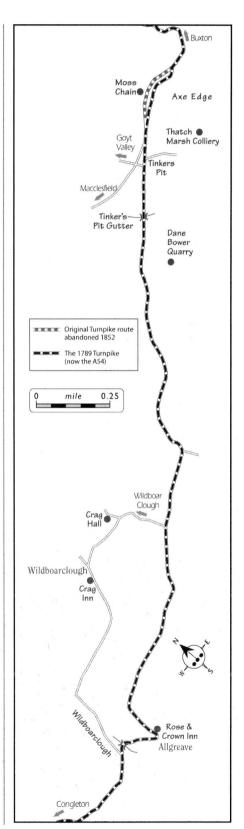

Map: Part of the Congleton and Buxton Turnpike, 1789.

A raised strip of altered vegetation reveals the original route of the Congleton Turnpike at the junction of the A54 and A537 near the Cat and Fiddle.

Authorisation was given for a small branch road to the Havannah Mills, Eaton, near Congleton, where Charles Roe of Macclesfield had expanded his copper and brass smelting business.

The maximum permitted tolls were laid out within the Act:

(1) For every Horse, Mare, or Gelding, drawing any Carriage whatsoever, the Sum of Four-pence.

(2) For every Horse or other Beast of Burden, laden or unladen and not drawing, the sum of One penny.

(3) For every Drove of Oxen, Cows or other Neat Cattle, the sum of Ten-pence per score, and so in proportion for any lesser Number.

(4) And for every Drove of Calves, Hogs, Sheep, Lambs or Swine, the sum of Five-pence per score and so in Proportion for any lesser Number.

There were of course toll exemptions, such as, for example, the carting of materials for road repairs to any road in the township, dung and fertiliser (other than lime), hay, straw, grain, or flour for storage (but not for sale). There were exemptions for the movement of farming equipment and beasts travelling to pasture or water.

The revenue collected from the users of the road, however, proved insufficient to pay the interest on the money borrowed to build the new stretches. A Parliamentary Act of 1830 therefore allowed the trustees to increase the tolls and to fence the moorland sections where the tolls 'may by reason of the great width of such moors and waste lands be easily avoided'.

The earliest accounts for the three known tollgates within the study area are from 1823 onwards. The first was for Moss Chain (1823–?), somewhere on Axe Edge Moor, being a chain across a side road leading from the Congleton turnpike down towards the Goyt Colliery, the actual position of which is uncertain but may have been near the now demolished Boothman's Cottages. The second gate (1826–32) was at Danebower Bank, near to the Dane collieries and quarries. The third gate (1822–32) was at Allgreave near the Rose and Crown pub.

Moss Chain may be confused with the Portobello ('beautiful gate'!) toll bar, or 'catch' bar, described by GH Ward in 1944 as 'a possible toll house of one storey inhabited until 1905 by a Mr. John Brindley, a Buxton Waterworks employee'. Its suggested position (see maps) was at the junction of the existing A537 and the old 1773 coal road from Ladmanlow to the Goyts Moss Colliery, not 50m from the modern pumping station. A heap of stone and exposed ground floor flags were all that remained but all traces have now disappeared.

This road, several stretches of which were constructed by Jack Metcalf, exists today as the A54, where its northern end terminates in a junction with the 1821 Macclesfield 'new road', now the A537, at SK 021 713. The turnpike originally terminated with the Goyts Moss Colliery branch of the Leek turnpike about 200m to the north-east of today's junction, where a raised strip of altered vegetation reveals the old route that was abandoned in 1852.

The failure of a plan of 1829 to drive a turnpike branch road from Allgreave through Danebridge to Hug Bridge on the Macclesfield to Leek road has thankfully preserved the seclusion of that part of the Dane Valley.

THE MACCLESFIELD AND BUXTON TURNPIKE ('THE NEW ROAD'), 1821–78

By 1815 the trustees for this turnpike had become dissatisfied with the line of their 1759 road which, although well suited to light traffic, was unsatisfactory for heavy horse-drawn wagons because of its long stretches of steep inclines. A largely new road was required, better matched to both wagon and stagecoach, with reduced gradients and, by implication, a longer route.

John Loudon Macadam supervised the construction of the road, which was laid out by William Johnson, a Macclesfield surveyor. With the passing of the 1821

ANNO PRIMO & SECUNDO

GEORGII IV. REGIS.

•••

Cap. xxxvi.

An Act for more effectually repairing the Road from *Brokencross* in *Macclesfield*, in the County of *Chester*, to the Turnpike Road at *Buxton* in the County of *Derby*, and certain Branches of Road to communicate with the said *Macclesfield* Road; and for making a new Road from *The Waters* in *Macclesfield* to *Buxton* aforesaid.

[19th *April* 1821.]

WHEREAS an Act was passed in the Thirty-second Year of the Reign of His late Majesty King *George* the Second, intituled *An Act for repairing and widening the Road from the Cross at Brokencross in Macclesfield, in the County of Chester, through Macclesfield Forest, to the present Turnpike Road at the South End of the Township of Buxton in the County of Derby:* And whereas another Act was passed

....; And whereas the Powers and Provisions of the said recited Acts have been found in some Respects defective and insufficient for the Purposes intended; and it is expedient that the said recited Acts should be repealed and further and more effectual Powers and Provisions granted and made instead thereof in one Act of Parliament, for making, amending, widening; turning, varying, altering, and keeping in Repair the Roads mentioned in the said Acts: And whereas the Course of the present Road is in many Parts thereof steep and mountainous, and it would be a great Accommodation to the Neighbourhood and Public if a new Road was made from or near a certain Place in *Macclesfield* aforesaid called *The Waters*, to or nearly to the Crescent in *Buxton* aforesaid; but as the several Purposes aforesaid cannot be effected without the Aid and Authority of Parliament;

Extracts of the Parliamentary Act of April 1821 to re-route the Macclesfield and Buxton Turnpike.

Renewal Act for this turnpike, accommodation was sought with the Leek and Buxton Turnpike Trustees for a shared branch of road leading to the coalfield. A length of about 300m was agreed upon – probably part of the existing road. A new tollgate (1823–33) was then erected somewhere on Axe Edge at the joint expense of the two Trusts just outside a 'no toll' area defined in the 1821 Act. Although a very convoluted arrangement, it appears to have been constructed and shared satisfactorily by the Trusts.

Other stretches of the Macclesfield 'New Road' proved less complicated, although a couple of options seem to have been tried at the high point of the road on which the Cat and Fiddle Inn now stands (see maps). Almost a decade after the road was completed, John Ryle, a Macclesfield banker and mill owner, built this isolated inn. Excavating down to bedrock and then resurfacing resolved early difficulties with the road sinking immediately east of the inn. This involved building an embankment of solid material 2m high with ditches on either side across Thatch Marsh. The opening of this new road, now the A537, resulted in the disturnpiking of the 1759 road in 1824, from which time no new turnpikes were constructed in this area. Ten years later, in 1834, a Mr George Shufflebotham of Macclesfield advertised an omnibus service to Buxton. To travel inside the vehicle cost 4s 0d; travel outside cost 2s 6d.

For this road the local tollgates were at the Duke of York pub crossroads at Burbage (1815–33) (the Gosling Bar becoming redundant); at Ladmanlow, where the toll holder 'Blind Jack' Metcalf applied for a rent reduction in 1823, and at Stoneyway on the crossroads formed by this and the earlier version of the road below Stake Farm, 1km north-east of the Cat and Fiddle Inn.

The few isolated cottages known to have provided homes for families involved in the later years of active commercial quarrying and coal production on this large area of windswept moorland are now pulled down. The footings of the five buildings on the 1759 Macclesfield to Buxton turnpike east of the Cat and Fiddle Inn that were demolished with the coming of the reservoirs in the 1930s are easily found; those of Boothman's Cottages and of 'Old Engine House', which were still occupied in the early 20th century, are less easily found. The footings of Boothman's Cottages, built for colliery use about 1850, can be located 1km west of the small pumping station above the River Wye below the Terret. These two cottages

The Cat and Fiddle Public House near Buxton.

were also called 'Half Way House' (halfway to the Cat and Fiddle), and sometimes 'Old Posting Houses'.

The area still retains a wild and remote look and, being exposed to strong winds with high rain and snowfall, the road network is still blocked relatively easily in winter. Prior to the use of snowploughs, wooden poles often marked the course of these high moorland roads. Even with the coming of the turnpikes, transportation with wheeled vehicles in winter must have been sporadic with quarrying and coal mining hard and dangerous undertakings in this most exposed industrial location.

THE TOLLS

The local turnpike trusts introduced a fairly general schedule of tolls on the roads they controlled and the schedule shown below for the 1724 Manchester to Buxton turnpike is quite typical of the charges for the other early turnpikes in the South-West Peak. Each had its own variations for different types of vehicles but, perhaps more significantly, as the threat of railway competition became more apparent, progressive changes were made to reduce or even exempt the tolls on the mineral traffic.

For the Manchester to Buxton turnpike, the 1724 Act contained the following schedule of tolls at completion:

1) For every Coach, Chariot, Chaise or Calash drawn by 6 horses or more – 1 Shilling.

2) For every Coach, Chariot, Chaise or Calash drawn by 4 horses – 8 Pence.

3) For every Coach, Chariot, Chaise or Calash drawn by less than 4 horses – 4 Pence.

4) For every Wagon, Wain, Cart or Carriage drawn by 5 or more horses or oxen – 1 Shilling.

5) For a Horse, Mule or Ass, laden or unladen and not drawing – 1 Penny.

6) For every Drove of Oxen or Neat Cattle, 10 Pence Per Score and in proportion for greater or lesser number = PER BEAST – 1 Half Penny.

7) For every Drove of Calves, Hogs, Sheep and Lambs, 5 Pence Per Score and in proportion for greater or lesser number = per animal – 1 Farthing.

Occasional exemptions (often during Trust disputes) were given to packhorses and to horses and carts laden with coal, lime or limestone, or returning unladen.

A further Act of 1730 for the Manchester to Buxton road allowed tolls to be increased because the road had needed diverting and widening with surface improvements to accommodate the new carriages and heavier wagons. As wagons became heavier, it was thought (wrongly) that narrow wheels were damaging the roads and such wagons were heavily penalised irrespective of the load carried.

It seems remarkable that, although the exemptions mentioned above regarding carts or horses carrying lime and limestone were removed by this 1730 Act, the exemption for coal was, at least for a while, withdrawn.

A 1751 Act for this road re-introduced the general exemption for lime traffic. Tollgates then seem to have increased and differing toll levels were introduced at different gates.

By the end of the 18th century, when the new roads network around Buxton was nearly complete, more general toll schedules were applied. Exemptions were given to mail-coaches, posthorses carrying mail, vehicles carrying road materials, local agricultural traffic, livestock moving between farm and pasture, military wagons and wagons carrying poor people needing treatment at Buxton Baths. Free passage was offered to traffic going to or from church, voters on elections, soldiers marching, clergymen and all pedestrians. Tolls were usually doubled on Sundays for ordinary commercial traffic. There was much malpractice, fraud and evasion of tolls and heavy fines were imposed in an attempt to counter these.

The local trusts seem to have employed many differing and complicated toll schedules. Normally, travellers could expect to pay only once a day for the use of the roads of any one turnpike trust, a ticket from one gate clearing them at the others. Regular turnpike users could purchase what we would call a season ticket, both a convenience and an economy. Many of the toll houses or toll bars who charged for the passage of goods by weight employed 'weighing engines', but there are no known surviving local examples. Although attempts to simplify the toll structure were put into practice in the early years of the 19th century, these attempts seem to have merely caused further proliferation of gates and, for a while, much frustration! Technological changes were reflected by the introduction of a toll into the Leek to Buxton turnpike tariff in the Act of 1852, of one penny per dog drawing a vehicle and 'two shillings and six pence for a carriage propelled by steam, or any other animal power'.

If we take the period 1750 to 1850 we find that, although a passenger vehicle with four wheels drawn by four horses had the heaviest toll, it rose by little more than 20% over the period. Some traffic tolls remained unchanged over these 100 years. For a horse, laden or unladen and not pulling a vehicle, the toll remained at one penny. The Peak District climate could also have its effects on tolls. From 1811, the turnpike trusts added extra half tolls to cover the

additional expense of keeping the roads open during the winter.

THE TOLL KEEPERS

Often in remote positions and requiring someone in attendance at all times, the life of a toll keeper, and perhaps his family, could be both lonely and restricting. Some toll keepers had a house and garden provided rent-free but, even so, the rates were hardly generous for a job requiring watchfulness on a daily basis.

Toll keepers would sometimes obtain the lease on the gate and retain the collected tolls while the Trust (of course) expected to receive a rent, quarterly and in advance. Such arrangements often resulted in these keepers getting into debt. These lessees – or 'toll-farmers' as they were called – were at first local people but, increasingly, professional toll farmers would bid for a number of gates and employ their own collectors. Fraud, intimidation and occasional violence became commonplace. Toll keepers who got into arrears would sometimes finish up in jail. There were other risks: in 1815, the Wardlow Mires keeper, Hannah Oliver, was murdered during a theft of the toll money; her murderer was hanged at Derby and his body hung on a gibbet near the toll bar. Surrounded by desolate moorland, many toll gates were especially vulnerable to attack and theft by desperate vagrants or highway robbers.

Although many travellers understood the collection of tolls, it was very unpopular with some of the local communities who felt aggrieved at being charged to use roads they were already helping to maintain by statute labour. The *Gentleman's Magazine* in 1749 reported riots throughout the country when gangs of men, some disguised in women's clothing and armed with staves, cut down the turnpike gates and destroyed toll houses. In 1765, two men were prosecuted for riotous behaviour at the Norbury toll bar in Poynton, whilst in 1838, a report in the *Macclesfield Courier*, headlined 'Riot at New Mills', recorded how the toll gates in the town were repeatedly torn down. Now recovered, and erected close to Bamford Station, are the sturdy Mytham Gate tollgate posts (SK 207 825) from the Sparrowpit branch of the 1758 Sheffield to Buxton turnpike. They show the arrangement whereby vehicles and animals passed through the main gate and pedestrians used the narrow side gate without charge.

A few old toll houses remain in the Peak District, although many have been swept away by road-widening programmes. They come in a variety of architectural shapes and sizes but the usual building is a small compact house providing accommodation on the job for the toll collector, with windows that gave a clear view both ways and with a board in front giving the toll charges. The Fernilee tollhouse was a typical example (see photograph p.148).

The building on the old 1759 Macclesfield to Buxton turnpike that was the Gosling tollhouse is one of only two survivors in the study area. On Smith's 1804 Derbyshire map, the building is shown and is spelled 'Gosling' although modern maps show the building as Goslin Bar Farm. It was known to be a 'catch-bar' for coal from the Goyt Collieries in one direction, and caulk (barytes) from the small Grin Low mines for the Goytsclough Mill in the other. In 1824, when the toll house became redundant, the Buxton School Trustees purchased it for £45 as it adjoined some of their land, converting it for use as a village school. The old toll house has been extended and is now a dwelling.

Bradley Howell tollbooth survives on the Goldsitch Moss branch of the Leek to Buxton turnpike at SK 0060 6585. The tollbooth and the house are on opposite sides of the road. The other tollgates in the area are long gone. Over the life of any particular turnpike, and for a variety of economic reasons, the position and therefore the names of the tollgates often changed. Investigation of any known sites may sometimes reveal the largely ephemeral stone footings of a small building or the remains of a substantial stone post.

THE HIGHWAYMEN

There have been robbers on the highway for as long as roads have been in existence but the stereotypical hero/villain appeared early in the 17th century. Their numbers swelled after the Civil War when massive unemployment caused by the demobilisation of large numbers of soldiers resulted in many 'taking to the road'. They were joined by all manner of other men with a variety of reasons for choosing this particular profession, including bold 'young blades' who robbed on the 'High Toby' for the sheer thrill of it. Many highwaymen followed respectable trades either before taking to the road or as 'covers' during their criminal career. Some were upper class and were described in the press of the day as 'amateur highwaymen' who would escape the gallows using bribery to secure blatant breaches of legal practice. However, much of the supposed highwayman activity lies in the realms of romantic fiction rather than historical fact.

The methods of most highwaymen did not attain great levels of sophistication – 'your money or your life' and a gun in the ribs usually achieved the desired result. In the pre-coaching days, postboys were employed to carry the mail in stages using fast ponies but were so vulnerable to attack that at one time the Post Office advised the public to send bank notes in two halves and to await for news of the safe arrival of the first half before forwarding the second! This type of mail robbery applied exclusively to these postboys and not to mail coaches; in fact there is no evidence in Post Office records that a highwayman ever held up a mail coach. Nevertheless, mail coaches, despite having armed guards, were sometimes robbed by opportunistic gangs of thieves, running a high risk of injury for the coachman, guard and passengers.

The peak of highwayman activity was 1680 to 1780 and although the main roads were now used more frequently, they were often poorly constructed and maintained. Until well into the 19th century, highwaymen lurking along their margins made them doubly dangerous. The bridle paths and minor roads – the 'Low Toby' – were also hazardous and were infested with footpads who would rob packhorse trains and foot travellers. Judging by weekly newspaper columns, the activities of highwaymen and footpads in the study area were considerably reduced by the late 18th century, when picking pockets and petty pilfering from coaches and wagons was far more common than vehicles being forced to halt so that passengers could be robbed.

In the early days of coaching, the penalties for highway robbery could be severe. If the condemned men were lucky enough to escape live gibbeting or dissection they were usually hanged. Many prepared themselves with new clothes in the latest style, but the more pessimistic donned shrouds. A hanging day was a public holiday, which was officially encouraged in the hope that the execution would act as a deterrent. Hangings and gibbeting of the more infamous highwaymen acquired a carnival atmosphere, with vendors and sideshows to occupy the enormous crowds, which would build up from early morning.

Chapter 19. STAGECOACHES, MAIL AND FREIGHT

COACHING SERVICES

Coaches carrying fee-paying passengers were quite rare before the late 18th century when, using roads where repairs had become unpopular and skimped, travel in these vehicles with their crude and failing suspensions was a slow, uncomfortable and often accident-prone experience. Such journeys could be very expensive, with timetables unreliable – schedules gave the day of arrival with the proviso 'God willing'. Early coach traffic was often seasonal, with fewer journeys in winter when the roads became even more hazardous. In such weather, on poorly constructed and rutted roads, passengers were frequently obliged to get out and push or wait in the disabled coach until a substitute arrived. Passengers who had elected to sit outside the coach paid half the standard fare. The total number of passengers allowed in and on a stagecoach seems to have been around 12 or 13 but this rule, especially in country districts, was regularly flouted.

With improving roads, the improvement of vehicles (previously a pointless exercise) became worthwhile, resulting in a startling reduction of journey times. The main technical improvements to coach design were the introduction of steel springs from 1754 but the biggest advance in suspension was the elliptical spring. These springs enabled the coach body to be lowered, reducing sway and making overturns less frequent. In the same period, lamps were introduced, providing a warning to other road users.

Brakes, which were unpopular with coachmen, remained rare until the very end of the coaching period. A coach was brought to a halt by the horses, controlled by a skilful coachman driving four- or six-in-hand and by the guard jamming a wheel with a 'shoe' or 'skid pan' when descending a steep hill or when stationary.

A Skid Pan.

MAIL COACHES

The introduction of mail coaches by an Act of Parliament in 1784 stimulated dramatic improvements in stagecoach performance and by the end of the 18th century the public long-distance coach had become an object of glamour, the most well-known symbol of the turnpike era. It was the first national transport system and, for the first time, offered a faster means of travel than horseback. People of all classes travelled by coach if only occasionally, on what was to become a well-organised national network of routes where journey times were reduced and punctuality was of a high order.

Mail coaches, which were exempted from road tolls, did not have to stop at tollgates and expected all other traffic to give way to them. Delivery time for letters was cut and journeys became measurable precisely in hours and minutes. The panache, punctuality and

Various horsedrawn vehicles at the Cat and Fiddle Inn.

sheer speed of the mail coaches must have been a real spectacle. Clad in their sober livery of black and maroon they scattered livestock, clattered through tollgates and exchanged village postbags, all without reducing speed.

An anecdote by Lady Newdigate, quoted in the *Buxton Advertiser* in 1937, shows that in 1781 'a mail-coach ran through Fairfield, probably one from Shef-field, and that the drivers were not very considerate of other traffic'. She says that she had 'half an hours trot on the little common by Fairfield. On our return, coming over the bridge, a mail coach and four drove full gallop against us, and had not the gentlemen obliged the postillions to stop, would have canted us down the high bank into the brook. They did lock our wheel, but as William stood firm and they stopped in time, we came off with a fright only'.

The mail coaches carried parcels on an ad hoc basis as well as letters, with passengers limited to four inside the coach and six outside. Prior to the use of mail coaches, the postal service, which had its ori-gins in Tudor times, had employed 'postboys' (often quite elderly men) on horseback to carry mail in bags but, as we have already seen, these carriers became increasingly vulnerable to robbery.

Two very direct mail-coach routes from London to Manchester were listed in 1786:

1) Via Derby, Ashbourne, Buxton and Whaley Bridge.

2) Via Derby, Leek, Macclesfield and Stockport.

By 1815, mail coaches were running between London and Carlisle via Leek and Macclesfield, and between Manchester and Sheffield via Bullock-Smithy (Hazel Grove) and Buxton. The usual distance between posting inns was about 10 to 12 miles with only four minutes being allowed to change horses.

Main-road towns enjoyed much prosperity in the early decades of the 19th century, when inns flour-ished with coaching business and travellers' custom. By 1835 the main inn of any market town might have 50 or 60 horses 'on call' in its yard to meet the year-round demand for stabling, with ostlers and farriers to care for the horses. A team of four horses could pull a coach at ten miles per hour on the flat for an hour at a stretch. It is significant that 'stages' are still marked by former coaching inns at roughly 12-mile intervals along today's main roads. In Buxton, The

Cheshire Cheese, The Sun Inn and The Queen's show the influence of the coaching and horse-drawn wagon days.

In the 1820s, a coach traveller recorded his expenses for his journey from Blackburn via Manchester to London:

	£.	s.	d.
Blackburn – London Fare	1	16	0
Tips to Coachman – 5 @ 1/-		5	0
Tips to Guard		4	6
Refreshments @ Manchester		1	6
Supper @ Leek		2	6
Breakfast @ Northampton		2	0
Total	2	11	6

In 1750, the stagecoach journey between Manchester and London was taking five days but by 1833 the same journey was taking 18 hrs including two 20-minute stops for breakfast and dinner. The stagecoach also carried certain goods, usually perishable luxuries and small items of high value.

Compared with the development of the railways in the 1840s, coach travel was considered both slow and expensive. It could not provide the mass transit system that the industrial revolution required and, crucially, it could not, unlike the canal network, carry freight in bulk.

THE GUARD

During the early years of the 19th century, the reputation of the coach began to depend also on its guard. His first care was the 'way-bill', i.e. the passengers and their fares. He must secure the passengers' luggage and the parcels. On the road, his duties included blowing his horn at the approach to tollgates (which would be promptly thrown open to mail-coaches) and upon arrival at coaching inns, where the horses were changed and passengers set down and taken up. It was also sounded on the road to warn wagoners, drovers and shepherds to clear the way for the

coach to pass. If the coach broke down or became stuck in deep ruts or snow, the guard had to help in such emergencies. In the event of a mail coach being unable to proceed, the guard was expected to continue the journey on with the mails, using the lead horses or by private transport if necessary. At the top of any steep hill he would lock a hind wheel with a chain or a skidpan and untie it at the bottom. A mail-coach guard's equipment included a timepiece, tools and ropes, while under his seat he carried his bugle or 'yard of tin' posthorn and a blunderbuss. Near at hand were two loaded pistols. Such guards were often ex-soldiers and well used to handling guns. It seems likely that mail guards used their firearms more often against rabbits or pheasants, even straying chickens, rather than against any highwaymen.

COACHMEN AND HORSES

Horses acquired by the coaching services were bought at auction, often hunters or carriage horses that had lost some of their value. They were schooled to become harness horses as distinct from saddle horses and were used in pairs that would tolerate each other on the road. If the road was known to be flat between any two stages, four horses would be sufficient to pull the coach, but in hilly country a team of six was the usual number, sometimes with a postillion riding one of the leaders. Much has been written and perhaps exaggerated concerning cruelty and floggings by coachmen using weighted whips. These were hard times both for the majority of people and no doubt for the majority of horses also. Despite having to adhere to the coaching service's timetable and suffer the wrath of passengers arriving late or missing connections, really serious and damaging cruelty to the coach team or individual horses in that team is somewhat unlikely. It should be borne in mind that each horse was considered as a 'work unit' and anything that compromised that work unit would result in loss of team efficiency and delays. What can be certain is that these teams were driven very hard by experienced horse-handlers and it is known that the working life of a mail-coach horse was about three to four years, after which they were sold, sometimes fetching extremely good prices. The analogy with modern second-hand cars cannot be ignored.

If the coach was to run comfortably, the horses had to be well matched to pull together efficiently and be strong enough to hold a two-ton coach on a steep hill. If the coachman knew these stage-horses he might change the pairing to obtain the right balance for the coach to be pulled smoothly. Some pairs performed better as 'wheelers' (those nearest to the coach front wheels) while others were happier as 'leaders'. A surprising number of coach horses, even 'lead' horses, seem to have been blind and yet performed well. Despite the gradual improvements in road surfaces and gradients and the development of lighter and better-sprung coaches there continued to be a great turnover of horses.

THE ROADS IN AND AROUND BUXTON

The pattern of the turnpikes terminating in or near Buxton, or passing through it, still control the present-day layout of the town where many of the old coaching inns and hotels continue to survive. The relative isolation of Buxton, the difficulties of the surrounding terrain and its unusual role as a spa resort combined to give these roads particular significance where journeys by public coach and 'fly wagon' (see Freight Carriers below) gave improved access and made possible the rapid development of the town from about 1760 onwards. By 1811 there were five stage-wagons a week through Buxton in either direction from Manchester, London and Nottingham and as the town developed, more of these services were introduced.

As for the quality of the roads themselves, which initially were good, there were few improvements to the system made after 1825 when even the minimum standards of maintenance were reduced.

Over a period of less than one hundred years, the stage wagon and public coaching trade with its associated stables and inns had risen to its peak around 1835 and then declined as the railways, which came late to the Peak District, quickly encroached on its business. Despite the demise of long-distance public coach services after 1837, Buxton continued to be served by both public coaches and mail coaches operating over shorter distances. By 1850, the days of the stagecoach were numbered, with tolls collected from the gates in the area reduced by more than one third. In fact, the main preoccupations of the Trusts over the final decades of the turnpike system were simply to maintain interest payments and repay loans. The dwindling coach trade was finally reduced to providing excursion transport for visitors. The romantic names given to the dashing long-distance coaches such as 'Royal Bruce', 'Peveril of the Peak', 'Lord Nelson', 'The Regulator' and 'The Enterprise' were adopted by the horse-drawn omnibuses and wagonettes which provided circular trips to Haddon Hall, Chatsworth, Topley Pike, Axe Edge and the Cat and Fiddle.

Having seen how the development of the one- and two-horse carts was to put the packhorse out of business, we find that the railways were almost as soon to put the larger draught horses out of business as a long-range carrier – a similar fate to that suffered by the stage- and mail-coach horses. Given that horses had figured so prominently in English life, the arrival of the 'iron horse'– the railway – and the road-going steam traction engine, was indeed a moment of truth, making people aware of minutes as a unit of time and that time could equal money. Horse transport, however, remained essential for agriculture and local journeys with the development of lighter carts and carriages continuing into the 20th century. The changeover to motorised travel was hastened when vast numbers of horses were requisitioned for the battlefields of World War I but was not complete until the 1930s. Pit ponies were to stay in the coal industry well into the 20th century.

FREIGHT CARRIERS

With the arrival of the turnpike roads, the majority of local freight, such as coal, lime or agricultural produce, was carried in fairly small carts of one or two tons' capacity, drawn by one or two horses and owned by local farmers, innkeepers or carters. Carriers also operated a regular service to and from market towns using horse-drawn vans. Long-distance freight movements were generally by stage wagons which were larger, covered, unsprung vehicles usually drawn by four, six or sometimes eight horses and carrying freight between stages. In some instances they also provided for low-cost and slow passenger services in lighter vehicles, but even these would have been quite uncomfortable. Much to other travellers' annoyance, the slow stage wagons were, by custom, given the right of way by other road users. At the discretion of the wagoner, 'drag horses' might be hooked onto the back of a vehicle descending a steep slope to act as a necessary brake.

THE PICKFORDS

The most famous name associated with this type of traffic was that of Pickford (a common local name). Local tradition has it that Thos. Pickford, who had moved into the area after being deprived of his lands and title in Adlington by Oliver Cromwell, resumed his business as a carrier. In addition, he was said to have acquired Goytsclough Quarry, 'carrying stone by packhorses for the repair of roads around Manchester' – an unprofitable enterprise one would think, for such a common and widely available material! No documentary evidence has been found to connect the 17th-century quarry owner Thos. Pickford with the later 'carrying' Pickfords.

Tradition also maintains that, rather than return through the villages and hamlets with empty panniers, Thos. Pickford would bring back such goods as people required, including perhaps greengrocery and hops for flavouring beer. Hops seem to have been a favourite item of back-carriage right through from the 16th century. Travelling in all weathers and bringing with him the latest news, a later Pickford was to become a well-known local figure. He eventually

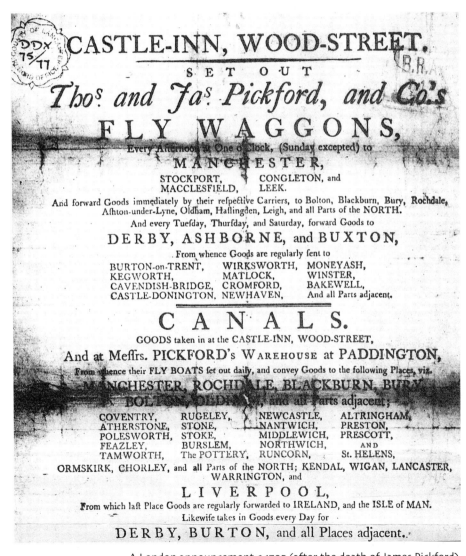

A London announcement c.1795 (after the death of James Pickford).
Faster, lighter, and better sprung than the heavy stage wagon, Pickfords
were using fly wagons on the road – and fly boats on the canals.

171

joined with other carriers already involved in long-distance journeys to Sheffield and London. A partial defence of local tradition might be established by an 1853 Errwood Estate map. It shows that a Mrs Pickford owned 70 acres of Wild Moor in the upper Goyt Valley in the mid-19th century, while a surviving contract shows that a Mr Pickford was providing stone to mend roads in 'the district of Macclesfield', a process that often consisted of tipping chipped stones into the dust or mud for passing traffic to consolidate.

Succeeding members of the Pickford family were equally progressive, and as road conditions improved they were quick to take advantage of the large stage-wagons that had been developed. These wagons now had steerable swivelling front axles, but would still take a day to travel 25 miles pulled by six horses, although a team consisting of one horse and eight oxen was sometimes used to move really heavy goods. It was known that oxen were regarded as 'sheet anchors' and had greater staying power than horses. The wagoners were forbidden to ride in case they fell asleep and were obliged to walk alongside. Following the completion of the 1724 turnpike between Hazel Grove and Manchester, the Pickfords were able to join the Carlisle route south to London. The *Manchester Mercury* newspaper of 17 August 1756 describes a James Pickford as the 'London and Manchester Wagoner', one of six such firms operating wagons between these cities. Twenty years later, using the main turnpikes, Pickfords did the London to Manchester journey in 4½ days, averaging 42 miles per day. In 1803 Pickfords provided this service six days

per week. Around this time, Pickfords also developed the use of the fly-wagon, a cross between the slow stage-wagon and the speedy passenger stagecoach. The fly-wagon was a light, well-sprung vehicle pulled by a team of four horses. By 1816 there were as many as 200 land carriers transporting goods to and from Manchester and London in wagons and carts.

Improved rural roads were also to bring advantages to agriculture and market gardening. Goods services operated by small local carriers proliferated and there was much competition for business. These local carriers often did the job in order to supplement incomes from their small farms or holdings. They sometimes brewed their own ale and then carried it to the local pubs. On days when the roads were impassable, they might weave on hand looms or dig coal from their small mines. A 'dual economy' is still the way of life for a few of the small working farms or holdings in, for example, Quarnford Parish. Even with farming grants in the early 21st century, it can be impossible to subsist by just grazing sheep on a few acres of impoverished high moorland.

Along the turnpikes, traffic flowed, bringing ideas, fashion and news. The scale of industry increased, assuring a supply of raw materials and a regular distribution of finished products. However, long-distance freight movements by road, already curtailed by the canal network where one horse could pull a narrowboat with a 30-ton cargo, were now facing a new challenge: the establishment of the railways.

Chapter 20. THE CROMFORD AND HIGH PEAK RAILWAY

THE MISSING LINK

This pioneering railway, designed and engineered by Josias Jessop, the son of the builder of the Cromford Canal, was at first built to employ horse traction but soon afterwards steam locomotives were adopted. At the outset there were nine inclined planes with static steam-engine haulage. Authorised by an Act of Parliament in 1825, the railway was single-line working on the level sections and double on the inclines. It 'opened to the public for general trade' (private carriers, briefly), at a cost of £200,000 in 1830–1. It was built to connect the Cromford Canal in the Derwent Valley with the Peak Forest Canal at Whaley Bridge in the lower Goyt Valley, where at each terminus there were canal wharves, storage and stables. The railway, which was to pass through the important limestone quarries south of Buxton, ran for a total length of 33 miles over a range of nearly 1,000 feet. The summit of the line was at Ladmanlow, 1,264ft above sea level. It was designed to fill a gap in the transport network where canal construction on the limestone plateau would have involved unreliable water supplies and huge flights of locks with their consequent delays.

The C&HPR, which was mainly a freight line, ran throughout the area, moving not only large quantities of coal, lime and limestone but also sand, grain, iron and lead, timber and raw cotton, bricks, milk and general produce. Another vital commodity was water in tenders to supply those winding engines that did not have their own supplies – and for domestic premises along the line. It was able to directly access collieries at Whaley Bridge, Shallcross and Burbage where there were branches and sidings. Limestone and lime were obtainable from branches to the Grin Low, Harpur Hill, Hindlow and Dowlow quarries, while gunpowder for blasting in mines and quarries could be picked up from the Fernilee Mills. Paving stones from the Goytsclough gritstone quarry were also transported out of the area on this railway.

From the outset, C&HPR efficiency was somewhat compromised by its canal heritage. The similarity was heightened by traffic being handled by private carriers who used both their own wagons and horses, or hired them from the C&HPR. The working methods followed canal practice: stations or halts were designated 'wharfs' and the men who worked at them 'wharfingers'. During the period when motive power was supplied by horses, it was found that one horse could draw a load of ten tons on the rails as opposed to one ton on a good road.

Faced with competition from more modern railways subsequently constructed in the wider area to connect with Buxton, the northern section of the line between Ladmanlow and the Whaley Bridge terminus closed in 1892, cutting out the Bunsal, Shallcross and Whaley Bridge inclines, with their inevitable delays, at a stroke. By 1894 the railtrack here (by now part of the L&NWR) and the winding engines had all been removed.

Considering its very early construction date, the railway was a considerable engineering achievement. The track was of standard gauge and had to negotiate sharp ascents and descents at either end of the line. The Cromford terminal and others, including the two-thirds of a mile 1 in 7 gradient of the Bunsal Incline in the upper Goyt Valley, were dealt with by the use of stationary steam engines with chain/cable haulage. The Whaley Bridge incline used a capstan and horses until the line closed. Horses were used for haulage on all level sections of the railway until a steam locomotive was delivered to Cromford in 1833. It took another 30 years, however, before horse traction was entirely replaced by locomotives on all the level

A 20ton water bowser, built c.1894 for the C&HPR.

sections. The first reports of locomotives in the study area appear in the 1850s, when one was described working the level section between Shallcross Top and the foot of the Bunsal incline along what is now the eastern side of Fernilee reservoir. During the same period, a lime company engine and wagons working between the limestone quarries and the colliery at Ladmanlow is described in a local newspaper article.

This railway, the route of which involved the excavating of deep cuttings and huge embankments, opened up the hills to the same massive industrial expansion that had been introduced to the valleys. Although these activities are seen by many as having damaged the Peak District landscape beyond repair, they are part of the price to be paid in the making of modern Britain. For others, such industrial relics are places of great interest and intrinsic beauty.

In its heyday, as a carrier of mineral traffic, the railway's impact on turnpike road tolls had been considerable. What remained of this fascinating old line gradually became unprofitable and it finally ceased working in 1967, since when many of the trackbed sections have become public footpaths and bridleways.

For rail enthusiasts, much remains near the Cromford terminus, with visitor centres both at High Peak Junction and at Middleton Top. The Middleton Top engine house and its restored engine survive in situ as a Scheduled Ancient Monument. Built by the Butterley Iron Works at a cost of £2,000, this winding engine was the last of eight such to be built by the company for the C&HPR between the years 1825 and 1829. The low-pressure, condensing, double-acting steam engine is in effect two identical single-cylinder rotative beam engines joined by a common crankshaft with the 16ft 2in diameter flywheel positioned between the engines. It produced a total of 40hp, steam being provided by two 'Cornish' boilers, supplied as replacements in the 1870s by the L&NWR. These served the winding engine until 1957 and are housed in the adjacent boiler house with its 80ft high, brick-built chimney. The frail engine is periodically run on compressed air for public demonstration.

In its 137 years of operation, the C&HPR suffered numerous 'runaways' on the inclines. Most resulted in the destruction of wagons and a great deal of debris, but others were more serious. Such accidents eventually resulted in the operators reducing the numbers of wagons on the incline at any one time.

Elsewhere on the line, accidents were frequent but seldom serious. Sheep and lambs appear to have been the most frequent casualties, with compensation paid to farmers.

THE NAVVIES

With the Act for this railway passed in 1825, construction of the line began in the same year. The contractor's men, the 'navvies' who built the line and who were 'fuelled by beef and beer', would not only have encountered practical difficulties with the terrain but would also have endured bitter winters and high rainfall. Much of the glory surrounding track construction went to the engineers and much of the profit to the entrepreneurs, but it was navvies with picks, shovels and gunpowder who made the railways.

Navvies were an anarchic elite of labourers who worked in constant danger, miles from civilisation, and lived according to their own laws. They were heathens in a Christian country; they drank, had many women but few wives, broke open prisons and were not received in good society. They were compared to an invading army. They came, made their earthworks and went, taking a few local women and leaving the ruin of a shanty town.

A navvy was not a mere labourer, although a labourer might become a navvy. They came from Scotland and Ireland and from the dales of Yorkshire and Lancashire. By 1825, they had already built many roads and canals and were expert at blasting and cutting, leaving the menial jobs and truck-filling to boys and locally recruited casual labourers. They followed the rail and travelled with one contractor until they heard of higher wages elsewhere. It took a year's solid work to turn an agricultural labourer into a navvy, by which time his wages rose, he could buy better food and was as strong as he ever would be.

The word 'navvy' comes from 'navigator'. It was a name given to the canal builders of the late 18th century and inherited by the railway men. To be a navvy was to be skilled in excavating, tunnelling, blasting and bridge-building. He must be able to live with others of his kind in encampments by the line and be able to eat and drink like a navvy. Two pounds of beef and a gallon of beer a day – and a man was accepted.

The dress too was distinctive. They wore moleskin trousers, double canvas shirts, velveteen square-tailed coats, hobnailed boots, gaudy handkerchiefs and white felt hats with the brims turned up. They would pay fifteen shillings for a sealskin cap and their distinctive badge was the rainbow waistcoat.

The life of a navvy was not commonly a long one. Many died young, sometimes violently, often during blasting operations, or else were run over by wagons they were leading to the tip-head. Most died at around forty years old; a good age for a navvy – but while they lived, they lived riotously.

THE C&HPR IN THE UPPER GOYT VALLEY

Railway features still to be found here include cuttings, embankments and branches to coal mines. There were branches with sidings to limestone quarries and kilns, an inclined plane two-thirds of a mile long with an average gradient of 1 in 7, the sites of two Butterley Co. stationary steam winding engines and their associated buildings and water reservoirs. There were 'halts' or platforms for transferring freight and passengers, a 580yds long tunnel and a number of overbridges. A few drystone walls still incorporate redundant sleeper blocks and various pieces of permanent-way furniture such as gradient markers.

Initially using chains for haulage, the Bunsal Incline had a vertical range of some 470 feet, and was worked as two separate inclines with a slight dog-leg at the changeover point opposite the engine house halfway down. The inclines were known as Bunsal Upper and Bunsal Lower, each worked by its own winding engine. When the two haulage inclines were combined in 1857 into one long incline worked by the upper engine, the dog-leg was eased into a curve to accommodate the continuous flat hemp rope and the later continuous steel rope. The redundant winding engine was sold to the limeworks at Grin to be used to power a stone crusher. The engine pit and associated reservoir can be found at SK 020 758.

Above: Looking down the 1:7 Bunsal incline.

Below: The Watford Moor double curve.

Near the foot of the Bunsal Incline, the two running tracks would widen out to pass either side of large sleeper-lined 'catch-pits' with gravel run-aways into which, via points, a descending breakaway run could be directed and brought to a halt.

The short overbridge near the foot of the Bunsal Incline has been filled in with the same disregard for railway relics as is evident elsewhere on the incline – the permanent way here is now full of trees. Similarly, both ends of the Burbage Tunnel a mile beyond the incline top can be found suffering somewhat from the ravages of time. The dressed stone portals are crumbling badly. A serious conservation effort by British Telecom, which has laid its cables through the tunnel, is long overdue.

From the top of the Bunsal Incline the track takes a more sinuous course, following the contour on low embankments or through shallow cuttings. There are two high embankments where the line crosses a stream (SK 032 748). One supported the original 1820s line, while the other was built in the 1860s to lessen the curvature of the bend.

By the eastern end of Errwood Reservoir Dam is a plaque recording the use of the old trackbed as a road to bring plant and materials into the valley to construct the dam. The plaque, erected by the Stephenson Locomotive Society, incorporates one of the original gritstone sleeper blocks with its central hole.

Because the horses used for pulling had to walk between the rails, cross-sleepers were never considered. Prior to locomotive working, therefore, the 'feet' of the iron rails were secured in short, square stone sleeper blocks using an oak plug and an iron spike.

Beyond the Errwood Dam it is possible to walk a near straight line of the old railtrack on what is now a concessionary bridleway running along the eastern side of Fernilee Reservoir as far as the dam.

An unusual linear feature can be identified downslope from, and parallel to, the incline above Bunsal Cob. Investigation reveals a channel with the lower half embanked, 3m wide and 90m long with a consistent gradient that overlies older braided hollow-ways that cross it at right angles. It has been interpreted as a probable experimental incline built before the course of the line was carefully considered. Not being long enough to have been a test track for locomotives, it was possibly an incline built to test the capability of horses to pull wagons up the identical gradient of what was to become the railway's steepest incline.

Three short single-track tramways in the upper Goyt Valley are associated with the railway. Two ran from a small quarry (at SK 027 734) that was used in the late 1820s to provide stone to line the Bunsal Tunnel and face its portals. The other ran from the Bunsal rail incline to a small coal mine at SK 023 757, known to have been active in the 1840s.

THIS ROAD WAS BUILT IN 1967 ON THE
BUNSALL INCLINE OF THE
CROMFORD AND HIGH PEAK RAILWAY
CONSTRUCTED 1831. ABANDONED 1892.
MAXIMUM GRADIENT 1 IN 7
PRESENTED BY MEMBERS OF THE
STEPHENSON LOCOMOTIVE SOCIETY
1972

Although the C&HPR was to depress the mineral traffic on the local turnpikes, the extra visitors who flooded into Buxton on two new competing railways (including The Midland) were keen to go in appreciable numbers on excursions in horse-drawn omnibuses along the turnpikes to view the astonishing countryside. New quarries generally opened near to railway lines where possible, but in other cases mineral products were taken by road to railway sidings for onward despatch. For a while, this feeder traffic boosted road toll income but the die was cast and tolls eventually fell to uneconomic levels. The railways had arrived and intended to stay.

THE TRIAL RAILWAY

At the Goyts Lane/A5004 intersection (SK 032 752), the Saltway crossing the upper Goyt (see Chapter 9) is briefly severed by huge spoil heaps and a mid-19th-century trial railway cutting at Longhill Farm. There is a further trial rail cutting and embankment immediately opposite Watford Farm. These considerable earthworks can be seen at SK 040 742.

Nineteenth-century documentation exists of a claim for compensation from a railway company driving a line from Ambergate to Buxton – for cutting the Longhill Farm property in half. The company was the Manchester, Buxton, Matlock and Midlands Junction Railway Company, who never registered their intention to build a railway over Long Hill. These earthworks must have been an early trial undertaken without official sanction, presumably as part of the planned Manchester to Matlock line in the 1840s. The company was seeking a high-level route over the western moors, perhaps with the intention of joining the Cromford and High Peak Railway at the top of the Bunsal Incline. In the event, the final line chosen was laid from Ambergate to Rowsley but was not extended to Manchester until 1860–7, when the Midland Railway laid the line up the Wye valley and through the long Dove Holes tunnel.

A VANISHED HAMLET AND A CHANGING LANDSCAPE

When the first one-inch to the mile Ordnance Survey map of the area was published in 1842 it showed a small winding road dropping down from the Buxton to Manchester turnpike towards the hamlet of Goytsbridge in the upper Goyt Valley. The road, known today as Goyts Lane, or Sandy Lane, has swathes of deep braided hollow-ways, some crossing it, while others run parallel to it on the open moor. The hollow-ways and the road lead to the hamlet, the hollow-ways having formed the basis for the road, parts of which can be seen down to bedrock. Also depicted on this map is the rail track of the Cromford and High Peak Railway that crossed Goyts Lane with a level crossing, from where the rails ran northwards down a two-thirds of a mile inclined plane with a 1 in 7 gradient as far as Bunsal Cob. The track then followed a level course to Shallcross, passing close by the Fernilee Gunpowder Mills. Other features of this railway, which opened in 1831, are shown together with a scouring mill and a number of farms, quarries and coal pits. Errwood Hall may have been built in around 1840 but is not shown. This might be accounted for by the delay between the mapping survey and the actual publication date of 1842.

The OS map of 1960 shows many changes. Fernilee Reservoir had opened in 1938; the valley farms had disappeared along with the gunpowder mills, the scouring mill and the C&HPR rails and stationary steam-engine houses. Errwood Hall is shown – but now as a ruin. On 25 June 1892, the London and North Western Railway had closed their line (the C&HPR) between Ladmanlow and Shallcross. Two years later the rails were removed, allowing the trackbed of the incline to grass over and sheep to graze around the stone sleeper blocks. The old road from the Long Hill continued to serve the little community of Goytsbridge and like other country roads in the area was maintained as necessary.

Current maps now show the Bunsal railway incline as a road. It had been resurfaced in 1962 to form a new spur to connect with the 'Street' to carry materials and plant into the valley for the construction of the Errwood Dam and to become, in effect, the new version of the valley road from the top of Long Hill.

With the flooding of the valley in the 1960s, the hamlet of Goytsbridge now lies under the waters of Errwood Reservoir and the largely redundant lower portion of Sandy Lane has itself become grassed over. From the level crossing at the top of the incline to the Burbage Tunnel, the old railway trackbed has been resurfaced and is now a dedicated wheelchair route and footpath, affording stunning views over wild moorland.

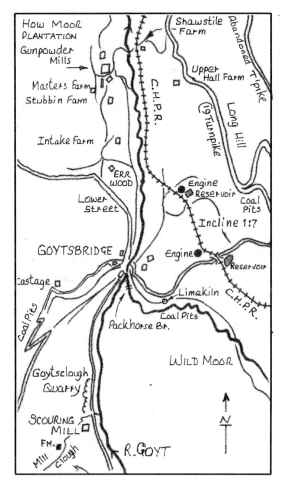

Left: A vanished hamlet and a changing landscape.

Below: The Bunsal incline above the Errwood and Fernilee reservoirs, 2007.

Chapter 21. TURNPIKE DECLINE

Several decades of activity by the turnpike trusts had ensured that, for the first time in centuries, Britain had a respectable network of adequate roads upon which, by the late 1820s, the stage and mail coaches were making very swift journeys between towns and cities. Such journeys, of course, still involved the changing of horses at regular staging points. Many skilled men were involved in caring for the thousands of horses and maintenance of the elaborate coaching system's vehicles. Coaching companies employed professional farriers, coachmen and ostlers at the inns, but by the 1830s, when Statute Labour ended, roads were probably at their best and the coaching services at their peak at just the time when the challenge of the railways began to make an impact. During the 1840s, as we have seen, turnpike incomes fell, coach and carrier services were abandoned and surviving turnpike roads acted increasingly as 'feeders' for the rapidly expanding railway system.

From the 1870s, local 'disturnpiking' was actively pursued; trusts were being wound up and replaced by local Highway Boards responsible to Quarter Sessions. Disturnpiking and the removal of toll bars brought much public rejoicing and by 1881 only 184 trusts existed nationwide. In 1888 came the Local Government Act that finally shifted the responsibilities of the parishes and turnpike trusts to county councils for the main roads – and to the district councils for other roads. By 1895 the last tollgate in England was thrown open. It was at this time that the roads, including the largely deserted country roads, experienced a sensational revival of fortune which continues to the present day, firstly by the vogue for the bicycle, followed by the introduction of the motor car. The early motor cars on the 'macadamised' roads caused huge clouds of dust which became an urgent public nuisance, and attempts to remedy it led to the development of new types of road surface, which usually involved some form of tar-mixing from which the word 'tarmacadam' is derived. Although the turnpike system had introduced a means of privatising a public resource – 'the common highway' – the concept of making road users pay, although sound in theory, was inefficient in practice and costly to operate.

The Local Turnpikes

Any improvements to the local turnpike system came to an end during the early decades of the 19th century as Trusts found it difficult to keep up the interest payments on their loans, funded by ever-decreasing toll revenues. Indeed, some roads seem to have been in financial difficulties permanently. As capital investment rapidly diverted to railway development, available funds for the Trusts dried up and Renewal Acts allowed interest payments to be drastically reduced or even written off. The Trusts were wound up, and by 1882 all the study area's tollgates had been removed. Perhaps the biggest impact of the turnpike roads had been to bring this south-western part of the Peak District fully into the national economy.

It is likely that most of the early trade on the local turnpikes was the transport of lime and limestone from Grin Quarry to Macclesfield and beyond, and coal from the Axe Edge, Dane and Goyt valley coalfields to Grin Quarry and to Buxton. This pattern of trade would change progressively from the early 1800s because of the following events:

1) In 1831, the Cromford and High Peak Railway opened and connected with Grin Quarry. Its southern terminus was at Cromford, and its northern terminus was at the Peak Forest Canal basin at Whaley Bridge.

2) Also in 1831, Telford's Macclesfield Canal opened to traffic and connected with the Peak Forest Canal at Marple and the Trent and Mersey Canal at Talke in Staffordshire. The Macclesfield Canal was thus linked to the main canal systems of England. However, this canal, together with many other old narrow barge canals, soon suffered a swift decline in commercial traffic and was too late to enter into effective competition with the railways after the middle of the century. The Macclesfield Canal continued to be used for a certain amount of coal, quarried stone, pottery and textiles until 1914.

2a) In the south, the Leek and Cheddleton wharfs on the Caldon canal.

3) In 1828, the Manchester and Buxton Turnpike Trust went into receivership. In 1837, the first rail link between Manchester and London was established, followed in 1840 by a link to Stockport, and in 1845 a link to Sheffield. These rail links caused a dramatic reduction in toll income on the turnpike. In 1860, the Trust was granted its final Act of Parliament, drawn up to focus efforts on reducing its outstanding debt of over £45,000. Despite the railways having reached Buxton in 1863 and all the debts being repaid by 1872, the Trust struggled on for another year, after which time it was wound up, the tollgates were removed and its responsibilities for the upkeep of the road were taken over by local government.

The Macclesfield Canal at Gurnet.

4) In 1845, the Macclesfield branch of the Manchester to Birmingham Railway opened, while in 1849, the North Staffordshire Railway linked Macclesfield and Congleton to The Potteries and London.

5) From 1831 onwards, limestone and its products would have been transported from the Peak District to Macclesfield and adjacent areas of Cheshire via the C&HPR, the Peak Forest Tramway and along the Peak Forest and Macclesfield Canals. These journeys, although longer than the more direct turnpikes, seem to have been somewhat cheaper. Similarly, the C&HPR link

enabled superior quality Whaley Bridge coal to be supplied more cheaply to the Grin Low kilns and probably depressed local coal production. All tolls on the Macclesfield and Buxton Turnpike finished in 1878.

6) The slow decline in road tolls at Grin after 1790 coincides with the opening of the Peak Forest Canal in 1796 and the opening of the Cromford and High Peak Railway in 1831, clearly indicating the diversion of mineral traffic away from the Leek and Buxton Turnpike and its branches to the local extraction sites. Like so many others, the turnpike slowly reverted to meeting agricultural and local needs. All tolls on this road finished in 1875.

7) In the mid-1800s, toll income on the Congleton and Buxton Turnpike declined, coinciding with a rail connection from Congleton to Crewe in 1848 and a direct link from Macclesfield to Manchester in 1849. All tolls on this road finished in 1882.

MILESTONES AND MILEPOSTS

An Act of 1744 made milestones compulsory on most roads and the General Turnpike Act of 1766 extended their use to all roads. Surviving milestones on turnpike roads are relics of a time when life moved more slowly. They were essential waypoints when maps were rare and travel was mostly by foot or horse. They were designed to allow accurate pricing and timing of journeys and enable coach drivers to maintain their schedules and timetables, but by the time the new 'local authorities' had been formed and had acquired the turnpike trusts' assets, some of the milestones and markers then in their charge had become illegible or had disappeared. The presence of existing mile markers is generally regarded as evidence of a turnpike road. The surviving markers in stone may have replaced any tall guideposts or 'stoups' predating the turnpikes, erected either by order of local justices or at the initiative and expense of local landowners.

With the onset of industrialisation, cast iron became increasingly available and in time a cheaper option. The presence of iron mileposts (again, with distinctive styles) usually indicates that they pre-date the dissolution of the Trusts. These iron posts often go

Cast-iron milepost, 1821 Macclesfield / Buxton 'New Road' (A537).

with new or diverted turnpike routes created in the early 19th century, while the short, stone markers are found on 18th-century routes. In some cases, stone markers have been replaced or supplemented by iron posts where the road continued in use. By the sides of many existing and abandoned turnpiked roads around the South-West Peak, surviving mile-markers in stone or cast iron from the 18th and 19th centuries can be found, often having unique designs. The mile-markers in stone are two to three feet in height and wedge-shaped in section. They can be found sometimes in situ, sometimes nearby if the road has been moved, sometimes hidden in overgrown grass verges or incorporated into stone walls by the roadsides. Similarly, many surviving iron mileposts can be discovered hidden by vegetation, rusting and in need of a coat of paint. A few of these venerable indicators of turnpike routes might still remain undiscovered.

A complete set of 18th-century milestones is to be found along the roadsides of the B5470 between Macclesfield and Chapel-en-le-Frith. A few similar milestones remain on the 1759 Macclesfield to Buxton turnpike, either incorporated into later enclosure walls or isolated in their original positions high on the moors alongside abandoned sections of the road. A very good example can be found 400m north-west

Milepost, Congleton / Buxton Turnpike (A54).

181

of the Cat and Fiddle Inn at SJ 9990 7230. A single unencrypted stone marker remains at the junction of two turnpike versions of the A5004 between Buxton and Whaley Bridge at SK 0190 7715. The symbol 'MS' on current OS maps may be used by the curious to perhaps unearth further examples. A complete set of 19th-century iron posts enhances the A537 between Macclesfield and Buxton. They are recently painted in white with smart black lettering. A mostly rusting and very incomplete set of 19th-century iron posts of a similar design remains by the verges of the A53 between Leek and Buxton. The iron mile-markers on the A54 have a V-shaped cross-section allowing place-names on two faces. Cheshire County Council erected these in 1896; one year after the last tollgate in England was demolished.

THE INDUSTRIAL LEGACY

The signs of past exploitation by man are everywhere. All the major gritstone quarries in the South-West Peak are long abandoned and the huge limestone quarry at Grin Low ceased working in 1972, after a period during the 1950s when the entire excavated area had been filled with stockpiled coal. It is now a caravan park, screened by the nearby lime ash tips that were landscaped and planted with trees to hide what the planners at that time saw as ugly scars. In 1790, coal mining, quarrying and limeburning would have been the main source of employment in places such as Burbage, helping to support most of the population. Burbage was never a mining village with terraced housing on the Welsh pattern; rather, the workers lived in scattered cottages and small farms or holdings, which had existed long before these industries became truly industrialised. By the end of the 19th century, these jobs had become strictly limited by the falling demand for poor-quality local coal and by the impact of mechanical brick and tile manufacture on traditional stone quarrying.

Few industries ravaged the landscape of Britain as badly as coal mining. In the South-West Peak, however, there are no large tips due to the narrowness of the seams, the mining methods employed and the very small scale of mining when compared with the lowland coalfields. Mining evidence in the adjacent lowlands at the heart of the coalfield has usually been swept away by later development. Only the minimum of material was dug out of the local mines, the miners sometimes packing waste rock back into the workings for support. This lack of large waste heaps makes it difficult to fully appreciate the extent of this mining, which dominated parts of the study area up to the beginning of the 20th century. The commonest surviving evidence is that of the hundreds of collapsed shafts, some surrounded by low mounds where some of the stone from their sinking was placed. Shafts can be found with their associated connecting barrow runs and raised causeways for transportation, in groups on the open moor. Ironically, while this mining was small in scale when compared with 19th- and 20th-century mining in coalfields to either side of the Pennines, what survives here is some of the best coal-mining remains in the country. Although some 19th-century mining of the area's deeper reserves used adits, these are now often lost or deliberately concealed, although traces of associated buildings sometimes survive.

The economic reserves of the collieries had become worked-out by the early 20th century and most mining ceased. Rumours abound about small mines reopening during the First World War of 1914 to 1918, the General Strike of 1926, the Second World War of 1939 to 1945 and during the bitter winter of 1947. Such reopening might have been quite unofficial – however, some small mines along the upper Dane were occasionally worked up to the 1950s, with the coal being taken for sale to Macclesfield by motor lorry. The coalfield's historical importance largely lay not in its production but in its proximity to pure Carboniferous limestone at Grin, Harpur Hill and Dove Holes, and the part it played in the regional expansion of the Derbyshire lime industry. Many of the older coal workings indicated on current maps can still be found. As part of a continuous process (i.e. not at the time of colliery closure), as various shafts became redundant they were sealed off with timber and back-filled as part of the lease agreement.

To attempt underground exploration of these shafts and any mine workings below would be foolhardy as collapse is always likely and deadly gases are frequently present. Injury and prosecution for entry are a likely consequence – assuming you survive.

The industrialisation of the area was accompanied at the time by environmental costs. Forges and kilns blackened buildings, industrial chemicals and mining killed off rivers and streams, while roads, railways and quarries cut through fields and ancient monuments, dislocating rural communities. Despite the healing processes of nature, there is still plenty of evidence of this earlier, uncontrolled development. Today, times have rightly changed away from the once-perceived need to remove all evidence of past industry. From our current perspective, this evidence enriches the historic landscape, giving fascinating insights into the endeavours of past generations who worked and perhaps lived in these sometimes harsh environments.

By the beginning of the 20th century, coal production in the study area had virtually finished and the limekilns were being fired by superior-quality coal brought in on the railways. Limestone quarrying and to a lesser extent the production of lime is still a predominant industry in and around the Peak District, providing important employment for people who live in the region.

THE TURNPIKES TODAY

Some of the local turnpike roads are now widened in places, have camber and surface improvements and some are classified as 'A' roads. While motorways and bypasses continue to proliferate elsewhere, with the exception of some minor forest and reservoir access routes, no new roads were build in the South-West Peak during the 20th century.

Especially interesting are the abandoned sections of turnpike such as those below the 'Long Hill' A5004 between Buxton and Whaley Bridge. Some still preserve their original surface, albeit somewhat rain-washed, and it is easy to imagine the fears of the carters and coachmen as their horses struggled to maintain a grip on the hillier sections. Many of the old 'coal roads' and 'lime roads' crossing the moors have become footpaths or now serve as maintained communication routes for the scattered communities of the area.

The modern roads network is a monument to the turnpike era, even though it has changed appearance because of tarmac, white lines, 'cats' eyes', reflecting road signs and, of course, motorised traffic. Of objects associated firmly with the turnpikes, perhaps surviving milestones are the most plentiful and lasting. On the Macclesfield to Buxton old road, the barn opposite what was the Setter Dog pub may be the Walker Barn tollhouse, while the 'Goslin Bar' in Burbage has been extended and remains in use as a dwelling. At the Ladmanlow road and rail junction, the white house at an angle to the road was the C&HPR level crossing keeper's house, while across the road, a red brick house stands at the site of the former Ladmanlow toll bar on a grass-covered length of Green Lane – the old Leek turnpike. Roadside inns developed in importance as they provided stabling for the many horses involved, and those Peak District pubs with large yards and outbuildings are characteristic of the coaching and horse-drawn wagon days.

Today, although the highways may be full of huge thundering trucks, tractors, tourists and tankers, ancient packhorse tracks and abandoned railways are now quiet routes for walkers and cyclists seeking freedom and fresh air. The footpaths and bridleways are beyond value; they belong to us all and frequently preserve important evidence of the past. Those who explore are likely to encounter abandoned coal or lead workings, deserted or ruined mills and disused quarries. They may be travelling on causewayed tracks, revealed perhaps only because of subtle linear vegetation changes, or will toil up the sharp 'vee' of a medieval hollow-way worn away by centuries of horse and foot traffic to such a depth that the surrounding landscape is briefly obscured. To explore these routes is a pleasurable and rewarding undertaking in itself, but it also affords glimpses of the lives and labours of the people of the South-West Peak stretching back towards prehistory.

GLOSSARY

Adit	Horizontal tunnel in a mine; a level; a sough
Assarting	Land grubbed-up for cultivation. Subject to fines
Barrow	A prehistoric burial mound
Bar	A toll or horseway
Bercary/ Burcary	A sheep farm
Brough	Fort
Cairn	Mound of stones
Calamine	The mineral, zinc carbonate
Calcining	An ore smelting term/Reduction of limestone to calcium oxide by roasting
Cart	A two-wheeled vehicle
Clough	Ravine or valley
Coe	A small mine building, sometimes over a mineshaft
Combs/Coombs	A valley/A basin of land
Commons and Wastes	Land areas within a manor where the tenants or tenants of other manors had the right to graze livestock
Coppice	To cut back deciduous shrubs or trees to near ground level, at intervals to provide a crop of usable and sustainable timber
Corfe/Corve	Box or basket sledge to drag coal from the face to the roadway in a mine
Culvert	A channel to take water under a road etc.
Demesne	Manorial land, untenanted, held by the lord
Dip	The inclination of geological strata
Earthwork	Prehistoric surface evidence. Man made of soil/or rock
Easement	Right of way over a property
Engine race	A walkway for horses at the gin
Engine shaft	A mine shaft for winding or pumping by a horse or steam engine
Fault	Fracture and displacement of geological strata
Field	Open land/an enclosure
Fogg	Poor grassland on which cattle could fend for themselves in the winter months
Frith	Private forest
Gate	Road / Entrance. Medieval method of pasture control
Gin	Abbreviation of engine. A horse-powered winding engine
Ginging	Stonework to stabilise a shaft at surface
Grange	A monastic farm
Greave	A grove (of trees) / a mining term; to dig
Grough	A peat gully
Greenway	A broad informal route manured by animal droving
Hag	A peat bank

Hagg	A place cleared of trees on a slope
Hay/Hey	An animal enclosure. Cleared woodland
Henge	A prehistoric monument with a circular bank and ditch
Hollins	Holly trees / haggs or boundaries of / winter fodder
Holt/Hole	Single-species woodland
In-by land	Farmland nearest the farmhouse
Intake	Land enclosed, usually from common or waste
Kibble	A large bucket used to haul ore or coal up a shaft
Lache/lech/lece/leache/leash	A pond or bog, a brook
Ladmanlow/Ladmanslow	Leadman's hill
Lea	Meadow or clearing
Level	A horizontal tunnel. An adit
Liberty	A township – but often a manor
Low	1) high; 2) a hill; 3) a burial mound
Marl	A fertiliser of clay and lime
Meadow	Where hay is grown and dried for winter livestock fodder
Meal	The soft part of grain; flour
Megalithic	Large stone structure
Mere/maere/meer/mair/mear	Pond or pool / a boundary / boundary stones
Metalling	Broken stone used in road making
Nab	Hillock
Neat Cattle	Oxen/black cattle
Nether	Further away/below – as in a place-name
Open Fields	Arable manorial land cultivated in large fields divided into furlongs, and divided again into strips worked by both the lord and the tenants
Pannage	The right to graze pigs in woodland, usually chargeable
Peak/Peac	Hill dweller (7th century *Pecsaetae*)
Pinfold	A pen for stray animals
Pitching	Stones laid on edge to make a floor or track
Plex	Where hops grow
Pollard	The hard pruning of tree branches to encourage growth
Rake	A steep village lane; a 'made' thing – not natural
Reeve	A local administrator responsible for roads, law and taxes. The reeve was elected by the villagers to act for them
Roaches	Rocks (Fr.)
Sitch/sytch/sich/sike/sick	A stream / a small watercourse
Slack	A shallow valley
Smelt	The extraction of metal from ore
Sniddles	Land with coarse grass
Sough	A mine(s) drainage level

Stoop / stoup	A post or marker
Tenter	To stretch and dry cloth
Thorn/Thorne	Thorn bush
Thorpe	Outlying farm or hamlet
Toot Hill	Lookout hill
Topography	Shape of the land
Tor	Rocky outcrop
Trundle	A wheelbarrow
Tunstead	Farmstead
Turnpike	A toll road
Vicus	Civil settlement around Roman fort
Waifs & strays	Any property found ownerless; if not claimed after a year and a day, it fell to the lord of the manor
Wain	A large, open, four-wheeled vehicle
Wash	Where ore, sheep or cloth were washed
Way	The track, or route
Whim	A winding engine (horses or steam)
Win	gorse bushes

ABBREVIATIONS

Fr.	French
ME	Middle English
OE	Old English
ON	Old Norse
OFr.	Old French

BIBLIOGRAPHY

(DAJ: *Derbyshire Archaeological Journal*)

Atkin MA *Hollin Names in Northwest England* Vol. 12 1988–9, pp.77–8

Baines P *Flax and Linen* Shire Publications 2003

Bagshaw RW *Roman Roads* Shire Publications 2000

Barnatt J *Archaeological Survey of the Goyt Valley* Peak Dist. Nat. Park 1994

Barnatt J *The Limekiln Complex at Peak Forest and Early Limeburning in the Northwest Peak* DAJ 2004

Barnatt J and Leach *The Goyts Moss Colliery,Buxton* DAJ Vol. 117 (1997), pp.56–80

Barnatt J and Smith K *Peak District* Batsford/English Heritage, London 1997

Barnatt J and Dickson A *Survey and Interpretation of a Limekiln complex at Peak Forest, Derbyshire; and a review of early limeburning in the North-West Peak* DAJ Vol. 124 (2004), pp.141–207

Barnatt J and Myers A *Excavations at the Bull Ring Henge, Dove Holes, Derbyshire,1984-5* DAJ Vol. 108 (1985), p.5

Barnatt J *Trial excavations at Silverlands, Buxton, 1984* DAJ Vol. 107 (1987) pp.18–23

Barnwell P *Anglo-Saxon Studies in Archaeology and History 12* 2003

Bede *A History of the English Church and People c.AD 731* Penguin

Bevan B *Peak Dist. Romano/British Rural Settlement Survey 'Peaks Romana'* for Derbyshire Archaeological Advisory Committee. DAJ Vol. 125 (1998–2005), pp.26–55

Bonson A *Driven by the Dane* Midland Wind & Watermills Group 2003

Borrow A *Valley of the Wild Stream, A History of Wildboarclough* Elderberry Press 2004

Briggs A *A Social History of England* Viking Press 1984

Buchanan RA *Industrial Archaeology in Britain* Pelican 1982

Burton RE *The Royal Forest of the Peak* Peak Park Publications 1966

Cameron K *The Place-Names of Derbyshire parts 1-3* (English Place-Name Society) Cambridge University Press 1959

Cameron K *English Place Names* Batsford 1996

Calladine A & Fricker J *East Cheshire Textile Mills* Royal Commission on the Historical Monuments of England 1999

Collins M and Stevenson M *Macclesfield: The Silk Industry* 1995

Cox JC *Notes on the Churches of Derbyshire* Vol. 1 1843–1919

Crocker G *The Gunpowder Industry* Shire Publications 1999

Darby HC *Domesday England*

Davies C Stella *A History of Macclesfield* 1961

Defoe D *Tour through the Whole Island of Great Britain* (1724–7; 1962 edition)

Dent A and Goodall DM *British Native Ponies* 1901

Darby HC *Domesday England* Cambridge University Press 1952

Dodd AE and Dodd EM *Peakland Roads and Trackways* (3rd Edition) Landmark 2000

Dodgson J McN *The Place-names of Cheshire* Vols I–IV Cambridge 1970

Dyer J *Discovering Prehistoric England* 2001

Earwaker JP *East Cheshire* (2 vols) London 1887–8

Evans KM *James Brindley, Canal Engineer – a New Perspective* Churnet Valley 1998

Edmonds M and Seaborne T *Prehistory in the Peak* Tempus Publishing 2001

Farey JM *General View of the Agriculture and Minerals of Derbyshire* 1811–17

Fiennes Celia (ed. Morris) *Northern Journey* (1697) 1982

Fitzherbert A *Boke of Surveyinge and Improvements* 1523

Fletcher JMJ *Notes on the History of Tideswell and its Manor* DAJ Vol. XLI

Gelling M and Cole A *Landscape and Place-Names* Shaun Tyas, Stamford 2000

Gascoigne M *English Customs and Traditions* Shire Publications 2002

Gaukroger S 'The Case of Quarnford – The history of a rural industrial township in the Staffordshire Moor lands' MA thesis, University of Sheffield 1995

Hart CR *The North Derbyshire Archaeological Survey* Wigley & Sons, Leeds 1981

Harris H *Industrial Archaeology of the Peak District* 1971

Heaf E *Tideswell Tracks* Tideswell Local History Club 1999

Hey D *Packmen, Carriers and Packhorse Roads in North Derbyshire and South Yorkshire* Leicester 1980

Hey D *Packmen, Carriers and Packhorse Roads* Landmark Publishing 2001

Higham N *The Origins of Cheshire* Manchester 1993

Hinchliffe E *A Guide to the Packhorse Bridges of England* Cicerone 1994

Hindle BP *Medieval Roads and Tracks* Shire Publications 1998

Hindle BP *Journal of Transport History* pp. 170–8 1975

Hoagies AG *Antique Maps* Shire Publications 2000

Hodges R *Wall-to-wall History* Duckworth and Co. 1991

Iredale D and Barrett J *Discovering Local History* Shire Publications 1999

Jenkins JG *The English Farm Wagon: Origins and Structure* 1972

Jones N and Bentley JM *Railways of the High Peak, Whaley to Friden* 2001

Kelly's Cheshire Directory, Various, 1878, 1878, 1902

Laughton J *17th Century Rainow* 1990

Leach J *Coal Mining Around Quarnford* (DAJ) 1996

Leach J *Grin Hill, Buxton. A Major Derbyshire Limestone Quarry* DAJ Vol.116 (1996), pp.101–34

Leach J *Coal Mining around Whaley Bridge* (DAJ) 1992

Longden G *The Industrial Revolution in East Cheshire* 1988

Longden G *An Historical Study of Kerridge Ridge and Ingersly Vale* report for Groundwork Macclesfield and Vale Royal, 2002

Marshall J *The Cromford and High Peak Railway* 1996

Mills AD *British Place Names* Oxford University Press 2003

Moreland J *The Bradbourne Cross* Current Archaeology 2005

Morris J (Gen. Ed.) *Domesday Book CHESHIRE* Phillmore & Co. 1978

Morris J (Gen. Ed.) *Domesday Book DERBYSHIRE* Phillmore & Co. 1978

Morris J (Gen Ed.) *Domesday Book STAFFORDSHIRE* Philmore & Co. 1978

Morris Cheshire Directory 1874

Mountfield D *Stage and Mail Coaches* Shire Publications 2003

Myers A 'An Archaeological Resource Assessment of Roman Derbyshire' for East Midlands Archaeological Research Framework 1999

O'Brien W *Bronze Age Copper Mining* Shire Publications 1996

Ormerod G *The History of the County Palatine and City of Chester* 1882

Prior F *Britain in the Middle Ages* Harper Press 2006

Prior F *Britain BC* Harper Perennial 2004

Prior F *Britain AD* Harper Perennial 2005

Philips CB & Smith JH *Lancashire and Cheshire from 1540* Longman 1994

Radley J and Penny S *Turnpike Roads of the Peak District* DAJ, XCII (1972), pp.93–109

Radley J *Peak District Roads prior to the turnpike era* DAJ LXXIII (1963)

Rayner D *Traction Engines* Shire Publications 2002

Rich B 'Manor of Macclesfield in the 14th century' unpublished paper 2005

Richardson J *The Local Historian's Encyclopaedia* Historical Publications 1993

Rimmer A *The Cromford and High Peak Railway* The Oakwood Press 1998

Roberts AF *Turnpike Roads Around Buxton* Scarthin Books, Cromford 1992

Roberts AF and Leach J *The Coal Mines of Buxton* Scarthin Books, Cromford 1985

Sharpe NT *Crosses of the Peak District* Landmark Publishing 2002

Sidebottom PC *Stone Crosses of the Peak and The Sons of Eadwolf* (DAJ) 1999

Slater's Cheshire Directory 1888

Smith H *The Guide Stoops of the Dark Peak* Halsgrove, Sheffield 1999

Smith H *The Guide Stoops of Derbyshire* Halsgrove, Sheffield 2000

Stanier P *Quarries and Quarrying* Shire Publications 2000

Sylvester D *A History of Cheshire* CCC Publications 1980

Thomas JM *Roads before the Railways 1700-1851* London 1970

Tonkinson AM *Macclesfield in the later 14th century* 1999

Victoria County Histories: Staffordshire, Cheshire and Derbyshire

Ward GH 'At and Around the Cat and Fiddle Inn and Axe Edge', *Sheffield Clarion Ramblers Handbook* 1946/47

Watts M *Water and Wind Power* Shire Publications 2000

Weston R *Hartington: A Landscape History* 2000

Watts M *Working Oxen* Shire Publications 1999

White's Cheshire Directory 1860

Winchester A *Discovering Parish Boundaries* Shire Publications 1990

Winfield J *The Gunpowder Mills of Fernilee* 1996

Williamson T *The Transformation of Rural England 1700–1870* Exeter 2002

Williams R *Limekilns and Lime burning* Shire Publications 1989

Wiltshire M, Woore S, Crisp B, Rich B, *Duffield Frith: History & Evolution of the Landscape of a Derbyshire Forest* Landmark 2005

Wolverson Cope F *Geology Explained in the Peak District* Scarthin Books 1998

Wright WN *Turnpike Roads* Shire Publications 1997

Wroe P *Roman Roads of the Peak District* DAJ Vol. 107 (1982) pp.49–73

Index